THE WAY IT WAS

Historical Narrative of Ouray County

by

David C. Bachman

and

Tod Bacigalupi

PRESS

Ridgway, Colorado

Published by Wayfinder Press
Post Office Box 217
Ridgway, Colorado 81432

Design, artwork and typography - Pat Wilson, Country Graphics
Cartography and printing - Marcus Wilson, Country Graphics
Copyediting - Doris Swanson

Cover: *A pawnshop in Ironton, 1885. This photograph has nothing whatsoever to do with this book. It was just too good to pass up.*

Third Printing
ISBN 0-943727-13-8

DEDICATION

To all these people who were willing to tell us their stories.
Without them, part of our heritage would have been lost.

TABLE OF CONTENTS

PREFACE

There are more people living in Ouray County with stories to tell. We couldn't get them all. We do think that we have collected a good sample. The stories in this book should give us a better idea of what living in this area was like in the early days of this century.

We do have a couple of major regrets. We were unable to interview Julius Sonza and Harry McClure. Julius died at age 90 just as we were getting ready to start the interviews. Julius was healthy, hale, and hearty right up to the time that he suddenly became ill and died. He was a wonderful storyteller and knew a lot of them, having lived in Ouray all his life.

Harry McClure owned one of the largest ranches in Pleasant Valley. He was in failing health during the time most of the interviews were made and has also died. All the ranch people knew, respected, and loved Harry. Thursday night poker games at Harry's house were famous.

We are grateful to all the people who cheerfully gave their time for these interviews. Most of them even provided coffee and snacks in their home where the interviews were conducted.

We would especially like to thank Mary Ann Dismant and Lyn Yarroll (Tod's wife) for typing all the transcripts for these interviews. Their job was difficult; our taping equipment did not provide stereophonic sound.

We owe a debt of gratitude to the Ouray Historical Society, to David Koch, the curator at the time we started this project, and to Vera Bremseth, the current curator. Their support helped to get this project off the ground. All of the photographs in the book are from the great Ouray Historical Society collection. Gerald Bremseth reproduced all the photos for us and we thank him.

Finally, our thanks to Jack and Doris Swanson of Wayfinder Press. We're grateful for their patience as they waited for the manuscript to finally show up on their doorstep and for their editing skills.

All of the tapes of the interviews in the book have been donated to the Ouray Historical Society. Although difficult to understand in some places, there are some great tales.

During its peak, in the late 19th and early 20th centuries, Ouray was a booming mining area with hundreds of working mines and thousands of people working in them. But like all mining communities, booms are followed by busts. The boom of the late 1800s turned into a bust in the early 1900s. Ouray County, however, was not only mining. The towns of Ridgway and Colona are now and were then ranching and farming communities.

The stories told in this book are the histories of the area from the perspective of those who lived in the county from the early 1900s to the present. The histories presented in this volume are ordinary. They are pictures of everyday life eighty years ago. And because they are ordinary, they are extraordinary. There are neither heroes nor villians; but, instead, we are allowed into the everyday life of people like ourselves. These people allow us to glimpse what life was like when things were perhaps simpler, and when people were perhaps closer and more in touch with their environment.

Their stories are exactly as they remember them, and for this reason, it is possible to occasionally see that not all people saw the same event in exactly the same way. This is the beauty of an oral history; it is history as people choose to remember it. It contains the feeling of life, that only the people who lived it can give to

a time long past. Each person has a different perspective on what went on in Ouray County, and what life was like in a time without many of the "necessities" that modern Americans treat as commonplace and necessary.

As a social history, we are given insights into a multiplicity of institutions and events, ranging from education to entertainment. We learn how people spent their time without television and how life on a ranch was lived from day to day. We meet the teachers in the one-room schoolhouse and the students who learned from them. As important as the obvious institutions, we learn about the ones now lost: the dance in the schoolhouse, the box social, and the silent movie.

A common thread that seems to run through many of the stories is one of independence and strength, from the teacher or the mule skinner in the middle of an avalanche, to the rancher and his wife working day to day to keep the ranch going. The strength of the women is as noticeable as the ruggedness of the men. But it was not only work, as one man told me, "Sometimes we just sat around and watched the clouds go by." But most of the time they worked, sometimes twelve- and fifteen-hour workdays in the mines, on the ranch, or in a hotel or boardinghouse. Children were adults often by the time they were eleven or twelve, often working as long and as hard as the adults.

And of course, there are the "girls." Most people would not talk about them, or would only after the tape recorder was turned off, the explanation being, "Their families and children are still alive." There is a sense of honor and solidarity in this group feeling, to not speak about this aspect of life. This is an aspect of our interviewees' shared past, but not a part they will willingly share with us. And yet, there are bits and pieces of information for us to glean from their comments. Several commented that "the working girls" were nicer than the strait-laced ones. They, of course, would never allow the children into their rooms; and, in that way, separated their work from the children who ran errands for them.

Another theme that seems to run through the narrative is the "shared sense of community" that used to exist, but, our informants imply, is now gone. People shared more, and made do with less. People met more and talked more, and played together more. Not only were there card games and dances, but people met downtown for coffee in the afternoon. That sense of community also appears in the way adults took care of the children, not just their own, but others' as well. There were no secrets. A child could not miss curfew or run errands for the "girls" without being caught. And when children worked, the adults made sure they spent their money wisely. We even find the local gamblers looking after the young sales clerk, so she would not be shortchanged by the other gamblers in town.

That sense of a shared life and lifestyle is something we heard referred to wistfully. Life was simpler and harder; but, as far as our interviewees are concerned, more fulfilling.

WORK

Some sociologists (e.g. Tausky 1984) suggest the history of humans is the history of work. In other words, our occupation defines our being. We are the job at which we work. Men in Ouray County were mainly in mining or ranching. At the turn of the century, and, until the late 1960s, women defined their position in the social hierarchy in terms of their husband's occupation. The women we interviewed frequently saw their lives in terms of their husband's occupations; and, for this reason, women's lives were frequently defined in terms of the occupation of their husbands. By this we mean what a woman did depended on her husband's job. We recognize that when we label a woman as a "farm wife," that is to designate a person in terms of another's occupation; however, to change the designation would be to change the reality of the life lived at that time.

This also does not mean that the women did not have jobs outside of the home, or outside of the kitchen. They did. They fully shared in the operation of the family farm, contributing in a variety of ways, each according to the needs of the farm. Many held jobs outside the home as teachers, postmasters, newspaper writers, and a host of other jobs.

In reviewing the content of the interviews, we find

that much of what is significant in people's lives is their contribution to the society in which they lived. Much of that contribution comes in the area of work. For this reason, much of the content of this oral history is about work. In the early 20th century, it was common to work far more than eight hours a day. For farmers and ranchers, work from dawn to dusk was common. For miners, ten- and twelve-hour shifts were normal, work was hard and occasionally dangerous. We get some insight into the hardships of working a mine from the ranchers who hire the miners who need to get out of the mine part of the year to regain their health.

However, if work is part of a dichotomy, then the other half of the dichotomy is leisure. A person may work seven days a week, from 6:00 A.M. to 6:00 P.M., but that still leaves twelve hours to rest and recuperate. Miners talk of running eleven miles on Saturday night to get from the mine to town in order to have time to take a bath and get to the dance at the Opera House. Following the dance they would rent a horse, ride back to the mine, and be ready to go back to work at 6:00 A.M. Sunday morning. They talk of other miners who never left the mines except occasionally. Some of these might spend six month's earnings on a weekend in Ouray.

During their leisure time people played cards, took walks in the mountains, went fishing, went to the movies, and filled their time in a variety of ways. When radio came along, they would listen to Amos an' Andy. Again, looking at the overall content of this oral history is the feeling that life moved slowly. Even with full days of work, there was time for most people to enjoy life.

METHODOLOGY

While the concept of "an oral history of Ouray County" was fairly straightforward, when it came to actual implementation, translating the concept to reality was a bit more complicated than just going out and interviewing a few senior citizens. Our first problem was determining just who we should interview. This problem was solved by doing a modified form of snowball sampling. Like a snowball rolling down a hillside that increases in size as it descends, a snowball sample relies on going to one person and having that person inform us of other people who would be good to interview.

We had several sources which we used to create our list of potential informants. Being residents of the county ourselves, we each knew several people who had grown up in the county in the early 1900s. We also talked with people in the local historical society and the curator at the museum. Our biggest problem, however, was the snowball soon became unmanageable. Our original list of subjects included almost fifty people. In the beginning, this seemed to be a reasonable number. However, reality soon replaced optimism.

All research conducted on a shoestring is limited by the length of the shoestring: time and money. The interview itself is perhaps the shortest and least expensive part of a project like this. An interview that lasts an hour and a half takes between twelve and eighteen hours to transcribe and here lies the expense of an oral history. Organizing the transcript into a readable form takes an additional eight to twelve hours. It became obvious that we would have to sample from our population of potential informants.

Several criteria were used in determining the actual people who would represent the whole of Ouray County. The criteria included occupation, locality, gender, continuous resident or migrant, availability, and, unfortunately, (at least from our point of view) willingness to be interviewed. Some people refused to be interviewed. Based on these criteria, our sample was chosen. We hoped to cover a wide range of occupations, locations, and, of course, the perspective of both sexes. We feel that within the limitations that we encountered, we accomplished these goals.

In sociology we have a term which expresses the point at which interviewing should end: the term is saturation (Glaser and Strauss 1967: 61-2). This is the point at which little new information is being gained and informants are repeating the same information but in different ways. In the beginning of a project such as this, all of the information is new; but, at the point of saturation, the information has been expressed before, but in a different style. In conducting the interviews, it became obvious when we had reached saturation.

It may be argued that we missed some of the best people. This point is moot as saturation, by definition, means even the "best people" at this time would only repeat the gist of what already is recorded. The number of people represents a dense sample of our population, as approximately 50% of our available informants were interviewed. To this extent, we feel we accomplished our goals of interviewing a wide variety of people who are representative of most of the major occupations and lifestyles in the community during the early 1900s.

The next step in the process was conducting the interviews. The interviews might formally be designated as semi-structured (McCall 1980:147), but a more accurate term would be emergent. I entered the first interview with a list of questions, which I soon found to be irrelevant. I was, however, "tabula rosa." This gave me the opportunity to see what was important to the interviewees and what was not. By allowing this to be their opportunity to educate me, I learned more than by entering an interview with preconceived notions as to what was "supposed" to be important. Because I had no idea of what was right or wrong, truth or fiction, we obtained information that was a candid portrayal of what the interviewees believed to be true about the particular situation.

Caution should always be exercised when interpreting information received in interviews. Schwartz and Jacobs (1979:64) warn that we should be careful when someone says, "We did X." This may not mean, I did X, but that others did X. For this reason discrepancies may occur in the narrative. That, however, is to be expected; and for the most part, we found that most accounts substantiated each other.

Returning to the concept of the emergent interview, I soon found that the chronological interview was easiest and allowed me to probe more deeply into subjects and concepts with which I was not familiar, and then return to the interviewee's "history." A normal interview lasted from one-and-a-half to two hours and started with, "Where and when were you born?" and ended when we had arrived at the present. Other questions that were typical included: How did you get to Ouray, what was school like, when did you first work, at what, what was the town like? and so forth.

Each interview was different and exciting, much like going to a movie or to the library for story hour. In each, I learned some new aspect of life from the early part of the century. All interviews but one were conducted in the interviewee's home which was a comfortable setting for the interview. As important for me as any other aspect of this research was being able to watch people's faces as they told stories that especially excited them. Often when speaking about the dances, faces would light up and I could see remembered joy at some instance or another. It was sharing this special excitement with people that made recording these histories so rewarding.

Tod Bacigalupi

REFERENCES

Glaser, Barney G. and Anselm Strauss, 1967. *The Discovery of Grounded Theory: Strategies for Qualitative Research. Chicago: Aldine.*

McCall, Michael, 1980. *"Who and Where Are the Artists." Pp. 145-147 in William Shaffer, Robert A. Stebbins, and Allan Turowetz (eds.), Fieldwork Experience: Qualitative Approaches to Social Research. New York: St. Martin's.*

Schwartz, Howard and Jerry Jacobs, 1979. *Qualitative Sociology: A Method to the Madness. New York: Free Press.*

Tausky, Curt, 1984. *Work and Society: An Introduction to Industrial Sociology. Itasca, Illinois: Peacock.*

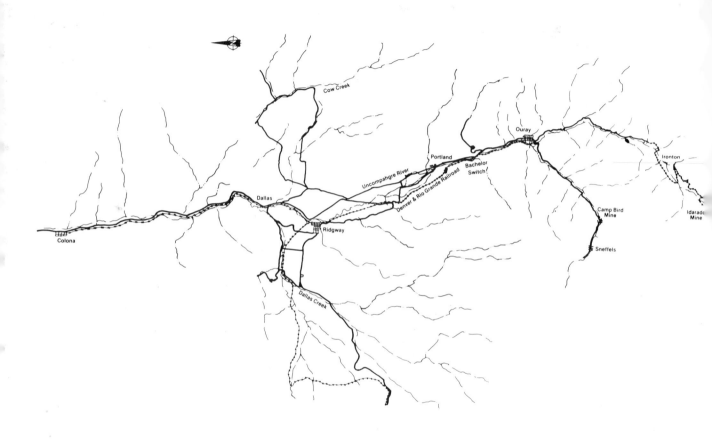

Ouray County, Colorado

Ouray County is located in the southwest corner of Colorado. As the crow flies it is about 75 miles to the Utah border on the west, 70 miles to New Mexico to the south, and 110 miles to the Four Corners and Arizona.

Ouray County is one of the smaller counties in the state with an area of 504 square miles in a roughly triangular shape. It is about thirty-three miles long, from north to south, and twenty-nine miles wide at its widest point. The permanent population is estimated to be 2100 people. During tourist season there are approximately 1500 visitors in the county every day. The table below shows population figures in Ouray County for the last 100 years.

Population of Ouray, Ridgway, & Ouray County

	Ouray	Ridgway	Ouray County
1880	864	*	2669
1890	2534	*	6510
1900	2196	245	4731
1910	1644	376	3514
1920	1165	400	2620
1930	707	239	1784
1940	951	354	2089
1950	1089	209	2103
1960	785	254	1601
1970	741	262	1546
1980	684	369	1925

*No Census Data reported   (Source—United States Census 1880—1980)

The dominant geographical feature in Ouray County is the mountains. Natural boundaries define the county on three sides. The San Juan Mountains form the southern and a portion of the western boundary. The other portion of the western boundary is made up of the beginning of the Uncompahgre Plateau. The Cimarrons form the eastern boundary. The only artificially drawn boundary is at the north end of the county at Colona. The altitude of the county ranges from 6300 feet at Colona to 14,150 feet on top of Mt. Sneffels in the San Juans.

Ouray County has only two paved roads and no stoplights. U.S. Highway 550 runs south from Colona through Ridgway to Ouray and then, as the Million Dollar Highway, continues over Red Mountain Pass to Silverton. Colorado Highway 62 starts in Ridgway and goes west over the Dallas Divide to Placerville where it joins Highway 145. Four-wheel-drive roads can take you east over Owl Creek Pass in the Cimarrons or Engineer Pass in the San Juans. If you are brave enough you can jeep over Imogene Pass to Telluride. None of these four-wheel-drive roads are open in the winter and winter storms and avalanches can close the two highways to the south and west. Sometimes the only winter access to Ouray County is from the north through Colona from Montrose.

The mountains are and always have been the reason for Ouray County's existence. To begin with there was gold and silver in those hills. Ouray was a mining town. It existed to provide services to all the miners working in the area. Ridgway developed as a railroad town to service the trains that carried supplies and ore back and forth from the mining towns. It was also a major shipping center for the ranchers' cattle. Before the railroad came to Ridgway the town of Dallas had been the starting point for the wagon trains that served the mines in the San Juans. As Ridgway grew Dallas declined.

The rivers and creeks flowing out of the mountains created the valleys where people settled; along the Uncompahgre, Dallas Creek, and Cow Creek. They also provided irrigation water for the ranchers and farmers around Ridgway and Colona. These people raised the food needed by the people working in and dependent on the mines. The miners and the ranchers have been the two major factions in the county. Their lives were different and they have had their disagreements but their relationship has always been symbiotic, each needed the other.

Today Ouray County is changing. Mining is no longer the major employer; tourism is. The mountains account for that, too. The San Juan Mountains provide some of the most rugged and spectacular scenery available in the United States. The 1500 tourists that come to Ouray daily in the summer come because of those mountains. The hiking and jeeping trails take people high into the mountains to see the scenery and flowers and to explore abandoned mining camps and claims.

Martin Zanin said that in the 1950s, 500 people were employed at the Idarado Mine. The Idarado had two mining sites: one near the top of Red Mountain Pass above Ouray and the other at Telluride. The two were connected by a series of tunnels through the mountains. Now only a skeleton crew works at the two mines, doing maintenance. Many of the old-timers claim that the Idarado still owns rich gold in their claims and that mining will come back in the San Juans.

In its heyday the Camp Bird Mine above Ouray employed 750 men and produced enough money to allow Tom Walsh's daughter, Evalyn, to buy the Hope Diamond. Now it is down from about 100 men last year to less than 20. That has been the history of mining in the San Juans; you can see the evidence of the boom and bust cycle of mining from the population changes in the county. The mines produce for awhile, then close down. The miners come and go. The miners have always been a transient population. The ranchers have been the stable element in Ouray County.

That, however, is changing too. It's more difficult to make a living as a rancher. The equipment is expensive and the price of beef has been marginal for a number of years. Land is getting more expensive. Part of the reason for that is the newcomers. Ouray County has been discovered by people who move here just for the beauty. Many are retirees with independent incomes that allow them to buy land for building sites that once was used as pasture. All but one of the small ranches in

Cow Creek have been combined into four large ranches that are owned by people who live elsewhere. Some of the large holdings are also owned by absentee landlords. Ralph Lauren bought part of the Marie Scott place and now owns around 15,000 acres west of Ridgway. His holdings run west from Dallas Creek up over the Dallas Divide and south to the base of the Sneffels Range. While these are still working ranches, it's a change from when families ran the small spreads. These changes have driven land values up in the county.

At one time there were six towns in Ouray County: Red Mountain Town, Ouray, Portland, Ridgway, Dallas, and Colona. It is said that there once were 2300 registered voters living in Red Mountain Town and Ouray. Not that many people live in the whole county now. Many more people lived at the Camp Bird and Bachelor mines and around the Bachelor Switch. Now there are only two towns, Ouray and Ridgway, plus two unincorporated communities at Colona and Log Hill Village, which is primarily a retirement community.

Many more people have expressed a desire to settle in Ouray County, but it's tough to make a living here. The population is small and the tourist season is only four months long. Many people who feel they can't move here now say they will when they retire. Some are even buying land to get ready for that day. Indeed, Ouray County may grow someday.

While the population of Ouray County has changed, you can still see some of the same traits in the current residents that come through in the stories in this book.

A "sense of community" remains. People are willing to help each other. The old-timers say it isn't as good as it used to be; but, for people moving in from other areas, it seems outstanding. You can also sense an independence and strength in the people living here now. That's essential if you are going to survive. This area is rural and residents are a long way from some of the services most of us were accustomed to when we lived in the city. For all of us that live in Ouray County, these inconveniences don't matter. This is still the best place in the world to live.

FRANK MASSARD AND ALBERT SCHNEIDER

THE PHARMACISTS

This was the first interview conducted and the only one done with two people. I remember going to the interview with a list of questions and finding, after a short time, that my questions were not relevant to where the interview was going. So I let them take me on a magical tour of Ouray during the early 1900s.

We traveled through their recollections of the mines, the town, the businesses, the dances; wherever they wanted to go. It was obvious that they were old friends and had been friends all of their lives. If one of them started a story the other one would either finish it, embellish it, or add another.

About a year after this interview Albert died of cancer. Frank is still active in town and in the church. You can still find him driving his jeep over Red Mountain Pass.

Frank: I was born in Ouray on February 4th, 1897. My family had come to the United States from Switzerland, and settled in Salt Lake City before coming to Ouray. I was the youngest of five children. My two sisters were born in Switzerland and my two older brothers were born in Salt Lake City.

My father was a chef and had cooked in Salt Lake City. I guess things weren't going too well there so an aunt, who lived on a ranch just outside of Ouray, wrote to him and told him to come here. Ouray was an upcoming mining boom town then. They moved and he got a job right away. He cooked at the Beaumont and several of the restaurants in town. When I was born he was the chef at the Office Cafe. That was in the back of what is now the bank building. There was a saloon, called the Corner Saloon, on the corner that opened right into the cafe. There must have been about 3000 people in Ouray at the time; it was a larger town than Montrose then.

Albert: I was born in Ouray on March 25th, 1898. Both of my parents came here from Germany. I don't know what brought my father to Ouray but my mother had an uncle who ranched down the valley at Hohl's Grove at Piedmont. My father was a mining man, a milling man. My parents met and married here in Ouray.

> "... the La Veta Hotel...used to advertise a free meal on any day when there wasn't sunshine in Gunnison."

Growing up here was fun. It was a different town than what we've got now. There were always teams going back and forth to the mine. I don't know how many six-horse teams there were, maybe twenty or thirty, that went back and forth to the mines every day. Then there were mule trains with twenty or thirty mules in a string, packed with lumber, powder, food, supplies, and what not going to the mines. And there were burro trains. They kept all the animals in town. With all the animals in town, there were many large barns. It made it a different atmosphere entirely.

Both of us went to school in Ouray and finished at the same time. We had an exceptionally good school here. The discipline in school was strict. There was no fooling around. They had good teachers and they had good discipline. But we had lots of good times.

As kids we used to ride the ore wagons to the Camp Bird and gather whiskey bottles and demijohns and bring them to town and sell them to the saloon keepers. We got a nickel apiece for the whiskey bottles and a quarter apiece for the demijohns. Those held about a gallon and were covered with wicker. Beer bottles sold for four-for-a-nickel. The saloon keepers refilled those bottles from big barrels and sold them again.

We kept busy all the time. We had to work; everybody worked. Everybody stayed here; nobody left. We also carried in coal for people, mowed lawns, chopped wood, any old thing. There was plenty to do if you wanted to do it.

We used to build cabins out in the woods around here just for our own enjoyment. In the summers we walked over the hill to Lake City to go fishing. We'd pack a couple of burros and be gone for a week or two. It would take us two days to get there and two days to get back. We took the same Engineer Pass road as you use today, only then it was more of a trail.

Probably the most fun we had as kids was to go swimming at the bathhouse. They had an indoor plunge. It was located where the Matterhorn Motel is now and the whole pool was covered. They used to have hot tubs in there, all natural hot water, and the miners would come in there to take their baths in the hot tubs. The plunge had a walkway built around the edge where you could run all the way around it. We used to play games on the walkway. They also had rings on which you could swing out and drop into the pool. But we didn't have bathing suits. It was one sex at a time. They used to rent it a lot to the girls on Second Street. On certain nights they would come up and use the pool.

Second Street looked just like an ordinary street but it came alive at night. There were saloons and dance halls and the teamsters, the single men and the married men, I guess, too, would go in there and dance and buy drinks just like an ordinary bar. If they wanted to go to bed with a gal, they'd just pick their gal and beat it on out and that's all there was to it. It was just part of life, that's really all it was.

Those people stayed in their area; they never intermingled. They never came to a public dance or anything. In the early days when we were in business, the red light district was still going. Those gals were just pretty decent people to deal with, some of them more so than people you'd respect. If they'd tell you a thing, you could believe it. They were right on the up and up. They didn't mix with people in town at all. They'd come into the store and buy their groceries, drugs, or whatever, and that was it. To see them on the street you'd never realize, unless you knew them, that they were anything different from anyone else. You never saw them smoking on the street or anything.

The red light district was right around the corner from the barns. The barns finally burned and were never replaced. Some of the buildings in the red light district burned, too. Some of the rest were torn down, some were wrecked, some of them are still there. There was no call for that type of thing any more; and they just closed it down, that was all. It just dwindled away. The old Coachlight was a bar with a brothel upstairs. Around the corner where the Mattivis live was the Monte Carlo, run by Lily and Louise Morrell.

The red light district was two full blocks on both sides of the street. It was pretty solid with houses and saloons run by different people. They'd each have their own girls. Down the alley behind the vacant lot across from what is now the Silver Nugget were a lot of little houses, called cribs, and a place called the Gold Belt. They had a bar and a dance hall and a little stage where they put on little shows. They had a band that would come up town every night and play. There was a violin, drums, a cornet; maybe four or five men, and they would march around town, up and down Main Street, and play

to attract people, and then go down to the Gold Belt.

There were a lot of big places down there; there was the Club, the Clipper, The Temple of Music, the Monte Carlo, and the Bird Cage. There must have been eight or ten girls in each place; thirty or forty altogether.

The Beaumont was a big attraction in those days. It was built in the 1880s, just before our time. The weather vane at the Beaumont says 1887. Many rich people would come into town on the train in the evening, and they took them to the hotel in carriages, and then took them back to the train in the morning. There were a lot of salesmen in those days, too. Every line of merchandise had a salesman, and they used to stay in the Beaumont. There was an exhibition room there to display their wares. The Western Union Telegraph Office was in there, too. It was a beautiful hotel for its time, but you'll never know because nobody gets in there now.

In those days everything had to be taken to the mines by horse teams. In the wintertime they used sleds. In the spring they'd run their wagons halfway to the Camp Bird and then transfer the load to sleds to take it the rest of the way. They brought the ore back into town on sleds or wagons and loaded it onto boxcars.

It used to be quite a thrill to get to ride the train from Ouray to the Bachelor Switch, just two miles north of town. There was a siding there where they used to load ore from the Bachelor Mine. The ore was trammed down from the mine which was up on the hillside across the road. After the cars were loaded, the freight would come and take the ore to the smelters. We used to ride down there and then walk back. It cost us ten cents to ride that far. That was expensive. A dime was a lot of money in those days.

In those days the trains were separate. They ran a passenger train every day and a freight two or three times a week. It was a narrow gauge, of course. The passenger train would come in every day about five o'clock, stay overnight, and leave about ten in the morning. It ran from Ouray to Salida; that was the end of the line for it. The other train would run from Salida to Ouray at the same time. At Salida you could catch the regular gauge coming from Grand Junction and go to Denver. It took all day to go to Salida; you would get in there about six o'clock in the evening. You would stop for your noon meal at the La Veta Hotel in Gunnison. It was a big, famous hotel at the time. We used to stay there when we played basketball in high school. The hotel was a three- or four-story building that used to advertise a free meal on any day when there wasn't sunshine in Gunnison.

Ouray had nothing like that. But when we were in business and went to Grand Junction for conventions, Mr. Woods, the head of C. D. Smith, used to tell us that when he arrived in Grand Junction, they used to call out on the train platform, "Change trains here for Ouray and Telluride." We were booming and they were just starting out. Things have changed.

In the early days the miners stayed at the mine. There was a huge boardinghouse where they served three meals a day. The men either had rooms or bunks, whatever the mine provided. Payday was every thirty days; and, when they got paid, the men would come to town to spend their wad and would be back up to work on their next shift. They never got a day off, only a night. They worked Sundays, holidays, all straight through.

When we worked at the Atlas, we only lost one shift, on the 4th of July, in the thirteen months we were up there. When we used to come to the dances, we would walk or dogtrot down to town, dance all night, then hire a horse after the dance, and go back on shift the next morning. It cost two dollars to rent a horse. When you got to the mine anyone who needed a horse to get back to town got one free. If no one needed the horse you just looped the reins over the saddle horn, turned the horse loose, and it came back to town on its own. We'd come down to the dances maybe twice a month if the weather was nice.

The dances were good, great. They had nice dances at the Elks, at the Opera House, and at what they used to call the K. P. Hall. That was a two-story building around the corner from where the telephone exchange is now. It was owned by the Knights of Pythias and had a hall downstairs as well as upstairs. It was a popular place for dances.

Most of the dances had an orchestra. Occasionally, our Saturday night dances only had a piano player such as Ned Bradley or George Chilcotte. We usually had a four- or five-piece orchestra with a violin, a clarinet, maybe a cornet, drums, and always a piano.

The popular dances were the two step, the waltz, and occasionally a schottische. We always had circle dances. Everybody joined hands and someone called the dance. You'd dance with your partner on the right, or you'd grab your partner across the hall; it was fun. You'd get all mixed together.

They charged the men a dollar for the whole evening of dances; the women paid nothing. You could come by yourself or get yourself a gal and go. There was a lot of intermingling. You knew everybody. If somebody came to town that you didn't know, you'd soon find out who it was or they would make themselves known. Now so many people are coming in and out all the time that you just don't know everybody. Then you knew everybody, even though the town was bigger.

We used to go to Ridgway to dances, too. We'd spend the evening down there. It took an hour to an hour and a half to go each way in a horse and buggy. When we went to funerals, we'd pack a lunch and take a team. It took all day to go to Ridgway for a funeral. Ridgway was a railroad town with more people than there are now and much more of a business town. It's sort of dwindled away—just like the rest of us.

At that time the Rio Grande Southern went through each day on its way to Telluride, over Lizard Head, and on to Durango. Another train would come through the opposite way each day. The freights hauled all the ore out of Telluride. It was quite a deal. Lots of stock from the Norwood area would be loaded at Placerville to be brought to Ridgway to be shipped on the D&RG. The railroad had a regular repair house for the engines in Ridgway; it took quite a crew to take care of that. The roundhouse was down by the track just across the way from the old depot.

After we got out of high school, we went to work in the mines. We worked at the Atlas; that's where the

The Atlas Mill in winter.

old wreck of a mill stands before you get to Yankee Boy Basin. The mine was on the hill above the mill and had a tram running down from the mine to the mill. Both of us worked at the mill for about thirteen months. The ore was brought down to the mill on the tram and the buckets were unloaded. Then the ore went through the crusher and then through the ball mill or stamps. We called them batteries, sophisticated you know, but they were just stamps that ground the ore. From there it went on into the Harding Mill which ground it finer, then on through the flotation and over the Wilfley shaker tables where the waste would be run off, and finally into the big, huge tanks. Then there were men who backed the ore cars under the big bins and moved the ore out to the chute. They put the ore down the long chute to the warming house that was steam heated and where the concentrate was dried. After the concentrate was dried, it was sacked and the six-horse ore teams took the sacks down to town.

I worked every job in the mill, started on the tram and then worked in the tram house. I ran the batteries and I ran the flotation. It was interesting work. I enjoyed it. I was making about $150.00 a month and I quit to take a $65.00 a month job driving a grocery store wagon. I remember the first time I had to put the hames onto the collar of the horse. I put them on backwards and I think everybody in town was watching. It was the first time I ever hooked up a horse and wagon.

Frank: My first job was helping empty the tanks. It was about as dirty a job as you could get and hard, too. We took the ore out of the tanks, put it down the chute, and raked it over the steam pipes to dry it; then it would be sacked. It was a rough job, you knew you had been somewhere at the end of the day. The tanks were half as big as a room and the concentrate was like wet sand. It wouldn't run down the chute by itself, it was so sticky. You had to rake it down with hoes. There were about one hundred long steps in the chute that you had to pull the ore down. I was stuck with that for awhile, several months, and then I helped my brother-in-law. He was the electrician there and I was the electrician's helper. That was much more interesting and a lot easier. We'd get out and around and be different places. From there I went to the Army in World War I. We didn't go at the same time. We went separately.

When we began working at the Atlas, it paid $3.00 a day with $1.00 for board so that left us $2.00. Then they took another $1.00 a month off for hospital fees which left you $59.00. That was it, and you worked every day of the month for that. As you got better jobs, as on the flotation, you got another 50 cents an hour. That was about $75.00 a month. Some of the natives were teaching school in the mountains at the Atlas, Revenue, or Camp Bird for $60.00 a month and they stayed up there the whole time.

I went to France for about eighteen months. I made it back all right with no problems at all. I enjoyed seeing France and seeing what I could see. I didn't get to see Paris which I felt badly about. We were quite close to Paris at one time, but they didn't allow us a pass to go so we were stuck. I was also close to Switzerland at the time. I'd hoped I'd be able to get into there, but I wasn't able to get a pass to go. I still had some relatives, my dad's sisters, living there and I'd hoped to be able to meet them but I never did. I don't know how I would have talked to them if I had met them. It was just one of those things. Then we got back home and went mining again.

We went to Paradox to work in the uranium mines. We had a lot of fun. We had a tent with a wooden bottom where three of us slept. When we were there, we were mining vanadium. They used that in hardening steel. That was a black ore and, of course, uranium came with it. We were just throwing that uranium ore on the dump. They were just using it for pigment in paint in those days. We handled that stuff, and now they've got to move it if they see a speck of it. We think that's kind of crazy because no one thought anything of it then at all, and no one seems to have been hurt by it. I think they just try to make too much of it. We've got a piece of yellow cake right outside the house and it's been there for I don't know how long. Doesn't seem to hurt anybody but who knows.

We kind of got tired of mining and had a chance to buy a drugstore so we formed a partnership and bought the Corner Store next to the Variety. It was a separate store then; they weren't connected. Both of us had worked in a drugstore before and kind of liked it. We opened on January 1st, 1920 and ran it for forty-three years, quitting in 1963. We ran a pharmacy, both of us are pharmacists. We chose that only because that was available. We had to make a living. Living in Ouray, the only other thing you could do was go into the mines and we had had enough of that.

We had a hotel above the store where we rented rooms for $30.00 a month. That included heat and lights, a stove, and what not. That was unbelievable. There was a restaurant in the building where Cecilia's is now. We put that in and rented it. It was successful while we were there.

We also ran a picture show where the Variety is now. We ran silent movies for three or four years. We used to have to crank the films through and we had an orchestra: three pieces with a piano, clarinet, and violin. They tried to play something that would match what was going on on the screen. If it was a wild horse race, they'd play something typical to go along with it. If it was something sad, they'd get into that. The movies would last one and a half or two hours. We cranked the film through and changed films, one reel at a time. If it was a seven-reel movie, you changed your reel seven times. It wasn't continuous at all. We charged 20 cents and for specials on Sunday nights we raised it to 35 cents. The special movies were the ones that were unusual: Jackie Cooper, for instance, or Tom Mix. We did a good show business. We'd have a fairly good house full regularly. The movies changed three or four times a week. We'd ship the old movies to Denver and they would ship us a new set. We had them booked ahead of time. Seven nights a week we ran a show at the Isis Theater.

When we were kids, there used to be a theater here. I remember Rico; he used to stand there and explain the picture to people, give a running talk with the picture.

Every once in a while, we'd have vaudeville. People would come through and we'd book them and they'd put on a show on the stage. They'd tell a few jokes, put on a little skit, do a dance with, maybe, somebody jiggling. Then they'd be gone the next day.

In 1926 they put in the Ouray pool. They sold memberships in the Ouray Recreation Association. They wanted to build a pool and they had problems doing it, so they went around to the different merchants and asked for donations. We didn't have much to give so we signed a promissory note for $400.00 that we would pay over time, at $10.00 a month. They were going to let us have free swims if we agreed to donate; but, after things didn't go well, they cut that out. The pool worked out but not as fast or as well as they hoped it would. The pool never closed down except the one time when they had the flood that filled it. The tent bathhouses for changing were floating around in the pool after the flood. That was the only time the pool filled up. The Skyrocket flood was in 1929. It came along with the crash.

When the depression came, we were already so far down that we hardly noticed it. Ouray had been deteriorating for a long time and it gradually went down. There just wasn't much mining anymore. It was getting worse instead of better. There were still some mines working, but it was never on the up. It was always on the downhill slide, never as good as it had been.

When the bank holiday hit in 1933, it was tough for everybody. Pretty slim pickin's, that was all. All the banks closed. Our bank closed for two or three days with the bank holiday everywhere; then it opened up again. Our bank was financially alright, or it took care of things alright. There was no problem, just tough on them, just like the rest of us.

The WPA started at that time and it tided a lot of people over for quite a long time. Quite a few good projects were done, too. They channeled the river down by the depot, all by hand labor. They built bridges and things of that sort. I think it would be a good thing today rather than just dole it out to them. They don't want it and we don't want it. They'd get a lot of things done that need to be done for the same money. All our streets and roads need fixing. There's plenty of work to do if they would just put people to work. The only way you have good times is when people are working.

Most of the men working for the WPA were single miners who had been laid off from the mines and were just hanging around town. There was no place for them to go. When temperance came in, bootlegging came in. That was a fruitful valley. That kept a lot of them going. There were a lot of stills. They sold liquor in town and hauled it out in cars. Nobody got rich on it. I don't think anybody made a fortune on bootlegging, they just made a living, that was all.

Ouray just hung on during the depression. A mine

would open up; another one would shut down. There weren't any mining booms at all. What really put us back on track was when the Idarado started. That was during World War II and they needed ore and minerals. The government came in and started a crew working and they found what they wanted. The Newmont Company was going to do the work for the government; but when they saw what they had, they bought out the government's lease and took it over and ran it. We think there is still ore there if they could get started again. Of course, as far as Newmont is concerned, they're just too big to want to fool with it any more. I think a smaller company could take it over and make some money on it. I believe they think so too because they're still keeping their skeleton crews on our side and the Telluride side to keep it open. Sometime, maybe, something will happen.

Both of us got married shortly after we opened the store. Both of us married school teachers. They were teaching here and would go to the dances.

Albert: I met my wife on the way to Gunnison, on the train. She was coaching the girls and I was coaching the boys. That's how I met my wife: basketball. I got married in 1921 and Frank got married in 1922.

Tourism became popular with the coming of the automobile. They had always had excursions in here with the train but the automobile is really the thing that brought the tourists in. That must have been in the thirties. It seems like tourism is growing every year. More motels are being built, more accommodations for them,

food, things for them to do, the rental of jeeps; that all adds to it, brings people here. As the population increases in the cities, people have to get out. That's why they come here, buy homes, and spend their summers here. That will continue; that's going to be our lifeblood. If we could find something to keep them here a little more in the wintertime, we'd do better. We always had big 4th of July celebrations and we had Elks conventions here that were big things. We had lots of big hotels: the Beaumont, the St. Elmo, the Western, and the Belvedere, where the Coachlight is now. Then there were the rooming houses; there were two on Second Street, the Mountain View and the Traveler's Home. There seemed to be plenty of places for people to stay.

Both of us have served as mayor of Ouray. It has had a good city government.

Frank: I was on the city council when we got the grant for the new emergency services building and auditorium. I was happy to have a part of that.

Albert: One of the best things that happened when I was mayor was acquiring Box Canyon. Some of the people were in favor of leasing it and others were not. We had public meetings and decided that if someone else could make a go of it, so could we. Once we controlled it, we started charging admission and that's been a profitable thing over the years. That and the pool. Someone told me they had 500 people here from Delta on the free day. I can't imagine 500 people up here in the winter.

There used to be a pavilion at Box Canyon where we

21

had dances and public meetings. It had windows that could be opened or closed. You could have it open for most things but still waterproof and windproof if you needed it. The people in town would go over there for dances or big parties on Saturday or Sunday. It was a lot of fun.

In the old days, people were all more or less on the same level. You didn't have the vast difference between the poor and the rich. There were both but not as pronounced as it is today in the cities. They were just people that specialized in their way of life; had something to give and they gave it.

We were close in those days. We never felt isolated, but we didn't have many places to go and couldn't go if we wanted to. Now you can get in your car and get to Grand Junction in a couple of hours. Then it was a whole day's trip to get to Grand Junction, maybe more, and it was a real effort. Even going to Silverton was a day's trip on the stage if you could do it. That was a rare thing to do. You were really stuck here all the time and I'm sure the sister towns, Silverton and Telluride, were the same way. You just lived here, that was all; this was your home. You knew everything about everybody else. That may not have been so good in some cases, but it wasn't that bad.

The communication between these mountain towns was good, especially in the summertime. In the summer months, we had intertown baseball games and every town had a band. We ran excursions every Sunday between Ouray, Silverton, and Telluride. If we got to Mon-trose once a year to the fair, that was a big deal. We'd save up all year to earn money to go to that. The first thing we'd do when we went to the Montrose Fair was run to a place where they rented bicycles and we'd ride all around town. Just think of what it meant in those early days to go up to Ironton or Red Mountain and to see that there were a thousand people in that area at one time. Now the whole town of Ironton is wiped out. Now no one even mentions that it was there and that was a big town. There was a big town at Portland, too. We used to go up to Ironton to hunt rabbits. They had their own school, a church, a fire department, their own waterworks, many, many saloons and grocery stores. It was quite a town.

We don't think anybody can really understand what life here was like unless they lived it; everything that went to make life go on, the things you did and the things people did, and the activity that had to go on to keep things going. We can't tell you the things we did as kids and we can't tell you about our schools and of the notoriety that this school has had over the years. Some prominent people have gone from this school here in Ouray and made their marks elsewhere. A governor of Colorado graduated from Ouray and several state officials. And think of the college teachers who have graduated from school here and gone on to teach at Vassar, the University of Kentucky and Minnesota. You have to know things like that to know what went on here.

We don't know if we want to compare Ouray to what it was. We like it the way it is or we wouldn't stay here.

We'd like to see mining come back but don't think it ever will; at least, we'll never see the mining town the old Ouray was. The only way we'll go on is with tourism; there is nothing else here that will bring people in. Just the scenery and a comfortable, decent place to live. When we were first married we always kind of thought, well, maybe someday we can move to California or someplace else, but we just kept getting in deeper and deeper here and this was it. Now we just like to live here and keep it the kind of place that it is.

BARBARA SPENCER

POSTMASTER

Barbara is a friendly, outgoing woman who lives just up from the lumberyard in a beautiful house that is surrounded by flowers. The house is full of pictures and furniture and has plenty of room for guests. It seems as if the coffeepot is always on and a place is ready for visitors who drop by frequently. Barbara is as warm and friendly as the house and has a way of talking that is both witty and self-deprecating. Her stories about living at the Camp Bird tell much about the effect of a woman in a mining camp.

I was born on November 20, 1916 in Rico, Colorado. My mother had been born in Rico, so I was the second generation born in that town. My father was superintendent of the Rico Argentine Mine.

When I was 18 months old, my father was given a job as superintendent of a mine in Georgia so we packed up and moved. In those days you moved in barrels and

"On the 4th of July there was a dance at the Elks Club and one at Box Canyon. You went to both. I tell you, walking down from Box Canyon at 2:00 o'clock in the morning after you'd been dancing since 9:00 in high heels was something. You just walked home on your ankles."

trunks and went on the train. You packed all your china in excelsior, those thin, curly wood shavings, and put it in a barrel. Mother said that almost everything got there safely; but one out of every set was broken: one cup, one plate, one everything.

For mother, a western girl who had been brought up in Rico, going to Georgia was something. She even had a pair of silk stockings to wear on the trip.

We were in Georgia during the flu epidemic at the end of World War I. Many of the people there were quite poor. Houses were built on little stilts and the epidemic was rife in the community. Mother put a mask over her nose and went out to help with the people. Finally my Dad got the flu and mother had to stay home with him. I never did get sick and neither did she.

From Georgia we moved to southern Illinois where my father worked at a fluorspar mine for several years.

My mother used say that for years, when she lived in Rico and came down through the valley on the train,

25

she would look up toward Ouray and wish she could visit there. In 1920 we came to Ouray in the summer, went back to Illinois, then moved to Ouray in 1921, and this has been home ever since.

We came west from Illinois in a seven-passenger Studebaker. Every night you would stop at a hotel or a rest home some place and exchange information with the group coming from the other way. There was no concrete highway, only dirt, and it was filled with bog holes. If you got caught in one of those bog holes, you had to be pulled out. The route we followed was the Pikes Peak Ocean to Ocean Highway. It was marked by colored rings on telephone or power poles which showed you where to turn in all the towns.

My dad had rigged a tarp for the side of the car and we had all the camping equipment packed on the running board so we slept out on the trip. It was fun.

I don't remember much about Ouray when we arrived, but we stayed in the Beaumont and the St. Elmo when my dad was looking over the jobs. He came here to work for the Camp Bird and was an agent for Evalyn Walsh Maclean's properties. He and a friend, Charlie Jordan, also worked the Hidden Treasure.

That summer when I was five we spent some time up in the Walsh cabin at the upper Camp Bird. One day my mother and Gertrude Jordan made some apricot sherbet. They were proud of themselves since there was little to work with up there, and they could hardly wait for the men to come home for supper. They served it with great pride but neither fellow was en-thusiastic. It turned out that Charlie didn't like apricots and my dad didn't like sherbet.

I don't remember much about living up there. The cabins were rough but comfortable. They had coal stoves. I remember playing out in the yard with a broken-down doll buggy. Going up into the hills with the odor of plants and flowers still evokes memories of that place in the high country.

That fall we moved into what's called the Homer Reed house. It was an Idarado property on Oak Street. I'd walk down a trail on the hillside and across the railroad bridge on my way to kindergarten.

We moved away when I was in the first grade but moved back for the second grade, and then I went all the way through school here.

The school then was square with four rooms on the first floor. One for the first and second grade, one for the third and fourth grade, one for the fifth and sixth, and one for the seventh and eighth. Then when you reached this exalted status, you went upstairs to high school.

There was no such thing as junior high school in those days. A lot of people went to the eighth grade and stopped. That's the reason they started junior high school. It was to be a bridge between grade school and high school so there wouldn't be a place to stop and so the children would be lured into high school and finish. But by the eighth grade, you were supposed to be able to know enough reading so you could read the classics; enough writing so you could write a business letter or social correspondence; enough arithmetic so you could run a business — all the fractions, all the decimals, all the equivalent parts — so you could really take over a business and run it with ability.

We had good teachers in the school; the faculty was small, but excellent. The eighth grade teacher had a great responsibility to make sure those kids knew enough to make a living. The teachers put an emphasis on music. There wasn't too much emphasis on science. It was presented, but the drive wasn't there for science education.

After we moved from the Homer Reed house, we lived in a house up on Third Street. Then when I was eight or nine, my folks bought the house Alvin and Marian Gray McCoy lived in on the corner of 5th Street and 5th Avenue. That was the house I really grew up in; that was home. The rest were just rented houses. My husband and I sold it after my folks died.

I remember pulling my sled all the way to the top of the hill and coasting all the way through town down to the depot. There were few cars, only the ore wagons to look out for. On the corners, you would drag one foot to turn your sled, and you could come lickety split down the hill.

The mail came in on the train at 5:00 o'clock at night. You'd know when to go for the mail because the whistle would blow down at the Bachelor Switch and again at the American Nettie Mill. Everybody would start congregating at the post office and lean against the wall and wait for the postmaster and her helpers to put up the mail. Everybody was down there. I would go down on my sled, especially at Christmas time, to get the packages. And if you got a package notice in your box, then you importantly walked around to the window, and everybody would start eyeballing your package.

It was fun; and, of course, in those days, you were sure-footed and the cold didn't matter. I remember walking up the hills; and, since you didn't wear slacks, my knees would be so cold, I couldn't feel them.

In those days, you wore skirts and heavy underwear. When I was younger, we wore leggings, too. They were soft fleece with a strap that went underneath the foot and they buttoned to the knee. There were lots of buttons; you used a buttonhook and you buttoned and you buttoned and you buttoned. I'm telling you, trying to get those things on and get to school on time, that was something.

I can't remember what we wore for boots but in high school we had galoshes. You didn't buckle them all the way; you turned the tops down and left the tops unbuckled. When you walked in them, they went swish, swish, swish; that was very in.

When you were a child, you held up your stockings with what was called a pantywaist. Your hose were hooked to garters that came from that, and your panties buttoned around the waist. Then elastic came in, and that solved that. I remember in high school a girl named Geneve came to spend a winter or two here. She brought in a lot of outside ideas. I was horrified. She would roll her stockings below the knees. My, did you ever hear of such a thing? She was immensely popular. Everybody thought she had all these wonderful ideas and she was an interesting girl besides.

In the first six weeks, when I was a freshman in high school, I had scarlet fever. There were only two cases in town. The other was a girl six or eight years older than I; I hardly even knew her to speak to her. We had no idea where those two cases came from. Quarantine was quarantine in those days. I was in bed and quarantined for six weeks. The only ones into my room were the doctor and my mother. She was up and down and up and down those stairs. I was spoiled. My hair came out and everybody consoled me by saying that it would surely come in curly. There were other lies told to me.

Curly hair was in. It was after I was a freshman that permanent waves came in. Oh, was that the answer to a girl whose hair was so straight that it bent back the other way. That was a big thing. When you got through, your hair was frizzy and your eyes were drawn tight; but, oh, you had this curl. It was great.

We always had fun when I was a child. I feel sorry for the youngsters who say, "There's nothing to do here, you must entertain me." We were a lively group. Picnics always. Eight or ten or fifteen of us would go hiking and take a picnic lunch and then walk back just for the fun of walking. We swam as soon as they built the pool. Every Friday the children in Ouray were permitted to go for free. All you had to do was bring your towel and walk in. So we swam a lot.

I don't know whose concept it was, but it took a lot of donated labor to put that pool down there with that hot water. A lot of people in town bought bonds to help and never cashed them in. My mother was the chairman of the celebration when they were going to open the pool. Just as they started, it began to rain but my mother said, "We're going to have this party, come hell or high water."

We had parties at each other's homes. We played; there would be excellent refreshments; there'd be music, and there would be card games. It was up to you to think up a little something different each time. Sometimes there would be dancing if the homes were large enough. There would always be birthday parties and some of them were quite elaborate. The mothers went to a great deal of effort.

The ladies also had a lot of bridge parties, big ones of four and five tables. And luncheons, the kind you read about that bring nostalgia. I wonder today how those women did it: the hot rolls, the fresh butter, and all the little extra touches to those tables. Mrs. MacLennan always said, "Mrs. Buskirk served doilies, but I served grub."

I played on the girls' basketball team in high school. I was chosen to be the center because I was the tallest of them all. But I was not a natural athlete; that was all too evident. We played schools like Telluride and Norwood. We usually drove to the games. Nearly everybody in town had a car, even though they cost $700 or $800.

I never worked much as a teenager; a lot of kids didn't.

I picked raspberries and I used to help at the swimming pool as one of the check girls. But my dad took care of us so I didn't have to work.

One of the women in town had a nephew who came to Ouray in the summertime. He had TB. He was from Mississippi where the moist air was not conducive to good health so the family sent him out here for help, which it did. One of his sisters was a dress designer, working in St. Louis. But all she did was work on kitchen dresses. A friend of my mother's wrote this girl and asked her if she would design my graduation dress. She was pleased to do it, but on graduation night we were still waiting for the train because the dress still wasn't here. I'd had a note saying hang tight until the 17th. There were phone calls to Anna Richardson at the post office who said, "I'll let you know, I'll let you know." And sure enough, there it finally was. Somebody flew down the street, got it, brought it up, and pressed it. It fit perfectly. It was an off-white, Grecian chiffon with heavy, double satin bands across the front, tied in a bow in back, and went down into streamers through the skirt. Absolutely beautiful! It's still downstairs in the trunk.

Our high school graduation was in the Opera House. Our proms were there also. Walter Wheeler would lead the grand march for the prom. He knew how from all the old rounds and square dances. He knew how to build a really grand march that gave everybody a chance to get up and walk around and blend. The ladies could get up and show their dresses and the men could show nice little bows, and everybody felt pretty elegant. The grand march would last for, perhaps, ten or fifteen minutes. It wasn't just once through lightly. This was an important opening of the prom. Mothers and fathers came to the proms. Younger sisters and brothers came; all the gay blades came. The music was good; it was live and lively. Usually there was a piano, a clarinet or saxophone, and a violin. Sometimes a drum-

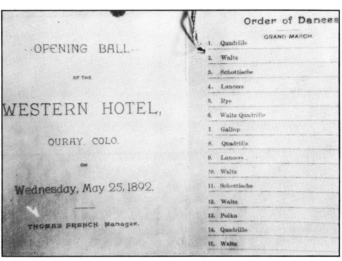

OPENING BALL

OF THE

WESTERN HOTEL,

OURAY, COLO.

ON

Wednesday, May 25, 1892.

THOMAS FRENCH, Manager.

Order of Dances

GRAND MARCH

1. Quadrille
2. Waltz
3. Schottische
4. Lancers
5. Rye
6. Waltz Quadrille
7. Gallop
8. Quadrille
9. Lancers
10. Waltz
11. Schottische
12. Waltz
13. Polka
14. Quadrille
15. Waltz

Dance card for the Opening Ball.

mer. You would watch the dancers like Tuffy and Thelma Flor and Frank Rice who was deaf but could feel the vibrations through the floor. He danced very nicely.

The Elks Club had lots of dances. They had a Christmas dance, a New Year's Eve dance, a pre-Easter or post-Easter dance, and the big Elks Annual in June which was a private affair, beautifully put on, and very elaborate. They did themselves well in those days. My father was an Elk and we went to all the dances. Everybody went: the Massards, the Schneiders, the Driscolls, the Franzs. People came up from down the valley. They were always well attended. Each lady had to have one or two gowns every year. It would never do to be seen wearing the same gown time after time. On the 4th of July there was a dance at the Elks Club and one at Box Canyon. You went to both. I tell you, walking down from Box Canyon at 2:00 o'clock in the morning after you'd been dancing since 9:00 in high heels was something. You just walked home on your ankles. There used to be a pavilion at Box Canyon with an enclosed dance floor. Those dances used to keep us busy, and you lost your heart many the time to some fellow who looked pretty nifty.

It was quiet in Ouray during the 1920s. The mines were down, building up to the Depression. Those were hard times. My dad worked on a fluorspar mine called the Cragmont, putting in a tram. There's no trace of it now. When I was small I rode in that tram with my mother. The tram line ran over towers in a continuous loop. As the heavy buckets, which were as big as a table, came down filled with ore they would pull the empty buckets up. You could ride up in the buckets or they could send up groceries, mail, tools, dynamite, or whatever was needed. I don't remember much about the tram ride except you had to be careful as the bucket swung in because it jerked a bit and then would go on up. I guess I didn't think much about it except that it's my dad's; one that he had built.

He had a cook up there, Mrs. Art Wright, a lady from England. She was small, delicately boned, petite, and tough as whang leather. She'd come from the working class, an excellent cook, and ruled her kitchen and boarders with an iron hand. My dad walked all the way around her. She had worked at the Camp Bird, too. If you went up there and the superintendent wanted to ask you to stay for lunch, he had to clear it with her first. She could use language that would melt the ears off a brass monkey. Oh, my. That's why they called her Mrs. Cussin' Wright. We used to borrow her shovel and dish pan and slide down the snowbank. When she'd have enough of that, she'd take her things; but we'd take them right square back. That was funny.

My dad later ran a prospect up at the Lucky 20 and the Guadalupe in Ironton Flat, in the gulch just before that old stone garage. They had a telephone up there so he could phone my mother every night. One of the fellows who worked at the Guadalupe had a very pious wife, an evangelist, as a matter of fact. She'd get out here on the street corner with her family and sing and hold meetings. She was respected but nobody paid her a great deal of attention. She would call up her husband and sing hymns over the telephone, play the organ, and read scripture. The other men wanted to get to the telephone to call their wives to hear what they had to say, but she would just go on and on. Finally, the fellows at one of the other mines learned to take the old receiver off the hook and put it against the mouthpiece. That produced a scream you wouldn't believe. That was the way to solve that problem.

My dad, at that time, had a pair of long skis, eighteen feet long, as I recall. One of the skis was hardwood and other was pine. As he would ski across Ironton, the hardwood ski would slide beautifully but the pine one would drag. He was short and square and it was hard work for him to ski, but that was the way he got home since the road wasn't kept open. He had to come down to town every two weeks or so for the mail. He had to take care of business dealings, since the lease was in his name; and he had to work with the owners and financiers to keep the mine going.

My dad was a great joiner. He was an exalted ruler of the Elks, worshipful master of the Masons, and president of the Rotary Club. He was County Commissioner for 16 years and was president of the State County Commissioners Association. He was into politics, a Democrat clear up to here.

My mother used to point out that none of that brought in any money. As he'd go out to one meeting or another at night, she'd say, "You're going out to save the world again." As we would drive past the poor farm down there by the cemetery, my mother would refer to that, with some apprehension in her voice, as the old prospector's home.

During the depression, my dad was running the American Nettie Mine which was going well so there was no problem for us. Some people were having hard times; but, really, the depression never really hit home. Everybody was poor; nobody had great, huge stacks of money, but we were able to eat. In those days it was customary for the prospectors in town to charge their groceries; then, when you made your shipment and the check came back from the smelter, you paid off the grocer. The bill might keep getting higher and higher, but that didn't keep people from entertaining. They entertained well even if there wasn't any caviar and a notable lack of champagne. There might be home brew, if you were into that sort of thing, but it was never served in my folk's home.

I never knew anything about 2nd Street when I was growing up. I was carefully reared, and it was never mentioned at home or in our groups. I think I was not the only girl in town that did not know anything about it, had no idea. There were stables and things down there; but, unless you needed a horse for something or other, you weren't down in that area. I guess I was married before I knew much about it.

When I was a teenager, Frank and Albert had the post office store. It had a soda fountain. At one time they had a line of phonographs. They sold magazines and the *Denver Post*. They had boys take the Post around to your home every day. I think it cost 65 cents a month.

Next to that, in the Variety Store, they had the Isis Theater. That's where you saw all the Saturday serials, all the cliff hangers. That was where I saw my first Walt Disney film; it was the "Three Little Pigs." I watched the wolf's face turn blue when he blew so hard; my dad laughed so hard that I thought he was going to fall out of that chair and roll down the aisle. There was music in that film; but, before that, Elsie Sonza and her sister Marie used to play for the silent films in the theater. They had had training so they could watch the screen and play; it was special. Elsie played for everything, funerals and all the organizations. She sang at weddings. She had won state-wide honors.

There was a dry goods store and a shop that advertised fashionable hats. Mr. MacLennan ran a tailor shop, Mr. McCaffrey ran the barbershop, and Mr. Witherspoon ran the jewelry shop. A. A. Moule ran a drugstore, he was a registered pharmacist while the post office store boys were not. Later, as medicine got to be a little more scientific and complicated, they studied on their own and took the tests to be registered pharmacists, too.

Julius Sonza ran a grocery store and the Nichol-Smith Mercantile was where Duckett's Market is now. There was a bakery next door. They had the best doughnuts and the best macaroons. The baker smoked cigarettes and wasn't always too careful so ashes got into the dough, but you always bought a loaf of bread. He made the best bread. That was where I saw my first bread slicing machine. You put the bread up in the top and gravity brought it down. It was nifty.

We used to go to Montrose to buy our dresses at Humphrey's. Humphrey's used to be in Ouray; but, because times were hard and there was a wider market there, they moved to Montrose. We still had that seven-passenger Studebaker with side curtains and a cloth top. My mother knew how to drive, and she could maneuver that big old bathtub down the road. She would drive it up the hill in the summertime to where my dad was working. There was one place in the Ruby Walls that is still kind of a sharp turn where she would have to back up to get that old thing around. The road wasn't very wide; but, on the other hand, there wasn't much traffic.

There was a cigar and tobacco shop and a barbershop in the Beaumont Hotel. If you had top guests, you took them to the Beaumont for dinner and, of course, that was where they stayed. It was beautiful inside. There was a big desk with a high arch over it. There were stairways coming from two sides of the mezzanine. After the prom, coming down that stairway in your prom dress, you were like Cinderella, the queen of everything. The dining room itself was lovely, the food good, and ambience special.

They used to have dinner dances at the Beaumont, but the balls were held in the Opera House. The Opera House was pretty much as it is now except there were two, huge, coal stoves in there then, one on the side where you went into the dressing rooms and one on the side where you came up the stairs. It's a wonder someone wasn't burned to death. Those things glowed red hot.

For my first two years of college, I went to Colorado College in Colorado Springs. Then my dad, who was a Mormon, said he would like for me to go to BYU to be close to his folks and find out what great people they were. You didn't visit back and forth like we do now. They were great people and I was treated well there. It was a great experience. . .but I'm Presbyterian.

I was upset when I found out there were no dormitories at BYU. We lived in private homes. Seven of us lived in this one house and there were seven daughters in the family, too. I found out that one of my housemates was dating a fellow, seriously dating, and he had taken her to meet all the wives of his father. My mouth fell open because I knew a law had been passed about that sort of thing years and years before. I wrote home to mymother and she said, "Oh, yes, the same thing happened to me." She had mentioned it to my grandmother who said, "That's true, the law went in; and we must obey the law; but what did you want us to do with all those extra wives when the law went in, take them out and shoot them?" I found out later that some of my grandfathers had plural wives.

After college I taught school in Montrose for a year; then I taught at the Camp Bird. I lived there during the week. There was a boardinghouse up there; upstairs, where the cook and his wife lived. I had a room of my own. It was just beautiful up there at the mine. There were no street lights; and, at night, there would be soft snow coming down through the trees with lights from the windows on that snow; it would be like some toy-maker's village in Bavaria or the Alps. After one of those heavy snowfalls, when the sun would come up in the morning, it would just be pink. It was something.

I taught kids of all ages. There weren't students in every grade; but, because all of them passed, I ended up teaching all eight grades in the two years I was there. That worked out fine because the little kids sit there and listen and learn from the older ones; it's a much better concept than what we have today. I had all the lessons set up and approved by the superintendent here in town and we had approved textbooks; so it was just a matter of progressing from day to day. The little folks understood what they were to do and I set up a certain amount of homework so the parents would know that I was really on the ball. There were never any rules for me from the school district. I was a local girl and had been well reared; they just expected me to conduct myself like a lady, which I did to some extent.

The school had outdoor plumbing, and I brought water in and filled a stoneware jar for drinking water. It was up to me to build the fires and get the wood although I was spoiled. The guys at the mine looked after me well.

The school was under the Schoolhouse Slide and I kept telling the kids what to do in case a slide came down. I told them to get under their desks; I thought that would be the only chance for them to have any air and protection from the weight of the snow or if the roof caved in; the only thing to protect those tiny little bones. It never ran while I was there. The kids went home and told their parents about my warnings, and it wasn't long before we moved out of that schoolhouse.

I ate with the men in the boardinghouse. The food was excellent. The mines always saw that the men had nourishing food, excellent food. Steaks were something special but were not uncommon. We always had cakes and excellent pancakes. I would sit and pour tea and coffee for the men from the pitchers sitting there, but I preferred milk. I offered milk to all the men and they got so they were enjoying it. One night Charlie Bell sat down at the table; his family had gone some place and he was eating with us. He was tall, slender, cadaverous-looking really, with big, black circles around his eyes. I poured the milk for the men as usual and he looked down there in horror at all his macho miners drinking milk. He said, "What's the matter with you? Have you not been weaned yet?" All the guys shrunk back and I was ready to take him on; but, fortunately, someone intervened.

There were a number of other women living at the Camp Bird; the cook's wife and there were a number of families living in houses at the mine. I played a lot of bridge with the women.

The miners were rough and sturdy but nice to meet and easy to get along with. There was a recreation hall at the mine. It had a piano, billiard tables, a library, card tables, all that sort of thing. You could go in there every evening. It was warm and comfortable; it was steam heated. The rooms were steam heated; there was hot water for baths, tongue-and-groove siding on the walls; this was top stuff.

The men could go into the recreation room to play cards, visit, and read. I was in there one time and one of my beaus was trying to teach me to play pool; that didn't take. A couple of fellows offered to teach me to play euchre. I just eyeballed those fellows and instinctively knew enough to say, no thank you. I got periodic offers to teach me to play and I noticed that they always came just after I'd had a payday.

I came down to town on the weekends and sometimes we would come down just to go to a show. I came down with the miners in a sedan. There would be so many of us in there so we could work our way back up with all that weight. One time Waterhole had run so one of the men and I took horses back to the mine. When we got to the slide, we had to turn the horses loose and walk across the slide and on up to Camp Bird. I couldn't walk; I couldn't catch my breath. But the man, his name was Freeman, waited for me under those slides each time as I caught my breath.

One Friday night I got on my skis and skied to town. It was snowing heavy wet flakes. This was along in the winter and the snow was so heavy and wet that I couldn't ski very well; I just had to slog along. I got down around the Drinking Cup when a big dishpan full of snow came off and went plop right in front of me. I moved out of there in a hurry and got on down. I met some men coming up to the Mineral Farm Mine. In those days, with no four-wheel drive, the men were standing outside on the car to hold it down in the snow so they could make it up. It was just beautiful with the car lights shining on the snow on the branches of the trees. When I came down Jim Brown hill, I had a hard time getting my skis to hit that little narrow bridge. I just dropped there but before long my husband-to-be and his brother came along. My mother had gotten nervous and sent them out to look for me. I had started at 4:00 o'clock and it was solid dark and storming hard by the time I got in. That was the last time I skied down, having got a little nervous about it. And every slide ran that night.

I met my husband, Don, in 1938. I was out of college and had been teaching and was semiengaged to another fellow who didn't live here. Don's folks bought the paper here; it was the *Herald* in those days. My father had been on some big junket or another and Don's father had written an article about it, so I went in to get some extra copies to send to dad's relatives. And here was this nice young man handing out papers over the counter. That was probably in the early fall because the Elks Charity Ball was held right after that. They held it in October in those days and it was always the night of the first snowfall. People from Silverton never knew how they were going to get home. Those things were jammed. There would be 300 people in there and everybody dressed. It was a big, big thing.

We were married in November, 1940. I was teaching in Salida at that time and quit at Christmas. In those days, you couldn't hold a job and be married. They felt that whoever was providing for the household should have that job, so women who married had to give up their jobs.

After Christmas we moved to Oak Creek where my husband and I ran a newspaper, or he ran it and I learned to run a Linotype. We stayed in Oak Creek until 1944 or 1945. Meredith was born in 1941, Mac in 1943, and Mary in 1945. Then we came back to Ouray to run the family's newspaper here. His folks were getting older and Don had been brought up on the newspaper; hated it, but knew it. I thought I'd married a newspaper editor and what I found out after several weeks of marriage was that I had married a prospector, a mining man in the guise of a newspaper editor. Talk about false pretenses. My goodness. He had been working up at a mine called the Rock of Ages, just below Twin Peaks. He would take a donkey up Twin Peaks trail with supplies on it and bring down ore. When we got married and went to Oak Creek to live he gave the donkey to my dad because my dad was still prospecting and mining. Frank Rice always laughed and said he thought my dad got the best of the deal. It was quite awhile before I was comfortable with Frank Rice again.

Don started prospecting again when we moved back here but then his folks retired and his brother, who was taking the burden of the paper, wanted to move to Moab, with his wife and family, because the uranium boom was on and he wanted to get in on some of that. He wanted to start a paper over there and some sort of printing company. So Don took over the paper so his brother could be free. We enjoyed it but Don said, "I won't live long if I keep this up." He wasn't the newspaper type.

It was hard for him. He could put out a newspaper but it was a lot of work for both of us. Joyce Jorgenson has a picture up at the newspaper office that's called "Hell on Thursdays." I can understand and agree with that title. Many times we worked all night to get that paper out and into the post office by Friday morning.

The paper wasn't as big as it is now, just four pages with a two-page insert sometimes. But Don and I had to fold all the pages by hand, set all the type, and Don had to set all the heads and then run the press. One of our big stories was the Idarado fire. There were birth and death announcements and there was always a personal column. We subsisted on the legal publications from the county and what ads we could get. That's the reason we had to close the Oak Creek paper and come home. The war had started and we could not get advertising. People wouldn't put in ads for refrigerators when they couldn't get refrigerators, cars, or anything. Don wanted to go prospecting anyway.

I did a little substitute teaching in the school here and was superintendent of schools for a short time, just a matter of months. Betty East had resigned and I filled in and stood for election. That was the year Eisenhower was elected. I was a Democrat and I went down the drain with all the rest of them.

After that my mother said that somebody was retiring at the post office and she needed me to come in and help. I wasn't sure that I wanted to do that but mother pressed the point; she was a forceful woman. We had four small children, the oldest one was five.

Mark was born some years after that, he was a tagalong. Don was working at various jobs and money was not that plentiful so I did go to work.

I worked in the Post Office from 1953 to 1976 and was postmaster for eleven years. Mother had been postmaster for 17 years, the longest of anybody in the succession of postmasters here. Prior to her tenure, postmasters came and went according to the political election. If your party was in, you kept your job. If your party was out, someone else took over. It was a patronage job in every post office in the United States. The postmasters got out and worked on elections, I'll tell you. Now you're not permitted to do that. You're permitted to hold your opinions but you're not permitted to work; something called the Hatch Act.

I miss it yet, I loved my job but it got very difficult for me. There were cutbacks and cutbacks, especially in the hours allocated to me for hired clerks. I was having to do more and more of it myself. I always was built for comfort, not for speed. I was working from 7:00 in the morning 'til after 10:00 at night to get out the catalogs, the 3rd class mail, and do the reports and the everyday work of the post office. It was a physical thing; I couldn't get the mail out fast enough so I retired.

The post office was at the Variety Store. That's why Frank and Albert called it the Post Office Store; the post office was in the back of the store. We were a 2nd class office. The 1st class offices were Denver, Colorado Springs, and Pueblo. The little rural ones were 3rd and 4th class. This was a top office and it still is. For one thing Idarado was sending bullion out to the mint. Somebody would bring it down after they were through up there and shove it through the window. We'd set it on an ice cream stool, an old stool with wire legs, and tie it up. We would have to have help to get it on the scales. Then we would put stamps on it. It would always go by registered mail. It was gold ready to be made into bullion; it was pretty pure stuff.

In those days we gave out silver dollars for change. Tourists liked them; they liked souvenirs. One day two well dressed men, businessmen, came in. One of the men bought stamps and gave my mother a bill. She gave him back a couple of silver dollars in change. He pushed them back and said, quite rudely, "I don't want that, give me folding money." Mother pushed the silver dollars back to him and said, "Fold that if you're man enough." She was a character.

ISABELLA MCDONALD

A MILLER MESA GIRL

Isabelle was one of the first interviews and, not to denigrate any of the rest, one of the favorites. Isabelle is a strong, gruff woman raised on a farm with language to prove it. Her voice sounded rough and gravelly and she let you know exactly how she felt about questions that had been asked. She never minced words and said exactly what she felt. At the end she was confined by illness and could do less than previously, but she lived by herself despite what others would have her do.

My family name was Zanon. My father came to this country first and then sent for my mother to come over to join him. I was born in Eureka, near Silverton in 1904. Shortly after I was born, my father homesteaded 160 acres on Miller Mesa so we moved over here. It was a beautiful place but all covered with brush. He cleared all that land by hand. He chopped the brush and then pulled out the stubs with horses. My father stayed up on that homestead until he died in 1922. My sister's kids still own that property and rent it out for summer pasture; there are no buildings left up there. The house burned down before Dad died. My mother and brother and sister were in Ouray when the house caught fire in the middle of the night. The only thing that woke Dad up was the window glass cracking in the fire. After the fire they fixed up a granary and lived in that. Mother continued to live in that after Dad died until she got sick. The granary was finally torn down to build an elk corral to keep the elk out of the hay.

"Ridgway was quite a place in those days... there were bars, saloons, hotels...a couple of grocery stores, a dry goods store, a jewelry store, and a butcher shop then. We had miners and railroad people living here and, of course, it was always a farming community."

My mother had a big garden. She had to water it by hand with a sprinkler can. Every night she watered down one row and up the next. She could not raise beans or corn but did raise cauliflower, cabbage, carrots, stuff like that. She never canned. She put all the produce in a root cellar. She made 50 pounds of sauerkraut

Riding sidesaddle.

every year. That would last us all year. By the time it got down to the bottom, the cabbage would be ready to make another batch.

My father raised oats, potatoes, and hay for the cattle. He plowed with horses. Part of the time I would drive the team and part of the time my brother drove the team. Dad would hold the plow. He mowed hay with horses, too. Part of the time he'd mow; other times we'd mow. I remember my brother and me mowing when we couldn't reach from the seat to the pedal. When we raked hay, we would stand on the pedal and drive the team.

We got up in the morning at 5:00, milked the cows, separated the milk by hand, and then walked five miles to school. After school we walked home again and then had to hunt the cattle. We had to find them out in the pasture to bring them in for milking. We had to separate the milk again, eat supper, and then we were ready for bed.

We had a nice log house that Dad built and a big log barn. Upstairs was one big room where all the kids slept. Mother had thirteen children but all but four died. Downstairs there was a big kitchen and bedroom combined where my parents slept. There was also a small spare bedroom. There was a big hall and a porch that ran the full length of the house.

We heated the house with a wood cook stove. Dad chopped down the trees for firewood but us kids had to saw it up every summer.

In the wintertime we would get up, milk the cows, and eat breakfast. Then we would turn the cows out to water at the spring and clean the barn out. If it had snowed we put the animals back in until 4:00 in the afternoon when we turned them out so they could drink again. We only kept six or eight milk cows for cream which we brought down to Ridgway once a week to sell. We kept twenty hens and sold the eggs at the creamery, too.

We planted about 70 acres of potatoes and would sell them in the fall. My job was to weed eight or nine acres of potatoes every summer. I had to pull every weed in there and pack the weeds out. We didn't have any machines. Hellfire, people don't know what it is to work now days.

We came down with Dad to Ridgway once a week. It took us about an hour with a team and wagon. After he got through at the creamery and had gotten his check, we went to the store to buy groceries. He usually gave us a quarter to buy oranges or cookies but never any candy. We were usually home by 12:00 or 1:00.

I went to school through eight grades. We had a pretty good-sized school in Ridgway. There were three or four grades in each room. We didn't have a teacher for every damn grade like they do now but she seemed to get along alright. We never had any homework. We went to school to learn. We didn't learn anything at home. When us kids went to school, we didn't know a word of English, we spoke Italian. It didn't take us long to pick it up. There were quite a few kids in school that didn't speak English at home. Most of them spoke Italian or German.

In the winter when the snow got too deep, mother rented a house in town and we stayed there until Friday night when we walked back up and stayed with Dad until Sunday. Sunday evening he'd bring us back down to town. He would hook the horses to a sled to bring us to town. Sometimes the horses would get tired going through the deep snow and just lie down. Then we would have to shovel the horses out before we could go on.

We used to butcher our own meat. We butchered pigs, chickens, and rabbits every year. Once in a while we butchered a cow if someone in Ouray wanted to buy part of the meat. Dad never hunted. He never cared for that.

In the wintertime Dad usually worked in one of the mines around Ouray. During that time two or three miners would come to the ranch to stay for the winter and get out of the mine. They helped Mother with the cows and hunted rabbits or grouse. They liked it up there because it was quiet and there was no damn saloon to run to. That way Dad could go to the mine because Mother wasn't alone with us kids up there. Then in about May when the ground was beginning to thaw and the snow was going away, Dad would write Mother and say, well, feed the horses their grain and plenty of hay because I'll be home to plow soon.

Miller Mesa was pretty well covered with hay farms at that time. We had all kinds of neighbors up there. We visited a lot. Sunday was visiting day for my mother. My mother never drove but she would get us kids ready and we'd walk. I don't care if it was five miles or two; we walked to see somebody. If we didn't go somewhere, two or three families would be at our place. Sunday dinner was chicken, potatoes and gravy, and some kind of vegetables. After dinner the adults talked and the kids went outside to play. Nowadays the kids run in and out of the house and you can't visit. God, in my time, my mother would look at us kids and we knew we'd better get out of there. If we didn't, we knew that we were going to get our hind ends tanned when our company left. Jesus, now people let their kids into everything.

Our folks never came to town on Saturday night. Hell, there was no such thing as coming down to town. People nowadays stay out all night. Then in the daytime, they can't do a darn thing because they're too tired.

There used to be a Catholic Church in town that burned down. My mother was a Catholic but my dad didn't believe in them so we didn't bother about the churches. You don't drive a team twelve miles to a darn church. When somebody died, my parents would get someone to stay with us, and they would go to Ouray for the funeral but that was the only time they went to church.

We always went down Coal Creek to Ouray. Mother used to take us to Ouray for the 4th of July parade. The band would be playing and two, great big white horses would lead the parade, dancing all the way up the street. The horses were beautiful, all decorated with medallions coming down their shoulders in front and on the bridles. I'll never forget those horses. Hell, they don't have a goddammed parade now. They just think they do.

I got married to a man named Smith when I was sixteen. We moved to a heifer ranch right where you start up the Dallas Divide. We raised hay and had a few milk cows and chickens. We raised potatoes and trapped muskrats for fur. In those days you got along with what you had. Later we moved to California but I wasn't there very long. We split up and I moved back here. My son was born on the Dallas and my daughter was born in California.

After I married again, my husband, Orie Imes, and I moved to Lake City. We had 500 cattle to take care of and did it all by hand. We didn't go out and hire half a dozen people to come in and help us.

We stayed in Lake City for about three years and then came back to Ridgway in 1937. My husband got the job of city marshal and waterman. He rode the ditch on horseback all winter long until he died, to make sure that it was open and that the town had water. He dug up all the pipes with pick, shovel, and bar. Now they have machinery to do that. That old system was so cockeyed, all the pipes were falling apart so he had a lot of digging to do.

When we moved into this house, we built some sheds across the road and kept the horse and six cows there. I sold milk to pay for them. We kept chickens, rabbits, and four pigs to butcher for the house, two in the spring and two in the fall. I finally quit delivering milk and cream because I found out that it didn't pay. I'd let the people have the milk and cream but they would tell me that, "Well, I just can't pay you this month, I don't have any money." I came home and told my husband, "I'm quitting".

People were just going overboard. Wade Carmichael had a grocery store in Ridgway and kept giving credit until he went broke. Some of the other store owners went broke, too, and some of the stores burned down. We had a fire department but they had a handcart that they had to push and pull to the hydrant to hook up the hoses. There wasn't any machinery in those days.

Ridgway was quite a place in those days. I don't know how many people lived here but there were bars, saloons, hotels, and three or four stores. There were a couple of grocery stores, a dry goods store, a jewelry store, and a butcher shop then. We had miners and railroad people living here and, of course, it was always a farming community. People used to go up to Ouray a lot. Ouray had a boom then. They had the saloons and the mines.

I remember when the Israels bought the first car in town when I was a little kid. People would get off the train here and want to look around for a while so Bob Israel would take them up to Ouray in the car after they were done.

When we first moved into this house in Ridgway it was so run down you could hardly live in it. I had a couple of guys come up from Montrose to check the wiring. They found out that most of the wiring wasn't wrapped so they had to fix that. Since they were here longer than they expected, I fixed lunch for them. When they came in, they went to wash their hands and found out that they couldn't use the sink because the sewer drain was plugged up. They said, "By God, we'll fix that for you." They went out in the yard and found a piece of rubber hose that belonged to a car or truck and dug down to the sewer line, knocked a hole in it, and stuck it in. It worked. I got electricity and sewer on the same day.

People today don't know how to work. Now everything is done by machinery. We used to do everything by hand. It was a job but we enjoyed it. If people would go back to that, they'd be a hell of a lot better off than they are today. My folks and the other old people didn't go into debt for machinery or this, that, or the other thing. Now they buy a piece of machinery and, next year, some damn salesman comes along and says you could do better with this new machine. So they invest and they haven't got the old one paid for yet. It's no wonder they're all going broke.

I married one more time to a man named McDonald and he died, too. He used to do a little of everything. As they used to say, Jack of all Trades, Master of None.

CLIEVE CARMICHAEL

GROCER'S SON

Clieve most recently lived in Montrose in a compact house full of pictures of life in Ridgway. Clieve was a quiet-spoken man whose father owned the Ridgway Grocery and Market during the boom times of Ridgway. Clieve grew up in Ridgway during the 1920s and 1930s and had vivid recollections of those times.

My Great-grandfather and Grandmother Carmichael came from Scotland. They moved to Ogdensburg, New York where my grandfather was born. Shortly after that they moved first to Kansas then to the town of Dallas. My Grandmother Carmichael moved to the town of Dallas from Nova Scotia. She was married to a man named William Smith who had moved here earlier because of his health. Her brother, who was bookkeeper for the Freighter, Dave Wood, had encouraged her to move here. After her husband died she married my grandfather in Dallas and they moved to Ridgway.

Dallas was the center for Dave Wood's freight operation

"In the upper grades . . . the principal who was an artist taught art. I was never any good at it. Only a mother appreciates those things."

which hauled to the mines in Ouray and Telluride. When Otto Mears built the Rio Grande Southern Railroad from Ridgway to Telluride, Dolores, and Durango, Ridgway became the shipping center and Dallas literally died. Ridgway was founded in 1890 and was named after the construction superintendent that built the railroad from Ridgway to Dolores; that's why it's spelled without an "e". They moved a lot of the houses from Dallas to Ridgway and my grandparents lived in one of those houses on Moffat Street.

My father, Wade, was born in Dallas and graduated in the first graduating class at Ridgway High School in 1915 along with my mother, Cora Israel, his sister, Gertrude, and Adam Miller. My father started working at age twelve for Frank Gay at the Ridgway Meat Market.

After graduation from high school, my mother went to Western State, a normal school, for the summer and then started teaching at old Dallas. There were several little country schools in the area then. There was one out toward Pleasant Valley that was called New Dallas, one in Cow Creek, Mayfield, (by Spud Hill) and Piedmont. In 1916 mother taught at Ridgway School. My parents were married in June 1917 so my mother had to quit teaching. At that time, when women married they were no longer permitted to teach. They were to become homemakers, I suppose. The teachers who came into the area were all single and usually only taught one year before they married.

When they married, my dad was working in a market owned by Snarr and Allen. That was on Clinton Street in a building that has now been torn down. It was next to the Pioneer Grocery which was owned by Leland Duckett. In 1921 my dad and Guy Lamb bought the market from Snarr and Allen and named it the Ridgway Grocery and Market. In 1928 Dad became the sole proprietor. He moved the market a block east into a building that has been torn down but stood next to an ice cream shop and hardware store on Clinton.

I was born in Ridgway in 1918 and went all the way through school here with the exception of my freshman year in high school. My parents thought that I should have the experience of a larger school system before I went away to college, so that year my mother took my sister and me to Phoenix. I think they thought I might want to stay there but I didn't. That was a little bit too big so I came back here and finished high school in Ridgway. I graduated in 1935.

At that time the Ridgway school was located south of Moffat Street between Laura and Mary streets. When I went there it was a one-story building. At one time it had been a two-story, brick building but it was damaged by an earthquake in the early 1900s. There were four rooms for the the grade school and each teacher taught two grades. While I was in school, they brought in manual training for the boys and sewing for the girls. In manual training you used coping saws to make little breadboards or bookshelves. In fact, one that I made in the fourth grade is hanging in the Museum. In the upper grades, sixth, seventh, and eighth, the principal who was an artist taught art. I was never any good at it. Only a mother appreciates those things. In 1930 the elementary school burned. It was arson but they never caught the arsonist. The grade school was moved into the Park Hotel, just north of where the True Grit Cafe is now. The new school was completed the next year and located in the old school building that is now the picture frame factory.

In the late twenties the high school began playing basketball in the Oddfellows Hall. That's the Rebekah Building now. The current lodge room is where we played basketball. It didn't meet requirements, but at least we were able to play. I'm sure that wasn't the first basketball team they had because I have a picture of my father and other boys dressed in basketball uniforms. They even had a basketball team for girls. The girls played in bloomers. It was quite something.

I went to high school in what is now the old fire station. They didn't add the high school addition to the new grade school until two years after I graduated. The fire station was two stories with one big room downstairs which was used for certain classes and for study hall. There were three classrooms upstairs. We met college prep in Ridgway at that time. We were required to have two years of foreign language, I took Spanish; a math background and I had algebra, geometry, trigonometry, and solid geometry; four years of English; and physics and chemistry. Not many went on to college at that time because of the Depression. I was more fortunate and was the only one of nine in my class to go to college. I majored in accounting with a minor in marketing at the University of Colorado.

I started working for my dad at the store when I was about twelve. He didn't want me to, because he had worked so hard so early, but I prevailed on him. I don't think I did much but sit around when I first went down there but it was different. At that time you had to be fifteen or sixteen to get a driver's license, but dad taught me how to drive when I was about twelve so I got a special permit and drove the delivery truck. Dad used to go out to the ranchers and buy cattle and bring them to his feedlot on the lower Dallas Creek, on County Road 5, and grain feed them to fatten them. He had a slaughterhouse there where he butchered them. He taught me to drive by letting me drive from the store to the slaughterhouse. We had an old Dodge delivery truck with an open cab. It ran beautifully. I wasn't permitted to drive on the highway, of course. In those days people didn't travel all that much. It took a good hour to travel from Ridgway to Montrose on the old gravel road. I think there was something like thirty-two railroad crossings between the two towns. The road wandered around along the river and was narrow with sharp curves. It must have been about 1940 when the present highway was built.

When I was delivering groceries, electric refrigerators were not too plentiful and food didn't keep too well in the iceboxes; so women would call in their orders almost every morning. We delivered about eleven o'clock in the morning and four-thirty in the afternoon. We filled the orders in little wooden crates and lined them up in order according to the route you were going to follow. We always delivered to the back door. We'd knock first and if there was no answer just go in and put the groceries on the cabinet. I remember one time going to a house and knocking. When I didn't get an answer I went in, put the groceries on the counter, and turned to go out and there was a ten-year-old girl taking a bath in a large wash tub. She was petrified and I was shocked. I guess that she was so frightened when she heard the knock that she thought whoever it was would go away.

We delivered pretty much over the whole Ridgway area. We went to the garage where the Sunset Station is now, up to Happy Hollow on the Elk Meadows Road, and out to Stringtown on the way to the slaughterhouse. When I had basketball practice my father was pretty lenient. He'd let me make the deliveries after practice. It only took about forty-five minutes to get them done. After I finished high school and left the area, Dave Wolford and other young people worked for my dad, delivering groceries until he sold the store in 1938 to work on his ranch full time.

Sherbino Theater in Ridgway.

The store was big, about thirty feet across the front and about seventy-five to one hundred feet deep. There was a warehouse behind the barbershop next door with a basement that had an elevator operated by a rope. Saturday seemed to be shopping day for the ranchers. We kept the store open until eight o'clock on Saturday nights but sometimes we never got out of there until ten. The ranchers would come into the Sherbino Theater to see the silent movies so we stayed open for the late trade. Sometimes they didn't go to the movie and just stayed in the store and visited. You'd think we were never going to close the store.

When I was in high school people danced a lot. Every month each high school class entertained the other three classes. We'd serve refreshments and have a dance. It was at that time that my parents and two other men decided to form an orchestra. My mother played the piano, my father played the sax, the roundhouse superintendent played the banjo, and another man played the drums. They started playing for the school dances and, when parents heard them, they suggested they play for some of the public dances. They decided they'd try that and called themselves the Carmichael Melodeons. When they needed five or six pieces, my sister, who was an accomplished violinist, played with them. Occasionally I joined them and played the sax, too. They would go all the way to Nucla to play or to Pea Green or Oak Grove near Montrose. They played at Cow Creek dances frequently. I used to go to the dances where my folks were playing but never had the idea that they were checking up on me.

I learned to dance when I was little. You always went to the dances with your parents. They used to have box suppers at the Sherbino before the Cow Creek dance hall was built. They would auction off the boxes at midnight and the men would eat with the woman whose box they had bought. At these dances the boys would dance with the older women. These older women were always nice to dance with, always willing to teach you how to dance. I remember dancing with Bruce Phillip's mother when I was in high school. She said, "Well, after you learn you'll probably never ask these women to dance again." I remembered that and when I was in college and came home to go to a dance I always made it a point to dance with Mrs. Phillips and the other ladies who had been nice enough to dance with me when I was young.

When I finished college, I went to Peyton, Colorado, east of Colorado Springs to interview for a teaching job. When I first saw Peyton I thought, oh, my, I don't think I can stay here very long. I went home and told my mother I thought I'd have to get a car. She agreed so we went to Montrose to Carrington Chevrolet. He had a good used car, a 1936 Oldsmobile Six coupe, that had been well taken care of. The price was $460.00. My parents put up $260.00 and my father thought this was a good chance for me to learn about borrowing money. We went up to see Ralph Kullerstrand in Ouray and I borrowed $200.00 and had my first car.

My contract for teaching that first year in Peyton was $900.00 on a twelve-month basis, $75.00 a month. I lived with the superintendent and his wife and paid $25.00 a month for board and room. That left me sufficient money to go into Colorado Springs, pay for my car, buy clothes, and things like that. At the end of the year, I hadn't saved any money but the car was paid for. The second year they gave me a $5.00 a month increase so I was making $80.00 a month or $960.00 a year.

At the end of that year, the war was on then, I enlisted in the Navy. I had applied for the midshipmen program in 1942 but never heard from them and was afraid I was going to be drafted, so when summer came I enlisted in the branch I wanted. When I was in boot camp in San Diego the company commander helped me get into the midshipmen program and I was sent to Notre Dame for training. After I was commissioned, I was ordered to the U. S. S. Swanson and billeted as a communications officer.

When I was young, Ridgway was a thriving little town, a pretty little town. In later years when I came home, I'd ask mother, "Did Ridgway always look this bad or was it because I was younger that it looked so different?" She told me, "No, it truly was a beautiful little town." The setting was so pretty and people kept up their places. It wasn't until they started talking about the dam and that Ridgway would be inundated that people began letting their places slide into disrepair. People took so much pride in the town. I'm glad to see that the organization, Ridgway Community Pride, has been formed. They have done a lot, I think.

ROSIE HALLS

CHILD LABORER

Rosie's life as a tough child seems so incongruous to the loud, friendly, and happy person interviewed that it was hard to reconcile the differences. She has both a wood stove and an electric range but uses the wood stove more.

Rosie is Italian in origin and somehow, without an accent, still lets you know that she is Italian.

Rosie is one of the few people who speaks specifically about what children were wearing to school and what school was like. Her brother, Mario, appears in Verena Jacobson's stories about being a schoolteacher.

My father, Matt Zadra, left Europe and came to this country when he was seventeen. I think he first moved to Minnesota and then to Ouray to work in the mines. He worked in the Bachelor and the Revenue. After he had saved enough money to pay for her passage, he sent for my mother. They had grown up and gone to school together in Tiro, Austria. They were married in Denver in 1912

> "They advertised dances by putting up little slips of paper in the drug stores or grocery stores. Sometimes they put them up on posts. That's how they got the name 'posters.'"

and then came back to Ouray and homesteaded just south of Ridgway. In those days you had to homestead a place to get it. Then you had to stay there a certain number of years and improve it before you got title. Later they moved to the Donovan place just east of Ridgway for a short time but left, and my mother moved to Ouray to the Belvedere Hotel.

I was born at the Belvedere Hotel on November 12th, 1913; delivered by a midwife. That's where the Coachlight is now but then it was a boardinghouse owned by Mary Fedel's mother. It had a dining room downstairs and rooms upstairs. My name is really Rosa but my parents started calling me Rosie. I always hated the name Rosa so I never tell anybody that's my real name.

Sometime after I was born, my parents bought the place along the highway between Ouray and Ridgway where my brother, Victor, still lives.

I started school at Piedmont and went there for the first five grades. When I was eleven I went to work at the Western Hotel in Ouray. I was the oldest child and had to help support the family. I washed dishes, set the table, scrubbed, and did all those things for Mary Flor, Tuffy's mother, who was running the hotel. I would come to the hotel after school and work until ten o'clock. We had all those boarders to feed. We had to get up early, too. I worked for my board and room.

I went to school in Ouray to the fifth, sixth, and seventh grades during that time. There were three or four grades in one room; the old school was where the playground is now. We played lots of games: baseball, andy-over, chop-up-sticks, poke-poke pull-away, and kick-the-can. In the winter when there was snow on the ground we played fox and geese. It was fun. We watched the fox because he was going to eat the geese.

For the eighth grade I moved back home and graduated from Piedmont. There were only two of us in the graduating class. That was a one-room school, all eight grades in one room. Irma Kullerstrand taught me in the sixth grade. Verena Jacobson taught most of the other kids at Piedmont. We had to learn our reading and multiplication tables which most of the kids today don't know. We had to learn writing and practice our penmanship. Some kids today can't read their own writing but we had to learn to write plain. We had history and geography and had to learn compound interest; I don't think I could do that today but we had to learn it. I always tell everybody the reason I'm so smart is because I went to Piedmont School. We had good teachers.

When I went to school at Piedmont, we had to leave at eight o'clock, cross the river, and go down Merling Lane to get to school. We seldom walked, we had a buggy. I was the driver. My horse's name was Beauty. The buggy was big enough to hold all the kids in the family; there were five of us, and other kids would jump on, on the way to school. When we got to school, we took the horse out of the shafts, took off the bridle, and put him in the barn, and fed him hay. He stayed there all day long. At the end of the day, at four o'clock, we hitched the horse back up and headed for home.

There were only four stanchions for horses in the barn at school. One boy, Kenneth Merling, used to get to school late so he'd take my horse out to put his horse in. If we both had a stanchion he would take the hay from my horse and feed it to his horse. If I found out about it I would take his horse out and put mine back in and hide his saddle back of the barn in the trees. Then I'd get a hold of him and, boy, I knocked the heck out of him. This was kind of a running battle that went on for a long time. He would turn my horse loose and I had to walk home or I would turn his horse loose and he walked home. There used to be a water tank for the trains just below the Hoskin Ranch, where the San Juan Guest Ranch is now. Ken and I used to meet over there to have big fights around the water tank. There were no teachers around.

My dad was on the school board but he used to tell me, "You got in trouble, you do your own fighting." I handled my own problems and I still handle them today. I always helped my brothers and sisters. If they got in a fight, I was there. We had to protect ourselves. Dad wouldn't stick up for us. He would for something serious but kids' fights he left up to us.

I always had to wear a dress to school. The boys could wear jeans but not the girls, they had to wear dresses. Sometimes the boys wore knickers and long stockings. I had one dress for school. I'd wash it on the weekend and then wear it again the next week. That dress had a great big bow on the shoulder and another big bow on the hip. The waist was way down on the hip. They're out of style now. I had long hair and had to wear a bow in my hair, too. Then I had to wear long underwear and long stockings. I hated long underwear. I'd roll it up and put my stockings over it but it would leave a big bump on my leg. I used to tell my girls they ought to wear long underwear. I think Judy did one time and she still talks about that long underwear and those long stockings.

Sometimes those dresses didn't survive the fights. I had to patch them and sew them or get hand me downs from other people.

After I graduated from the eighth grade, I didn't go to high school, I went back to work at the Western in Ouray. Mrs. Flor was still running the boardinghouse for the miners. She cooked breakfast and supper, it was our main meal. And I had to fix lunches, too, about forty or fifty of them. I hate them today. Nobody likes lunches; they always complain about lunches. We would fix them in the evening after dinner and pack them in paper sacks in the morning so they could take them to work. The sandwiches would be peanut butter and jelly or lunch meat. Sometimes, if Mrs. Flor had a roast, we made roast sandwiches. Then we'd put in an apple or an orange.

Breakfast was at six in the morning. I had to get up at three-thirty or four. I did that for a long time, that's why I sleep until eight in the morning now. We would set the table, fix the lunches, and then serve breakfast. Breakfast was usually pancakes, biscuits, and bacon and eggs. After breakfast we cleared the tables in the big dining room, washed the dishes, and set the table for dinner in the evening. We served lunch to the men hanging around in the daytime. For lunch we had soup and sandwiches. Maybe she'd fix some spaghetti. After lunch we'd have to finish up the dishes and pile the dishes and glasses. We had to dry the glasses and make them shine. I hate glasses today. I don't dry mine now. Then I had to go upstairs and make the roomers' beds. That took most of the afternoon. She had about thirty rooms. Then it would be time to fix supper. After supper we worked until about ten or eleven o'clock, then I'd go to bed. When morning came I wouldn't want to get out of bed. It was the same routine every day. I didn't get many days off.

When I was eighteen or nineteen, I went to work in Telluride for Mrs. Rock. I remember that Mrs. Rock; she was mean but we won't tell anybody about her. I worked at the Pandora and the Smuggler. They had a big boardinghouse on the hillside; it's still there. The miners had their own little houses in back of the boardinghouse but they ate there. I worked there two or three years doing the same thing, making lunches.

I came back to Ouray to work for Sam and Mary Aker

Dining Room at the Western Hotel.

who owned the Columbus. That was one of the bars in town. I was taking care of their five children; I wasn't allowed at the bar, I was too young.

Later I went to work for my dad. He had a beer parlor where the New Nugget sits today. We were selling 3.2 beer. I had my own room and Dad had his own room. Mother was staying down at the ranch with the two boys who were farming the place. It wasn't a big place, maybe forty acres or so, but a nice place to live. Dad had a little car by then so we'd drive down to the ranch occasionally.

Ouray was a nice, homey little town then. There were a lot of miners around then. There aren't many now.

I met my first husband, Pete Christant, while I was tending bar for my dad. Pete came from France to herd sheep for Van Hughes, a Montrose lawyer. He got tired of herding sheep and decided to go into partnership with Joe Seiborn so they bought the Columbus in 1937 or '38. The Columbus was next to the Cascade Grocery. There was a bar along the south wall with another little room on the other side and a big kitchen in the back. A lot of the miners used to go in there. I didn't meet my husband; he met me. He used to come across the street so we got acquainted. I liked him and he liked me so we just got together. We were married in Ouray on May the 18th, 1940.

After our marriage, we moved to the Hoskin place. I call it the Hoskin place; it's now the San Juan Guest Ranch. We lived there a couple of years, farming the place and raising hay. Then we moved to Hesperus where Pete worked in a coal mine.

There was a cute little village there. Pete had a heart attack so we moved to Montrose. We weren't there long when he had a second heart attack so we moved in with Mom and Dad. He didn't do well, developing dropsy, and had to go to the hospital in Ouray. He lived for about a month but the water came up and filled up his heart. He was just a young man, forty-two.

I stayed with Mama at the ranch for five years after that. In the meantime, Dean Halls had lost his wife. He was married to Myra Kemp who I grew up with. She had a brain tumor and passed away. It was a sad thing. So I was there and he was there and we got together and got married. We were married in Aztec, New Mexico; we didn't want a church wedding. I was married to Dean for about, well, must have been about ten years. He had a heart attack, too.

We moved into this house and I've been here for about thirty-six years. It was the Kemp's house originally, but Dean and Myra got it when they were married. I don't do much to my house so I'm happy.

Dean and I had two boys, Ray and Ronnie. Both of them graduated from high school in Ouray and from BYU. Both of them went on missions for the Mormon Church. Ronny went to Guatemala and Ray to Vienna for two years. They both live in Provo, Utah, and are married with families and good jobs.

Pete and I had two daughters, Judy and Wanda. Judy lives in Littleton and Wanda in Golden. I spend my winters with my family but always come back here in the summer.

As a young girl, I used to go to the dances once in

a while. The dances weren't like they are today with the girl over there and the boy over here. We used to dance together. We did the waltz and the two-step; once in a while, we did the beer barrel polka. Today they do twirls and shake. I think it's awful. We had lots of good bands, not like today. Some of the families had their own bands. The Zanetts had a family band with a piano player, a saxophone, a clarinet, and an accordion. I never asked the boys to dance, they'd come over and ask me. Now the women ask the men to dance.

I never went to a dance by myself. Sometimes I would go with a guy, sometimes in a group. We had dances at Cow Creek and at the dance hall where the Tipi Shop is in Ridgway now. Once in a while, there would be a dance at the school. I don't dance anymore, not since Dean passed away. I couldn't dance these dances anyway.

I only went to the Orvis Plunge once. I'm not a swimmer; I swim like a rock. It was something else. It had a built-in swimming pool and beaches. Right across the road, where the two chimneys still stand, was an old log cabin where we used to have dances. They advertised those dances by putting up little slips of paper in the drug stores or grocery stores. Sometimes they put them up on posts. That's how they got the name, posters. They tacked them up on telephone poles.

I used to get off work to go to some of the dances, but I was taught to work. I still like to work. I liked to work because I was taught to work. My parents could do that, boy. They taught us to work, taught us to be honest, not to tell lies, not to steal, not to take things that belonged to someone else.

Sometimes I thought it was a hell of a life. I know what it is to be hard up. Kids today don't know what to do if they're hard up. During the Depression, we didn't have enough to eat. My folks didn't have enough money to send us to school or pay for clothes, and eats, and shows. If we wanted to do that, we had to do it on our own. Then we couldn't do it all the time because we couldn't afford it. That was why I worked all the time.

VERENA JACOBSON

SCHOOLTEACHER

Verena returned to Ouray after a long absence and now lives with her uncle, Frank Massard. She is a wonderfully open person with lots of remembrances of growing up in a mining town. It is especially interesting to notice the similarities and differences in the life of a young woman growing up in Ouray compared to a young man. While her uncle, Frank, went to work in the mines, she went to teach. For everyone, the mines and the miners were the focal point of life.

My mother's parents were named Massard. My mother, Ida, was born in Switzerland along with an older brother and sister. When they emigrated to this country, they first moved to Salt Lake City. My grandfather, we called him Ami, decided to move to Ouray because he had some cousins, the Krafts, who lived out in what is now Idlewild. When grandfather first moved here, he cooked at the mines: the Smuggler, the Atlas, the Revenue, and a number of other mines. When he got tired of that, Grandma and Grandpa opened the City Steam Laundry on the corner where the Ouray Chalet is now and ran it for a number of years.

After that he opened a little cafe, the Twin Peaks, where Benjy's rock shop is located now. He had a lot of business; he served soup for ten cents a bowl and pie for fifteen cents. My uncles, Henry and Frank, and a little girl who died at birth, were born here in Ouray.

My dad, Fred Rucker, was born at Libertyville, Texas and came up here to work in the mines as an electrical engineer. I don't know for sure but I assume that my parents met at a dance. Dancing was the thing in those days and they both really liked to dance. We never discussed that much; "Roots" and that sort of thing never came into being at that time. Now, all of a sudden, everybody wants to know where they came from. We accepted it and let it go at that. We were here and so we

> "*One of the ladies who sold Avon products came to the house one day and, when Mother told her that I wanted to be a teacher, she said, "Oh, don't let her do that, they're always such messy housekeepers.*"

had to make the best of it; that was it. Often you hear people say, "Oh, we were so poor." Well, we were poor but it didn't bother us any. So was everybody else in town so everybody just had a good time. Ouray was in on a couple ups and downs; whenever the price of metal went down, so did Ouray. During the Depression, some of the mines closed but everybody was having trouble then, including the farmers.

I was born on July 5th, 1907, in that blue house right by the ski tow. Mother had a doctor but there were always ladies, midwives, that would come to help the doctor and stay for ten days after the birth, to do the housework and that sort of thing.

People always ask me, "What was it like growing up here?" I don't know. We were just like Topsy, we grew. We went to school, we had picnics, we did a lot of climbing in the hills, we played games like kick-the-can, tag, and "No Bears Out Tonight", that was a game like hide-and-seek; not big things. We accepted things just as they were. Maybe that's what preserved us. Now people complain that there is nothing for young people to do. There are more things for the kids to do than when I was growing up. Back then there were twenty-three saloons up and down Main Street, not counting the ones on the Row. It was just a saloon haven.

We used to take picnics up to the Box Canyon after school. There's a lovely park in back of the Box Canyon sign. We'd decide during the day to have a picnic so everyone was assigned to bring something and we'd build a bonfire and roast wieners.

During school we had dances and everybody went to the basketball games. We had school plays. Everybody had to be in them since there weren't enough of us; in fact, some of us would have to take two parts instead of one. The school didn't have an auditorium so everything had to take place at the Opera House. We thought that was really something, stepping out of the wings onto the stage of the Opera House.

Our proms were held at the Opera House, too. We always had an orchestra with good players. Johnny Foreman played the drums, Bud Croft played the piano, Mr. Faussone played the clarinet, and Mrs. Faussone played the violin. Mr. Faussone worked at the Cascade Grocery with his dad. Mrs. Faussone's mother, Mrs. Tuttle, was one of the ladies who went around as a midwife but all I ever saw Myrtle do was play the violin. She was an excellent violinist. When my youngest sister was born, Mrs. Tuttle came up to stay with Mother. Mother told her what needed to be done but said, "Don't worry about the dishes, Genevieve, my next older sister, would do them; and, if you do the washing, Verena will do the ironing." I was only fourteen and Mrs. Tuttle couldn't get over the fact that I could iron. Her own daughter, who was much older than I, couldn't iron. She was married by that time but I think Mrs. Tuttle did a lot of the work.

When we were kids, we could play until curfew time. At eight o'clock a big bell on the tower behind City Hall would ring. You could hear it all over town, which wasn't hard to do here. When the bell rang all kids from freshmen on down headed for home. If you didn't, the marshal took you home. Woe to you if the marshal took you home, you got no sympathy there. Our parents said we told you, you were supposed to be home. Of course, we were grounded for a while if we didn't get home on time.

I must have been about in the seventh grade when I started to work in the store for Frank and Albert. I know I could barely look over the counters. They had this long ladder on rollers that I used to get things off the high shelves. I waited on customers and, of course, they had the soda fountain there where you made ice cream sodas, banana splits, and ice cream sundaes. Both of them worked in the store but they took any odd job around town they could find to support their families and pay for the store. They were bound and determined to make a go of it.

They ran the theater, too. During high school, my sister and I worked there. Sometimes one of us would sell tickets and the other would take them at the door and then we'd trade off and either Frank or Albert would run the film.

When I was growing up, Ouray had a lot of grocery stores and even more saloons. It wasn't twenty-three saloons, it was thirty-two. Not long ago, I wrote my sister, who still lives in Minnesota, and said now we have as many motels as we used to have saloons. She wrote back and asked where they put them. I said, "Well, all the old saloons are now motels." A couple of years ago a dear friend, who had grown up with me here, came down to visit and I took her to the Coachlight for dinner. That used to be a house of ill repute. While we were there,

she said, "Verena, this used to be a no-no." I laughed and said, "Yeah, but look how it's been upgraded."

The only kids that went down on Second Street were the boys that delivered papers. They knew that they couldn't pull anything. The girls were good about that. If anything was going wrong, they sent the boys on their way. For the reputations they had and how they made their living, they were protective of young people. My grandpa cooked for a woman, who was a prostitute, and her husband in a restaurant. Over the Fourth of July, when excursion trains brought people from Montrose and Grand Junction for the celebration, they always put on extra help. Nell asked me to work as an extra cashier. She said she'd call my mom and just have me work during my grandpa's shift. The restaurant was uptown and Nell was burned out but she wanted to be sure to preserve my reputation.

The restaurants used to hire girls to work as waitresses in the summer. I remember one girl, Mabel, who was working her way through college at Greeley. She stayed with Mrs. Herring, a staid and serious Presbyterian lady, so it was alright. That Fourth of July weekend when I came to work, Mabel was in tears. She had been short-changed and was feeling just terrible. Just at that time the gamblers, who had worked the night shift on Second Street, were getting off and coming up for breakfast. They got wind of it and came over and said they were going to show us how to keep from getting shortchanged. In ten minutes they showed me twenty-five ways I could be shortchanged. I couldn't get it, they did it so quick and fast. Lester **Clark, Jack's** father, told me to put the bill on the register, make change, and then put the bill in the drawer, and not open the drawer again. I said, "I've always done that. I learned that at the post office door." They were anxious that Mabel and I not be shortchanged again. It was funny. Here they had been shortchanging people all night, gambling like crazy, but they were willing to tell us.

There were professional gamblers all up and down Second Street. They played cards for the house. Every house on Second Street had a professional gambler. It was just like it is now over in Nevada.

Second Street was just like any other street in town. There were just a bunch of houses down there. Some of them are still there. The other night when we went down that way, I noticed that a couple of them are about ready to fall in. It wasn't a big area, just a couple of blocks long. Second Street had a big reputation because of the miners, but that was it. None of us paid any attention to it. It was a way of life in a mining town and that was it. You had no business down there so you didn't go down there.

The girls used to come up to Frank and Albert's store. They were always real nice, the easiest people to wait on. They weren't as demanding as some of the others. As a rule they were always very generous. The girls always dressed in nice dresses. I remember one girl, Rosie; she was a tiny little thing and always came dressed in a lovely suit. It was nothing outstanding or pushy. When they came walking up the street, you'd never know what they did. They worked in gambling houses and that was their business. I guess they got sidetracked.

After the big Crash in Twenty-nine, everything dropped. People left town to find work and so did the gamblers. The houses on Second Street just dissolved. One or two of the gamblers went in for bootlegging and did pretty well but that was about it. The rest of us just went on living. It was just one of the things we knew about but it didn't astound us.

I remember one minister we had who, it seemed to me, just discovered the word "prostitute". We had more sermons about it; I couldn't believe that anybody could dwell on that subject so long. One of the other ladies said, "I think he's just discovered what it is."

After high school I decided that I wanted to become a teacher. One of the ladies who sold Avon products came to the house one day and, when Mother told her that I wanted to be a teacher, she said, "Oh, don't let her do that, they're always such messy housekeepers." But I became one anyway. I went to Gunnison. I only went to college for one year. Then if you took a test at the county superintendent's office and passed with a B-plus you could teach. I taught in three different areas in the county.

The first year I taught up on Log Hill. I taught in an old one-room log house. We only had school in the summer, from June to October because of all the snow they have up there. I had fourteen or fifteen students in all twelve grades. We had readin' and writin' and 'rithmetic, taught to the tune of the hickory stick. On my first day one of the youngsters said, "Can I get the water in?" We had to carry water in from the well in a pail and used a dipper hanging on the pail to get drinks. He said, "You know, Dad and another fellow cleaned out the well and they got out a rat and a skunk, and a..." I said, "Oh, fine, you go get the water. They cleaned out the well, so the well is clean." They were easy youngsters to teach, they were anxious and I think it was almost easier to teach all twelve grades in one room. When the older ones would run out of something to do, they would help the younger ones. Discipline was never a problem.

I stayed with a widow lady who had two children going to school. That was another experience, it was really something. The house looked nice enough but it was almost a shack. It was just boards with tar paper on the walls inside. Since it was summer, it got warm up there at night. One night it was really uncomfortable and I felt something crawling on me. I thought, what in the world? Since we didn't have any lights, just lamps I just grabbed it and twisted it like I was killing a wood tick. Pretty soon something else was crawling on me and I found out I had bedbugs. I was a mess. I guess this happened in a lot of the old houses. The bedbugs hid in the cracks of the paper in the day time and then came out at night. When I went home, my mother wouldn't let me bring my clothes in the house. She made me strip so I wouldn't bring in any bedbugs. The widow lady was an awfully good cook. I was always fortunate when I was teaching; I had good board.

In my second year, I taught at Piedmont. I had about fifteen kids in eight grades. One day I came into the schoolroom and looked around; everybody was kind of edgy, looking at everybody else. I thought, well, it's got to be gum on my chair or a pin because the closer I got to my desk the more apprehensive the girls got. I pulled the chair out and stood by it for a little while, trying to see if there was anything on it. I couldn't see anything. I pretended to pull out the second drawer in the desk so I could get a close look to see if I could see any pins on the chair. I couldn't see anything so I sat down. Just as I was going to lift up the top of my desk, one of the girls went "unnnnh." When I looked in I saw a little water snake in there. Of course everybody just roared. I was just miserable but I picked the snake up. I had it by the back of the head and the tail was winding around my bare arm. I asked, "Who put this in my desk?" Nobody said anything but they were all looking at one boy. I said to him, "Mario, did you?" He said, softly, "Yes, Ma'am." "Would you take it out?", I asked. He said, "Wait'll I get my glove on." I told him, "I don't have to have a glove on, why do you?" So the snake went outside and never came back in again. Mario Zadra was Rosie Hall's brother. They were awfully good kids. Their father was on the school board and he was one of the nicest guys I ever worked for, he was a prince of a fellow.

Each school had its own school board, with usually four members. They were the ones that hired the teachers. The county superintendent had a list of people that were available to teach that she would give to the boards or she would tell you to apply to a certain school. Then the

Log Hill Mesa School.

board would interview you and you would either be hired or you wouldn't. That was it.

I taught at Piedmont for three years and stayed with a couple named Burkett. They lived near the schoolhouse. They were a lovely couple but rather depressed the first year when I lived there. The had just lost their only daughter, a young girl, to appendicitis. We became good friends and had a good time together. I remember Mr. Burkett saying, "Teacher, you've helped us through the year." It was a good feeling to have done something for somebody.

The kids there were good kids. When I was teaching, you were expected to mind the teacher. What the teacher said, went. That made teaching easier. Now, you hardly dare look at a kid cross-eyed; you're liable to get sued. That's so ridiculous.

After three years at Piedmont, I transferred to the Sneffels School. I really don't know why, it just happened. It was cold at Sneffels, really cold, with lots of snow. I stayed at school all winter, only coming down for Christmas. I only had four kids in school up there, all from the Kuck's family. Mr. Kuck had the commissary at the Upper Camp Bird. At one time there had been more kids there, enough to open the school. At that time, once you opened a school, you kept it as long as anybody was there to go. When the last ones moved out that closed the district.

The schoolhouse was a regular country school with one long narrow room. At one time it had been a saloon. It was located on this side of Potosi Creek, right below the Schoolhouse Slide. That slide ran one time while I was there. It parted and went around us but it didn't get us. It was kind of eerie. When we heard it coming we knew we couldn't do anything about it. I just told the children to bury their heads in their arms so the mist couldn't get in their nostrils and throat. The whole room filled with fine snow and mist. There wasn't much wind, more like a concussion that was sucking air out of you. That's what happens to people, I think. When we heard the slide coming, we didn't know what was going to happen but there was nothing we could do so we just took it.

I stayed with the Kuck family in the big house up against the cliffs opposite the Revenue. It was about a quarter of a mile down to the school from the house. I usually walked down early in the morning to get the fire started and get ready for the day. I took all my meals with the Kucks. In fact, I did that in all the places where I stayed. Board and room for a dollar a day.

You didn't see many other people when you were up there. The mailman came up every day and there were some people at the Camp Bird that we visited on special occasions such as birthdays or something.

When I came down to Ouray for Christmas, I walked. I walked back up, too. I didn't need snowshoes or anything; the road was so well packed by the sleds and horses. I wore high boots with hobnails that kept me from slipping. It was a ten-mile walk with a two-thousand-foot gain in altitude. Pretty good hike when you're pulling up.

In the spring I stayed until school closed on the 21st of

May. One year I thought maybe I should take a horse down to town because we had had a lot of snow and the men at the Camp Bird said the water in the ditch was pretty deep from melting snow. I called the mailman to see if he was coming up early so I could go back down with him. He was a grouchy fellow and said, "No, I'm not coming up early — no way I'm coming up early." He asked if I wanted a horse. I told him I wasn't going to wait for him to bring me a horse. The day before he hadn't come up until about eleven o'clock. By that time, the icicles were dropping off the ledge above the road, and one had fallen on his horse and broken its neck, killing it. I wasn't going to wait for that. I said, "Forget it, I'll walk down."

Mrs. Kuck fixed a thermos of coffee for me and I had a bit to eat before I started. It went pretty well but I had to crawl over the bridge at the Camp Bird because it was so icy. Now they have a pipe that ducts the water under the bridge there. Then the water just ran over the bridge. I got chicken but I had to crawl over the ice that had built up there. Afterwards, I thought that was dumb. I had wool gloves on and couldn't have saved myself if I had slipped. Past the Camp Bird I had to get down in the ditch. I was walking on fifteen feet of snow. I broke through every step I took. It looked like ice and I'd think it would hold me but it wouldn't. By the time I got down to Jim Brown Hill, I was wet clear up to my waist. That was my last time up there.

After I had taught at Sneffels for three years, I married a Minnesota farmer. My sister had married a fellow who had come to work here and they had moved back to Minnesota. She was expecting a baby and asked me to come and help her. I did and married her husband's brother. I lived there for about forty years.

When Frank's wife became seriously ill, Frank asked me to come back to help care for her. I stayed the summer and then went back and sold the place in Minnesota and came back to stay. Frank's wife was reluctant to have anybody come in the house. She'd rather have somebody she knew. We got along well together.

I didn't notice many changes when I came back. I met different people but that didn't surprise me. Through the years, miners had always come and gone and so had the business people. So we were used to that. One lady told me that Ouray was changing so much she didn't like it anymore. I said, "Well, that's Ouray." It's just one of the things that is. I think all the mining towns were the same. I'm sure Leadville was the same. Camp Bird was the same. When I was growing up, Camp Bird was a real town. Two of my cousins were born up there. There were a lot of little houses, a store, a post office, and a school. Most of the houses are covered up by the tailings pond now. Ironton and the towns farther out, Mineral Farms and Animas, were all good-sized mining towns. The miners stayed there and brought their families. There were some lovely houses built for the managers of the mines. They were beautiful inside. Mule trains with as many as fifteen mules or donkeys brought the supplies in and the ore out.

A couple of years back, they were going to have a tour

up at the Camp Bird. Environmentalists were doing it. Someone asked if I was going. I said, "I should say not." They asked, "Why not?" I said, "I remember it when it was pretty. If I'd meet an environmentalist, I'd kill him. So I'd better stay home."

PAPER HANGER

Bill's house is full of furniture that he has made. The craftmanship is beautiful. Bill is a tall and lanky man with the look about him of someone who has worked hard all of his life. Like many others in Ouray, he has held a variety of jobs in order to make his living. He is happy with the work he has done and feels that boys should grow up quickly and strong.

My mother's family were miners and came to Silverton in 1878 by ox team. Later they moved to Red Mountain where my grandfather was superintendent of one of the mines.

My father came to Ouray in the early 1890s to work for his uncle, who was a truck farmer. In the fall they brought their potatoes, cabbage, carrots, and rutabagas to town in an old farm wagon to sell. After a couple of years, he learned that the miners were getting two dollars a day plus board and room so he told his uncle that he

"Camp Bird had quite a town . . . two or three hundred men working there at one time. The cooks were all men until the Atlas hired a woman to cook at the mill. After she broke the barrier, several of the other mines hired women.

was going to try his hand at mining. That was an awful lot of money in those days. He worked in several of the mines, finally ending up at Red Mountain where he met my mother.

We have the family Bible with all the records in it. Mother and Dad bought it the week they were married and Mother kept a complete record in it. I had one brother and two sisters; they're all gone now, so I got what's left of the family heirlooms.

I was born in Ouray in 1903 in that little house right around the corner that is now Frank Massard's garage. We lived there until 1917 then we moved to a nine-room house where the Wiesbaden is now located. That was where all the hot water for the indoor pool at what is now the Matterhorn came from. There was a regular bathhouse down there with tub baths and a pool. That's where all the kids in town learned to swim. It had a nice big pool, about 35 by 60 feet. Upstairs there were rooms that the miners rented by the month. Most of them just left their clothes and belongings there and would come down once a month. Others would stay in the hills four, five, or six months at a time.

When I was a child, the town must have been between eight hundred and a thousand people. Kids were of all denominations, all classes. Naturally, you had your kid fights and everything; but, all in all, we grew up together and had a lot of fun.

We had parties, the same as any other kid growing up. The parties were on Friday nights as a rule because on Saturday nights the children had to go to bed early so they could get up for Sunday School at nine o'clock the next morning. There was a Catholic Church, an Episcopal Church, and the Presbyterian Church, and they were all pretty well filled every Sunday morning and evening.

We were ready to go to Sunday School at nine and went from nine-thirty to ten-thirty. Then Mother met you at the door and you sat in church until noon. Sunday afternoon, after you came home for lunch, you read the Bible. It was up to us to read it ourselves; then we'd discuss various passages. We had dinner at five-thirty then went back to Christian Endeavor from six-thirty to seven-thirty. After that we came home and went to bed. The great majority of families did the same thing. There was no Sunday afternoon football, that was before football was ever thought of.

We did have some pretty good baseball teams around here in the early days. In the summertime, we must have had half a dozen kid's baseball teams that played each other. Somewhere around the early twenties, we had a Presbyterian minister by the name of McConnell. He was active with the children and built a couple of bobsleds, one for the girls and one for the boys. He would go out and play baseball with the boys. A couple of elderly ladies in the church thought it was just terrible for him to be doing that. But he weathered that and stayed until he retired.

As kids we hiked all over these mountains. When I was in high school, we were fortunate to have a young teacher, named Eva, who was a graduate of the University of Colorado. She formed a hiking club and took us on hikes all over this area. Your grades had to be above C before you could join. She was ambitious and would figure out where we were going to go during the week and announce, "On Saturday, we'll leave at such and such a time and we're going to do some hiking." We went to the top of Twin Peaks, we went all over the Amphitheater, right up Bear Creek Trail, up to the Bright Diamond, over to the Bachelor Switch, and the lake over there. Our parents would fix us a nice lunch; at about one o'clock we would stop by some good stream to eat. We had good clean water to drink, no coffee, or soda pop, or any of that stuff. We knew where the wild raspberry patches were so we would gather the raspberries and our mothers would make jelly and jam. That would be two-thirds of our jelly and jam for the winter.

In the winter, each of us had our own little sleds and we went sleigh riding. Third, Fourth, and Fifth avenues were coasting tracks. We could start up on the east side of town and go clear down across the bridge, past the lumberyard, and start up Oak Street. We weren't allowed to sleigh ride from three-thirty to six. That was when the ore teams were coming into town.

In those days, all the ore was brought down by six-horse teams. The team would come into town between three and four and then go down to the Donald barn, in the block below the Opera House, or to the Ashenfelter barn where they had scales. After they weighed the ore, they took it down and put it in the cars at the depot, then back again.

When I was in the fifth or sixth grade, skis came into use and we skied on the hill east of town. The boys would go down to the lumberyard and work all summer for Frank Rice. We'd take any lumber we could handle and stack them in proper piles. At the end of the summer, he'd give us some one-by-fours, six or seven feet long. We'd drill some holes in the boards about a foot from the end and then soak them in a barrel of water. After so many days, we would thread a wire through the holes and around a nail at the end. Every couple of days, we would twist the wire to make the board bend. You kept that up until you had the tip the way you wanted it. Then you left it until it was thoroughly dried out. We put candle wax on the bottom to finish the skis. We cut up the upper part of an old leather boot to make straps. When we skied, we used an old broomstick to guide ourselves. When you got going too fast, you put the broomstick between your legs and sat on it to slow down. Of course, in those days you had to walk to the top of the hill. Nowadays, you have quite a chore to make a kid walk from here to Main Street and back.

We didn't do much ice skating, although we did make a pond at the old milk ranch where the state highway garage is now. Later the city made a skating rink on the flat area just north of the theater.

When I was in high school, we had an old Chevrolet sedan, and we would drive down to the Piedmont Bridge to fish in the Uncompaghre River. We'd park the car there and fish up and down the river as far south as the Hoskin Ranch and as far north clear down, darn near, to Ridgway. We used to catch a pretty good mess of fish. I haven't fished for a good number of years. Now I don't think you'd eat those fish or give them away. I don't believe in catching them just to throw them away.

When I was about twelve or thirteen, I got my first job as a printer's devil for the old *Ouray Plaindealer and Herald*. I had to get up at six o'clock every morning to go down and start the fire under the Linotype machine so the metal would be hot for the Linotype operator when he got there at eight o'clock. After school, I would go home and change and then go back and clean. I learned how to run the small press so I could do some press work. I think my wages were two dollars and fifty cents a week, working two hours on week days and nine hours on Saturdays.

In the summer, you made most of your money mowing lawns and running errands for elderly people. A lot of us kids had eight or ten lawns around town to mow;

Single-pole skiing.

70

and that was with old hand mowers, long before your electric machines. Some of those lawns could be pretty steep. We would get groceries for the old people or get their mail or mail packages for them. They would make out a list and put it in an envelope with the money and tell you which grocery store to go to. Then you would go in and hand the envelope to the groceryman and he would fill the order, take the money out, and if there was any change put it back in with the bill. We usually got ten cents for doing that.

When I was in high school, I got a job hashing and washing dishes at the Atlas Mine. We would leave the day after school was out and go up there. We came back down on the third of July and went back on the fifth then stayed there until Labor Day when we came back down to start school again. There were usually three or four of us waiting on tables and washing dishes; each one had certain duties. We got up about five-thirty in the morning, before the men, to get ready to serve breakfast at six-thirty. As soon as breakfast was over, we had to clean up the dining room and then take your turn at being a dishwasher, a week at a time, or bring in supplies for the cook and baker. I think we got sixteen dollars a month plus our room and board. That was a lot of money in those days.

The food was good, you got the best food on the market. All the mines had good cooks and they knew different merchants and the merchants knew doggone well that they hadn't better throw in any inferior meat or vegetables or anything or they'd sure come right back at them and they'd lose their business. They didn't want to lose any of that mining business. For breakfast there would be ham and eggs, bacon and eggs, sausage, potatoes, and there was always a big pot of oatmeal. A lot of them liked old-fashioned oatmeal.

The men would go into the mine at seven or seven-thirty and come out at four or four-thirty. The men would bring in their lunch buckets and the dishwashers had to wash them and set them on a certain table. After dinner you had to fix the lunches for the next day. The cooks were right there to tell you what went in which pail. There were always meat sandwiches, a piece of pie or cake, and a little fruit of some kind. Most of them carried a thermos of coffee but they always sent in a five-gallon can of coffee at about eleven-thirty for the fellows that wanted it good and hot.

After the fellows came out at between four and four-thirty, they would go to their lockers and put their mining clothes in the lockers, take a hot shower, then rest for dinner. In the evenings the men would have cribbage games and poker or sluff games. We used to watch them until eight-thirty or a quarter of nine and then go to bed.

The mines were running three eight-hour shifts at that time, so meal times lasted for an hour and a half or longer and it depended on which shift they were working as to how many meals the men ate in the dining room. There was always food in the dining room for them to fix before they went to bed when they got off shift.

We worked seven days a week and didn't have any particular rules. You were treated as a man but you had to act as a man, too. You couldn't pull any kiddy stuff or mama boy stuff or you didn't last long. All the boys wanted to get a job in the kitchen or working as a roustabout, helping empty ore cars as they came out. They didn't let the kids go underground, you had to be eighteen before you could go underground. That was the state law.

There weren't any women up there, it was all men. Down below, at the mill at the little town of Sneffels, there were twelve, maybe fifteen women. A lot of the bosses had wives there and then there was the schoolteacher and the man that ran the store had his family there. All the west hillside had houses for the bosses and some of the married men. Camp Bird had quite a town, too. There must have been two- or three-hundred men working there at one time. The cooks were all men until the Atlas hired a woman to cook at the mill. After she broke the barrier, several of the other mines hired women.

The Mountain Top Mine was two miles straight over the hill from the Atlas. The cook over there made the best pies. A lot of evenings, as soon as we were done with dinner, us kids would take our shadowgees and hike over the hill to the Mountain Top for a piece of his pie or cake. A shadowgee was a two-gallon can with a hole cut in the side. You'd stick an ordinary candle in there and that was your light. We'd stay for a couple of hours and then hike back, about half an hour, and be in bed by nine.

In those days the men went back and forth to the mines on horseback. They would rent a horse from one of the two livery stables for two dollars and ride up to the mine. When they got there, they would tie the reins around the saddle horn and the horse would come back to town.

A lot of the miners were single but some of them had families in town. In the wintertime, about the only time anybody would come off the hill would be in case of an accident or for Thanksgiving or Christmas. A lot of the men would come down for Christmas and go up on New Year's Day and wouldn't come down again until the next May or June.

The mines got mail and supplies every day, brought up by six-horse teams. The road was kept open with a V plow pulled by three to six horses. Those plows were eight- to ten-feet wide. The town used them to plow the sidewalks. The road on Red Mountain was kept open, too. Until around World War I, there was a town at Red Mountain and Chattanooga as well as Silverton.

I went to school in Ouray all twelve years, graduating in 1922. School here was the same as in any other small town. You enjoyed it; you had to. You went to school to learn but only one or two in the graduating class had a family financially able to send them on for higher education. Graduation was always held in the Opera House. There was always a main speaker, then you would stand up and the speaker would give you your diploma. After that you would go down the steps and line up and each mother had to kiss you and congratulate you. There was usually a big party of ice cream and cake at one of the homes afterward, then we'd all go our separate ways.

There were the usual pranks pulled, I suppose the same

as in any school. The worst one I can remember was on a teacher — I can't remember her name — who wasn't well liked. At recess time, one afternoon, some kids put glue in her overshoes. By the time she got home, walking through the snow, she couldn't get them off. There was holy getout raised the next morning but nobody ever did know who put the glue in her overshoes. Kids were as they are today.

In 1916 we had an earth tremor that put a crack in the old school wall. That was when they started thinking about building a new school. It happened about one or two o'clock in the afternoon. We had a teacher, a tall thin woman by the name of Miss Holliday, and a fellow by the name of Cochran was the superintendent. He opened the door and said, "We've got an earthquake, get out of here." Boy, the teacher was out of the room before any of us kids. The old high school was where the present building is now. They decided to combine the schools and built the present building.

I got my first car in 1925 or '26. It was a 1920 Model T coupe. Cars were getting pretty popular around here by then. Before that it was all horses and buggies. When I was growing up, if you wanted to go any place in town, you walked. Few people went to Montrose unless you were leaving town for some reason and then you took the train. There were plenty of doctors and dentists and drugstores and grocery stores; you had plenty of everything you wanted here.

Once a year, around Labor Day, they had Labor Day rates, our family would take the train down to Colona.

An old Swedish family by the name of Soderquist had homesteaded there after the Camp Bird had closed. The man had worked with my father at the Camp Bird. We would spend the day with them and then in the evening pick up the train and come back to Ouray.

There were a lot of people coming in and out of town on the train. The highway wasn't built until the twenties so that was your one way out. The train was due in about five o'clock in the evening and, I think, leaving time was about nine-thirty in the morning. You stopped at Colona and Montrose and then at Cimarron for lunch. After lunch you went on to Gunnison and got to Salida between nine and ten that night. At Salida you changed trains — I think you had an hour — and then got into Denver around seven o'clock the next morning. There were sleeper cars from Salida on but you had to be rich to have one of them. I can't remember what the fare was to Denver but it didn't seem expensive to us. In the beginning, both trains rode on narrow-gauge rails. I can't remember when they made the track from Salida to Denver broad gauge.

A popular event in Ouray in the early days was the old-fashioned box social. The ladies would take a shoebox, put in a nice lunch for two people, wrap it up all fancy, and then take it to the dance. You would dance until eleven or eleven-thirty, then they would auction off those shoeboxes. You would eat with the lady whose box you bid on. The women tried their best to keep their boxes secret. You seldom got your girl's box unless she told you which one it was. That's how everyone met everybody else. Within two months you knew ninety per cent of the people in town if you wanted to. People were always friendly; always had a hand out to help you in case of necessity. That's the kind of friendship you can only find in a small community.

I started going to dances when I was a freshman in high school. I went as often as I could. It cost a dollar to get into the dance so if you had a dollar you went, if you didn't, you stayed home. Everybody from eighteen to eighty went to the dances. They always used to have an old waltz, called the Sweetheart Waltz. Three judges would judge the dancers. They would get down to ten, then to five, then three and two, and finally, one. The prize was a great big cake, a three-layer homemade cake. It paid to be a good dancer. You didn't have regular dancing partners for this dance. You could dance with any girl you liked if she would dance with you.

Ninety-nine per cent of the dances in those days were program dances. There were twenty dances on the program. You gave your girl the program and she would pick out the ones she wanted then you'd start, going around and trading. Before the second dance was over, you had your program filled. Then you would look at your program to see who your next partner was. No one couple was dancing together all the time. Everybody intermixed and everybody had a lot of fun. Actually, your girl would take your program around and get it filled. She'd choose the person she wanted you to dance with. There was a dance practically every Saturday night at the Opera House or the Elks Club.

The dances usually started at nine and quit at one. Sometimes, after the dance you would go to one of the restaurants to have something to eat; other times you'd just go home. The restaurants were open twenty-four hours a day then. Men were working various shifts in the mines and would come in after their shifts to eat and make up their lunch for the next day.

They used to have dances in the dining room of the Beaumont. There were two or three dance orchestras around town years ago. As a rule there were four or five members in each band. You would book them two or three weeks in advance and agree to pay them so much if you wanted them to play at a particular dance.

The Beaumont was open then along with the St. Elmo, the Wilson apartments above the Variety, and the old inside swimming pool had rooms. The Beaumont was *the* hotel in town. At one time there were two banks in the Beaumont Building. The Merchants and Miners Bank was on the corner. Right next to the entranceway, as you went into the lobby, was the old Bank of Ouray. After Prohibition came in, the owners of the Bank of Ouray bought the building where the bank is now and changed the name to the Citizens State Bank.

The Beaumont was a nice, old-fashioned hotel. You walked in through a hallway into a nice lobby that had soft chairs all the way around for people to sit on. The registration desk was at the east end. They always had a bellhop to carry your luggage upstairs. Next to the desk was a doorway to a hall that led you past the second bank to the old Beaumont Saloon. They had a nice dining room that served three good meals a day.

In 1922 I went to work on the Moffat Tunnel. I worked as a waiter in the dining room. I stayed there until 1924. About the first of December that year, I got a letter from my brother who said the 16th is your 21st birthday, why don't you come home for Christmas. Later I got a letter from my mother who said, why don't you come on back here, I'm sure you can find some work. While I was home my brother said, "Why don't you stay here and join the Elks, and I think you can get a job." He had an application in for me at the Elks since I had turned 21. I joined the Elks in 1924 and went all through the chairs there. I was district deputy and state trustee, five years, and State Chaplain. Finally retired. The Elks had the only bowling alley in town, which they still have. They had various card tournaments and a billiard table, and, of course, the dances. The day after Christmas, I went down to the power company and asked if there was any chance for a job. I got a good job there, reading meters and repairing small appliances. I worked there until the late thirties when they closed the place down.

After that a fellow came to me and asked if I wanted a little extra work, helping him hang paper and paint. I worked with him one year and started up my own business the next. I stayed in that business until I finally retired about five years ago. I think I worked in about 95 per cent of the houses in this town. Back in those days, they didn't have the glazed paper they have today. You bought your own paste in five-pound packages. You just mixed it in water each time. A ten-pound pail would usually last you about a day.

I helped build the pool in the summer of 1925. I was on the bull gang; that's what they call the help. I put the rock in place, did pick and shovel work, and helped build the forms for the cement. They built the pool in one summer. They sold stock to various people in town to pay for it. The stock has all been paid off although I think one or two people in town still keep one or two shares as mementos. Didn't need the money. People were paid fifty cents an hour to work on the pool; worked eight hours, four dollars. That was top money. Fifty cents an hour for common labor was top wages in those days.

I met my wife in 1937. She was a nurse at the hospital when one of my nephews had an appendix operation. I went there to visit him and that's how we happened to meet. We started going together and the next thing I know we were married. She got me to the altar that same year. We had two boys. One of them is in Colorado Springs and the younger boy is in Minnesota. Both of them graduated from school here and Bruce went to Western State and Bill went to CU.

My brother was one of the original members of the old Gun Club Ranch down by the Orvis Pool. They formed it to teach the young fellows to handle a gun. They had an indoor range and an outdoor range. Each fellow that belonged had to be pretty doggone proficient in the art of having a gun. Each summer they would take one or two kids down there and show them how to take a gun apart, how to clean it, how to put it back together again, how to carry it, how to load it, and how to unload it. I would say that 98 per cent of the kids, before they were 21, could handle a rifle as well as anybody on earth. There are a lot of these young lads today who will tell you how my brother taught them to handle a gun.

When I was growing up, Ouray was strictly a mining town. Up until World War I, when all the mines closed down, the town was between a thousand and twelve hundred people. When the war came everything was shut down. Most of the younger fellows went into the Army and prices went down. Mining declined and the town went downhill.

Even then the 4th of July was the big day of the year. Along about six o'clock in the morning they'd shoot off some of these big sticks of dynamite and wake everybody up. At about ten o'clock they'd start lining up on Second Street for the parade. In those days all the floats were all on wagons drawn by horses. I think it was 1911 or '12 before the first automobile hit town. All the merchants would put in their float, advertising their business. They'd have two or three bands and special trains would come from Grand Junction, Delta, and Montrose. After the parade there would be all kinds of street games for the boys and girls. There would be all kinds of races for both boys and girls and a tug of war. In the afternoon there would be a big baseball game. It would always end up with the water fight. Then everybody would go home, have their dinner, and get ready to watch the fireworks. Then they used to set off the fireworks on the corner right down from the bank. They shot them right up against the hill. Some of the volunteer firemen would be scat-tered around up there with fire extinguishers in case any little fire started. It was only in the last twenty years, after they started the flare parade, that they started shooting the fireworks off up here on the point.

In the twenties and thirties, there was a little more doing than there is now but it was a good, quiet, neighborly town. Everyone seemed to know everyone else. No matter who you were, if they heard that you had had a fire or if someone was sick, the people of the town and the various churches were there to give you a helping hand. As far back as I can remember, that's the one thing I've heard people say that they loved about this town. Everyone is so friendly and has a helping hand out in case of necessity. I don't think a higher thing could be said about a town than that. To me it's more like one great big family.

MARTIN ZANIN

MACHINIST

Martin lives in a neat frame house on a corner in Ouray. The house is compact, comfortable, and bright. The thing that stands out most about this interview was the process of apprenticeship to become a machinist. It began in the blacksmith's shop where Martin spent much of his time as a child. Here he learned the ways of the blacksmith and found his interest for the rest of his life.

This interview was one of the first and told about the time when Ouray was still thriving. The early interviews gave the first inkling of the excitement to be found in learning about Ouray's past.

Both of my parents came to this country from Austria, at least it was Austria then; it became part of Italy after World War I. My dad came to this country in 1898, looking for work. He spent a few years in Trinidad, Colorado, working in the coal mines, and then moved to Ouray to work in the metal mines because he heard they were paying more. My dad was a blacksmith around the mines but he was always going out to find a mine for himself. He never did find his own mine but that's what found a lot of the mines around here. One individual went out and prospected. About the time he was ready to find something he would have to give up because he ran out of money and one of the big companies would come in and take over. Then he would start over again. Prospecting is a disease that gets in the blood.

My mother came to Ouray in about 1901. She had a sister who was married to a miner and living in Ouray. My parents met here in Ouray and were married in the Catholic Church in 1903. That was the old church that has since been moved to Nucla. They moved the whole building intact and set it up in Nucla. It wasn't very big but it was a nice church. Both of my sisters and I were baptized in that church.

My dad became an American citizen in 1903. I still

> "In those days in the machine shops, they would come in and say we want this made or that made. You couldn't get out a catalog and order it. You designed it and made it ... We even built an 18-ton diesel electric motor."

have his certificate. At that time, the wife automatically became a citizen at the same time as her husband. Dad always said this is my country and he became a citizen as soon as he could.

I was born at home in 1911. I grew up here and have spent my whole life here with the exception of two years away at school, a couple of jobs that took me away, and a tour in the Navy.

Ouray was still a busy town then, although the heyday of Ouray was winding down. There were still a lot of mining operations with maybe one thousand miners scattered around in the hills. This is a mining area and, at that time, that's all there was.

I remember Ashenfelder's, one of the biggest freighting outfits in Colorado. Their barns were down on 2nd Street, in back of the Western Hotel. At one time they claim they had about 1200 head of animals: horses, mules, and burros. They used them to supply the mining operations in the hills. Although some of the mines were accessible by wagon, most of them had no roads so they had to use these animals to bring supplies in and haul ore out. The ore was brought down into town and then shipped out by rail. When I was small, we still had three freight trains coming into Ouray each week. At one time there was a freight train every day bringing in hay and grain for the stock.

There were two other freighting outfits in later years: John Donald and the Fellin Brothers. They were the first ones to haul ore from the mines in trucks. I remember the first truck, it was a new Buick. To find out how much ore they could haul they loaded bags of concentrate on it down on Main Street and drove it up the hill. If they could make it they brought it back down and loaded more ore until they finally found out how much tonnage they could carry. Some of the old freighting outfits were not too happy about using trucks to haul ore. There was some resentment when they tried to modernize freighting by using a truck.

In the 1900s the price of silver dropped, so mining started to go downhill. That meant the end for most of the freighting outfits. The only thing that kept them alive was hauling to the mines. Even after that there was always some mining. Some of the big mines like the Camp Bird, the Atlas, and the Revenue were still hanging on.

In the early years, the only school in Ouray was a grade school. Then they added a high school where the present school is. When the population started to dwindle, they combined all the grades in one building. That was where I started school. When I started, they still had all the country schools. The superintendent and the principal in Ouray were in charge of all the schools. There never was much rivalry between the schools back then. In fact, I don't think there is much rivalry even today. The students all get along well, they always have. I think the rivalry starts with the parents.

I graduated from high school when I was sixteen. It was a lot different than it is today. For one thing, when you graduated, you didn't get a car. Of course, now they get them when they start their freshman year. If you were lucky, you had a nice suit and that's what you graduated in.

They did have a banquet for just the class and the teachers. There were a lot more poor people than rich ones then but everybody was happy.

When I was a kid there was a shoe-shine stand at the barbershop where I used to shine shoes. Sometimes I made more than the barbers. They didn't like that very much. When a miner had a pocket full of money, he'd come for a shoe shine and give you a $5 bill. Maybe in two weeks he'd come back and be broke, but you would shine his shoes anyway because you were well paid the first time. The miners were

Train at the Wye at Red Mountain Station.

always good to the kids, always gave them money. They liked the kids.

As kids we played ball; we had the same sports as today. Of course, we didn't hang around the pool halls or soda fountains. We'd generate our own games. At night we'd play kick-the-can or hide-chief-hide. Just about anything for entertainment. At that time, all the streets had an arc light out in the middle of the intersection so we would play under those lights.

Those arc lights were actually carbon lights; they used carbons instead of bulbs. They made a terrific light; they were too bright to look at. They made a little hum as they burned. The lights were hung from two poles diagonally across the street from each other. There were two carbon sticks, about eight or ten inches long, in each lamp. They kept feeding together to make the arc. Every three or four days they had to pull these lights down on a cable to change the carbons as they burned down.

They had these lights on all the intersections on Main Street but they had them on 2nd Street, too. That was the area they called the red light district. Some of the places did have red lights, either at the entrance or in a window. If they had business, they'd turn the light out. That area wasn't at its peak when I was a kid, but

I remember several of the girls down there. The kids in town would go down and run errands for the girls. They would never let you in but they would come to the door and ask you to get them a malted milk or a magazine or something. It was always good for a 25-cent tip. If you had a few of those, you could buy a ranch. At that time, that was a lot of money.

The sporting girls were always restricted; they couldn't come up town. If they wanted a loaf of bread or something, they had to send somebody after it. All the girls smoked, most of them rolled their own, but you would never see them smoke in public or anyplace where there were kids around. Most of the girls had polly parrots that they would put out in the sunny part of the day. The kids would teach them to cuss and the girls would get mad. I suppose I was helping, too.

We never went into the cribs or into their rooms. I still say they were all ladies. They had their good parts about them.

I remember Main Street. There were ruts a foot and a half deep from the ore wagons. The only pollution on Main Street then was horse droppings and they didn't last long because the town was full of pigeons and sparrows. They kept that part cleaned up.

At Halloween there was a lot of mischief. At that time every block in Ouray had an outhouse and one of the big things was pushing them over. Kids always amused themselves.

If you were lucky you got a dime to go to the picture show. The old Isis Theater was next to the Variety Store.

It was great for silent pictures. In later years they had sound but the building wasn't constructed for it. For the silent pictures, there was always a music box or some woman playing the piano. The women tried to play music that would fit the picture. If it was a hilarious show, they'd have hilarious music. Elsie Sonza played at the theater for, I suppose, 25 years. They'd tell her what the picture was and that was all she needed. She played by ear, she had a knack for it. She was terrific.

In those days if you had a nice big dinner, that was Christmas. It wasn't a house full of toys that got broken and thrown out the next day. We never had Christmas like that. I don't even remember toy shops like they have now. My folks always had a goose for Thanksgiving and Christmas, not a turkey. For one thing, a goose was cheaper than a turkey, and I think if it's cooked right, it tastes better than turkey.

Christmas was one day. The family would be with the children. Now Christmas starts before Thanksgiving. By the time Christmas gets here, it's worn out. Now it's a big commercial deal. You go into debt until next Christmas then you're ready to splurge again. We never grew up like that. We always lived within our means but I was dressed warm in decent clothes and never went hungry.

When I was a kid, I used to hang around the blacksmith shops. That was quite a privilege because they didn't want kids around but they kind of took a liking to me. There were four blacksmiths and I knew them all. There was also a wagon-maker and helpers. They used to build all their own wagons. The blacksmiths did all the welding in the forge and those welds never let go. They would last forever. Now when you weld, you just run a bead and you have a heat line on each side. When you weld something in a forge, you fuse the iron and it's all in one piece.

I remember one time when I was watching them make tires for the ore wagons. They had just heated a big strap of iron to cut it and I went in and sat on it. I burnt my. . . and I thought they had jobbed me. I went home and wouldn't go back. I thought maybe they were telling me to stay away. After about a week, three of the blacksmiths came to our house and asked my mother why I hadn't been going down to the shop. They felt so bad that they gave me candy. That made me real happy again.

There is still a need for blacksmiths today but they don't have them. The mines always have a blacksmith because there is iron to bend or to shape or something. But the real blacksmith is a thing of the past. There's a few left but they are getting ancient. There is a blacksmith over in Aspen that does iron work, the fancy stuff, for my son but he must be 75 or 80.

When I was 14, I started working in the garages. We didn't have engines and parts like we have now. In those days you bored the blocks and scraped the bearings. You'd take them down, glue it, put it back up, and scrape the high spots. When you had a perfect glue on the top and bottom the bearing was ready to cinch down. It was slow. When I was 16, I could do a good job on an engine.

I worked at Croft Brothers where they sold Studebakers and at the Ouray Garage where they sold Dodges. We worked on other makes, too, like Rickenbacker, Norman, and Stutz, really ritzy automobiles, but mainly we worked on our own makes.

There weren't many cars in Ouray at that time. They were just starting. There was a Dodge dealership, and then Chrysler came in. The old Dodge people used to say they don't make them better than Dodge. Then the Croft Brothers started the Studebaker agency and got pretty competitive. They had a good product and they were good salesmen. There used to be an advertising sign below town at the city limits that said, "When you cross the streets in Ouray, be very careful. You might be run over by a Studebaker." The Crofts worked under Shaw in Grand Junction who was the head dealer on the Western Slope. One year they outsold every other car dealer in Colorado. The Croft Brothers lasted about six or eight years in Ouray. They were both gamblers and gambled it away as fast as they made it. They gambled it away.

After high school I started working at the Bachelor Mine. I started working in the kitchen as a pearl diver. That was what they called someone who washed dishes. I waited on tables, too. Later I helped in the blacksmith shop, dumped cars, just about anything that was available. In those days you did anything that gave you a dollar in your pocket. You were never fussy because if you were you wouldn't be working. That was my only experience of living in a boardinghouse. That mine was accessible; you could walk to town and back to work but all the miners stayed up there.

Later I went to Denver to school to learn to be a machinist. I knew what I could do but went to get a little smarter. Then I worked for American Lead and Zinc, for the Franz Brothers for one year, for Denver Equipment, and for Gardner Denver. I kept on learning from the old machinists, the shop people. They wouldn't tell you anything. They were the crankiest so and so's you've ever been around but I kept my eyes open and learned a lot. I swore that if I ever knew anything in the shops, I'd tell anybody that wanted to know and learn. That's always been my philosophy. If you take a secret with you, it doesn't help anybody. There were a lot of secrets in machine and tool and die work.

In those days in the machine shops, they would come in and say we want this made or that made. You couldn't get out a catalog and order it. You designed it and made it.

In 1941 I went to work at the Idarado, running the shops up there. I put in 29 years at the Idarado. I made a lot of machines for them. We even built an 18-ton diesel electric motor. I put hydraulic brakes on all the battery motors up there. These were three- to twelve-ton locomotives that had mechanical brakes initially. They always caused problems. When a miner was running one of those motors and wanted to stop it, he'd plug the controls and reverse the motor. That would burn up the controllers and points and got to be quite expensive. One of the supers came to me and asked if we could put some other type of brakes on the motor. I said sure, we'll put

our heads together and design new brakes. It was quite an operation; we had to design and make new motor shafts for both motors on each locomotive.

A lot of the mining equipment was old equipment; you might say it was obsolete. If you wanted to run it, you had to make parts for it. Parts weren't always available. Even when you ordered parts for some of the newer models, they wouldn't fit; and you would have to modify them to make them work. There was always a lot of work to do.

I commuted back and forth to the mine. We'd pool rides to work. Later the mine gave me a pickup to drive to work since I was on call 24 hours a day. Sometimes when I had to go back to the mine at night during storms, I think the pickup knew where it was going because I didn't. They didn't start paving the road until the early '40s, and it took six or seven years to get the job completed.

They didn't maintain the roads like they do now. After a big storm, it might take two or three days to get the road open again. We might have to stay in the boardinghouse a couple of nights once or twice a year because you couldn't get down to town. The roominghouse was huge; it accommodated 100 men. The boardinghouse had top food. Those old mining cooks were tops. They had a commissary where you could get 3.2 beer and play pool or cards. All the old mines accommodated the men the best they could. They kept the men happy.

The men stayed up at the mine for a week or two at a time. The mines paid every two weeks and many of the men stayed until they got a paycheck, then they came to town to have fun. I remember Freddie Biltz who cooked at the Camp Bird for years. At that time they were paying once a month, and one time he came to town with 21 paychecks. The red light district was going strong, and I think there were 32 saloons in town, so in about two weeks the miners would be broke and would have to borrow $5.00 to rent a horse to get back up the hill. Most of the miners were single, and that was the caliber of the men then.

During Prohibition, the bootleggers kept Ouray going. There wasn't any income or anything. The town would go to the bootleggers and say we want so much money to buy cement or some equipment. That's what paved the streets and built the swimming pool. People bought bonds or stock in the Ouray Recreation Association. After four or five years, they gave the stock to the city. My dad had a $1000 certificate. That's why the city owns the pool, but it first belonged to the Recreation Association.

When they first built the pool they had tent houses. They were wooden frames with a covering over them. That's where you changed to go swimming. In 1929, the year of the big flood, the river came over and took the tents down the river. The townspeople went up to the Revenue and tore down an old building and put it back up at the pool. It was used lumber to start with and it finally fell apart, but it lasted for years. In those days that's the way all things got done. The people would get together on a weekend and do whatever was needed; they called it Booster Days. The women would cook hamburgers or hot dogs for lunch and men would clean up the park or paint the sidewalks. We had boardwalks then. When they started putting in cement sidewalks they would do maybe half a block on one side of the street and then wait until they got financing so they could buy more cement and gravel. They might hire a man to oversee the job but the people would do it. That was the way they did things. Now they get grants and scratch their heads over the grants.

When City Hall burned, the town people rebuilt it. It isn't nearly the building it was, but there wouldn't be a City Hall if it wasn't for the people of the town. Kullerstrand, the bank president, loaned money for the materials. You had to have a good banker then, a fellow who was willing to cooperate, because the town pinched their two bits. They had to, you know.

I've always had a successful life. I had a wonderful family. My wife was a Chicago girl. We were married six months short of 50 years when she died. We had a girl and a boy. I lost my daughter in June 1986. She lived in Albuquerque. The son is in Aspen. He's a builder.

WILMA POTTER

RANCHER

Wilma is proud of her family's place in the history of Ouray County. Her grandfather was the first president of the Citizens State Bank. He had a house across from the cemetery on the road to the Sunshine Valley Ranch. It has been empty for many years but remains a place of strong memories for Wilma. Her home is on Merling Lane which led to the Piedmont Schoolhouse. Her story is a bit later than some of the others and gives a perspective on modern ranching to contrast with the earlier stories.

My grandfather, David Boyd, was born in Canada in 1863. When he was a small boy, his family moved to the United States, stopping first in St. Louis and then moving to Omaha, Nebraska. He used to tell about going long distances in a wagon to compete in spelling bees; he was a good speller. In 1882 he moved to Greeley, Colorado where he learned about farming and the cattle business. In 1887 he married my grandmother, Harriet Hudson, a great niece of Henry Hudson, the explorer.

"Ridgway had crank telephones at that time... The telephone operator, Rita, who weighed about three hundred pounds, was really a character... I know she used to listen in."

My grandparents adopted my father, Ralph Emerson Boyd, in 1892. My grandmother went to Denver and brought home my father. His mother had died the day after he was born and his father had been killed in a mine accident in Creede.

My father remembers how well his father got along with the cowboys when he ran a store in Snyder, Colorado. The cowboys would come into town on Saturday night and shoot holes in the roof of the large porch on the store. Sometimes the cowboys even rode their horses into the store.

Grandfather Boyd founded the Bank of Hillrose, Colorado, and ran it for a number of years. In 1912 the family moved to a small farm at Delta. In 1913 grandfather moved to Ouray, leaving the family to dispose of the farm, and started Citizens State Bank. He was the cashier of the bank. In all the years of its existence, the bank has had only four presidents; my grandfather David Boyd, Ralph Kullerstrand, Harry Lowe, and Dave Wood, the current president. Five years later, in 1918, the bank bought and moved into the two-story brick building that it occupies today. It had previously been a saloon that they remodeled.

Grandfather Boyd was a short little man that looked like Santa Claus. He had curly, red hair that never turned gray; it was still red when he died at 86. He was an ambitious man. He bought and studied law books and taught himself to type. He did all of his letter writing on the typewriter using two fingers. He was elected mayor of Ouray in 1918 and elected to the state House of Representatives in 1925. He had a great interest in Ouray. He had the trees planted along the walk to the swimming pool and spent a lot of time improving Box Canyon.

He loved to build things and had a building at the bank that he used as a shop. He made doll furniture for me that I still have today. He shod his own horses and remodeled the house at the Sunshine Valley Ranch. When he bought that ranch, the house, which had been built in 1876, was dilapidated; it was the oldest ranch house in the valley. He would come down after banking hours and work on the house until he got it livable.

When I was little, my grandparents lived right across the road from the cemetery. I practically lived in the cemetery and got to know all the families buried there.

Grandfather Boyd wanted my father to be a banker but he didn't want to do that. He worked on the Million Dollar Highway when he was young and then worked as a mine assayer at the Atlas. During that time he and my mother lived at Lake Lenore. My sister, Minnie, was born while they were living there. In the 1920s my parents bought the old Raleigh place in the valley, north of the Sunshine Valley Ranch, and he started ranching.

My mother's maiden name was Kennecott. Her ancestors started the Kennecott Copper Corporation. She was born in Delta where her family had an apple orchard. Mother taught school in Maher, near Crawford, before she married my father.

At Christmas time in 1926, my mother went to visit her parents in Delta. She became ill and stayed there until I was born on January 31st, 1927. My grandfather, William Kennecott, died the morning I was born so I was named after him. Besides my sister, Minnie, I had two brothers; one died from appendicitis when he was fifteen and Kirk was killed when a tree fell on him while he was running a backhoe near the Camp Bird Mine.

When my sister, Minnie, started school, there was a school at Portland but there were only two boys going there and they were sort of roughnecks so my mother wasn't happy about sending her there. Dr. Kemp, the dentist in Ouray lived in what is now the Hall house just north of the cemetery. He had a daughter, Myra, that he took to school in Ouray every day so Minnie rode along with them. He brought her home at night and she often fell asleep in the dentist's office waiting for him to be ready to go home. When she was in the second grade, she went to school at Piedmont which was just over the bridge west of our place. I went to the Piedmont School for a few years and then went to the old grade school in Ouray. It was an old two-story building where the school playground is now. It got to the point where it was not safe so they had to tear it down, and we moved into the new building when I was in the fourth grade. The Piedmont School opened in the 1800s and closed in 1948. There were about ten kids going to school there in a one-room schoolhouse.

Piedmont was named after an area in Italy. At one time there was a railroad stop at Piedmont before they changed the tracks. There was a water tank for the train there and a pond where they used to cut ice to fill the icehouse in Ridgway. They supplied ice for all of Ouray before refrigerators were in use.

I rode the school bus to high school in Ouray. We had a grouchy old driver who would not wait for you if you didn't get to the bus stop on time. Most of us didn't grieve too much if that happened. Times were hard while I was in high school. It was during the war and you didn't go places or do things because of gas rationing. The school did have a ball team that played Norwood and Nucla. We didn't go to Silverton. Our superintendent didn't approve of our going over the Million Dollar Highway; he used common sense. The school had a good band that had about 20 students in it. It had uniforms and even got to go to Grand Junction to play despite the gas rationing.

I graduated from high school in 1945. Our graduation banquet was at the Western Hotel. Tuffy Flor's mother ran the Western and she let us have our banquet there. I was the valedictorian and got the Reader's Digest Award.

When I was in school, the town was full of elk. Now it's full of deer. There didn't used to be a deer in Ouray.

In my grandfather's time, mountain sheep were around the depot. The trains brought in hay for all the mules that hauled freight to the mine, and the sheep, naturally, showed up to get what they could.

After I graduated from high school, Ralph Kullerstrand asked me to come to work in the bank. Grandfather was so pleased that I had gone to work in his bank. I still have the letter he wrote me about it. I kept the books until December that year when my husband, Jack, and I ran away to Gunnison to get married.

Jack and I met when we were going to school in Ouray. He quit school when he was fifteen to work on the ranch. Jack was seventeen and I was eighteen when we got married. I'm not sure why we ran away. Why do people do stupid things? Anyway, Jack kept insisting that we get married. I think he needed someone to do his dishes so we ran off.

Jack's father was a railroad man who had asthma and wasn't well. They had had a store in Gunnison and then bought a ranch here in the valley in 1937.

The first house we lived in had nothing, no water and no electricity. We had a well but it would go dry in March or April every year.

We started raising registered Herefords. We're proud of our cattle; that's our life. It was pretty rough in the beginning. We bought most of our original registered stock from Governor Dan Thornton, Bobby Edwards, and Jim Sanders in Gunnison. We sold a lot of our bulls locally to people like the Zadras, Harneys, Fourniers, and Israels. Marie Scott told us that she bought more good

The hay stacker.

bulls from us than anybody else. That was a real compliment. Often, when Jack was too busy, I would load bulls in the truck and take them to the sales in Delta or Grand Junction myself. Sometimes we would take as many as fifty bulls to the sale in Grand Junction. Things aren't what they used to be since they started crossbreeding. Now we don't fool around with bulls like we did.

We kept a few chickens and milked a few cows. We separated our cream and put it in cream cans, five or ten gallons. We'd get it down to the station and get it going to Denver. When we got a check back we thought we were rich. Fourteen dollars for a five-gallon can of cream.

Jack and I were one of the last people in this valley to work with horses. We put up tons of hay ourselves. We'd take the kids out with us and they would play and we would put up hay. We put up about 200 acres of hay every year. Finally we got a doodlebug. That's a car that's turned around and is used to push hay on the stacker. That was fun.

We did most of our shopping in Ridgway but our kids, all five of them, rode the bus to school in Ouray. Ridgway had crank telephones at that time. The telephone office was upstairs in the building where the hardware store was. The telephone operator, Rita, who weighed about three hundred pounds, was really a character. When you rang the operator, she would answer and say, "Number, please," or" What do you want?" if she was grouchy. I know she used to listen in. Jack's mother ran a store after his father died. Right after the war, you couldn't get silk stockings, but when Jack's mother would call and we would be trying to talk, Rita would break in and say, "You got any silk stockings?"

A man named California Frank used to live in the house just east of where the new highway joins the old highway at the north end of the dam. His last name was Hafley. I scarcely remember Mr. Hafley but he was a huge man who was a friend of my father. He had a wild west show that went to Madison Square Garden and even went to England to perform for the queen. He even had a midget that performed in the show. When they put in the new road, they were going to cut down that huge, old pine tree that stands beside California Frank's house, but all the school children from Ouray and Ridgway wrote letters. They caused such a stink that they moved the road and left the tree.

In 1970 we were haying the land in Idlewild. That was the Dalpaz Dairy. There wasn't a house there. When the dairy was sold they cut all the land up for houses. It upsets me the way the valley is changing now. I know someday it will all turn into homes. You have to give people like Ralph Lauren credit. At least they are keeping the land as ranches rather than chopping it up. If people want to get out in the country, there is a lot of marginal land around where they can build houses without picking the good farm land. It's the bankers that have done all that. They bought up the ranches and had them chopped up.

There has always been competition between Ouray and Ridgway for as long as I can remember. I've even seen people get in a few fist fights, a few hair pulling matches. They've never consolidated the schools because the people in Ouray never wanted their children to ride the bus. In the old days kids in Ouray never had to ride a bus to school. Now some of them do. The competition in the old days was just nonsense. But, you know, I don't think people are quite as narrow-minded as they used to be. I think they're advancing.

MARGE ISRAEL

NEWSPAPER WOMAN

Marge lives in Ridgway in a house next door to her daughter, Addie. She is still active, doing notary public work for people who stop by. As you can tell from her interview, Marge was and is one feisty lady.

I was born on May 29, 1909 in Lake City, Colorado, just 36 miles over Engineer Pass from Ouray. When I was about eleven years old, my grandfather, Franklin Sherman Williams, my dad, Stanley Williams, and his brother Lee built the road from Lake City over Slumgullion Pass to Creede in Mineral County. The whole family stayed up there living in tents. I had to get up at five o'clock to help Mama serve the men before they went out to work. Half the men were close enough to the road camp to come in for lunch, but we had to pack lunches for the other half. I baked five cakes every day. When the road construction moved too far from the road camp, we had to move the camp. We moved quite a few times during that period in horse-drawn wagons. The men would work on the road until the snow drove them out

"In 1953...some people in Ridgway called me and asked if I would run for town clerk. I thought it over and decided I would... That year there were 53 votes cast and I got 52 of them. I always wondered who didn't like me."

and then we would move back down to Lake City and stay with my grandmother to go to school.

One time we were camped in a little dale with a sharp incline running up to a plateau above it. A fellow by the name of Dabney ran cattle up on the plateau. One day two, great big white-faced bulls got into a terrible fight on the plateau. I think their horns must have locked because they rolled down that incline right into camp. Just Mother and us kids were in camp at the time. Mother said, "Come quick," so we ran outside and climbed up on a big old truck and watched the fight. Mother picked up a crowbar in case she had to do something to protect us, but the bulls finally separated and one bull went one way and one went the other way. That was the end of that little episode.

The cook's shack was a big cattle tent with doors on each end, wide enough for a vehicle to go through. All the men ate there. There were a lot of different types of men working there. I remember one fellow who was fond of peanuts. He would buy great big tins of them.

Us kids weren't used to any delicacies. In a camp like that we didn't have many good things to eat, just a lot of food, most of it canned. When the men would go out to work, us kids would slip up to his camp to help ourselves to a handful of peanuts; tasted awfully good. I bet he wondered where they went.

Grandpa always hired a handyman. He worked around camp chopping wood and digging holes to bury garbage and stuff. When we left a camp, everything had to be buried. Once when we were on top of a divide, a terrible thunder and lightning storm came up. The handyman, Mr. Wendt, was out chopping wood and lightning hit his ax. Blue flame came out of it; he got so scared he started running. All the kids laughed at him. That night he came and told my granddad that he was going back to town; so Mr. Wendt went.

There must have been fifty men working on that road. It covered forty or fifty miles. You go up from Lake City to Lake San Cristobal and then turn off to the left to go over the Pass. At the top there is a memorial to the partly eaten bodies that Alferd Packer killed. There's a little iron fence around it now. That wasn't there when the road was being built; it was put in later.

I can't remember how long it took to build that road, but there were a lot of swampy areas where they had to corduroy, put in logs and stuff to get over it. It was a big job. There were a lot of switchbacks, too.

Right at the lower end of the road, my grandfather, my dad, and my uncle owned a little mine, The Belle of the West Mine. They got in a boundary dispute over the mine so my dad hired Carl J. Seigfried, an attorney in Ouray, and the other side hired Moynihan from Montrose. My family lost in court. Before the lawsuit, they had shipped out a carload of ore that was full of gold and silver. It was a rich mine. Years later, my aunt in Lake City paid the back taxes on the mine and wrote me that she wanted to reopen it. We never did. I was afraid I might lose again. I don't know whatever happened to that old mine. I don't think anybody ever reopened it.

When I was in my early teens, I went to work for Mrs. Millen who ran a privately owned telephone company in Lake City. The telephone switchboard was in the front of a store on Main Street. In the back there was an ice-cream parlor and candy store. I worked for them for quite awhile and then Mother and Dad took over the store. We lived in quarters behind the office. I don't think we made any profits the first month. We ate up all the profits in ice cream and the good syrups you put on it.

I learned to drive when we lived in Lake City. We had an old Model T Ford with the spark and the gas right on the steering wheel. You had to crank that old car. When we'd get stuck on a hill, Dad would say, "Chock it." I'd run and get a rock and chock the back wheels so it wouldn't roll back down. Then he'd say, "Well, twist your tail, kid." And I'd go crank it. I could slip it over pretty good. Mother kept saying, "You cut that out now, she's going to break her arm one of these days." When we came up in the world a little bit, Dad bought a

Chevrolet and taught me how to drive that in Lake City. He went with me and taught me and then turned me loose and let me drive by myself.

When I was sixteen, my dad was working as a millright and helped tear down the old Lily Mill in Lake City. They brought it over to Ouray and he helped install it at what became the Banner American Mill. It was up near Ouray and has since been torn down. I finished my last year in high school here in Ouray.

I didn't think I would ever want to leave Lake City but I made a lot of friends here quickly. I like people. I don't remember much about the town at that time. There was a lot of mining going on. The Idarado and the Camp Bird were going full blast.

I do remember the move from Lake City. Dad hired a great big truck; we moved everything we had. Mama drove the car and it was loaded to the brim. We made the move in one day. It was only about 115 miles up to Gunnison, then to Montrose, and down to Ouray.

When we got to Ouray, having had telephone operator's experience, I put in my application with the telephone company. In a short time, I was hired as a relief operator. When anybody wanted time off they would call me in. Of course, since I was going to school, most of my work was night work.

After I graduated from high school, I would have given anything if my parents had had enough money to send me on to college. I wanted to be in commercial work and stuff like that. I had a job gathering news for the *Ouray Herald* in my last year in high school. After high school, Roy Young, the editor taught me how to run the Linotype, so I worked as a typesetter for three years until I got married in 1929. I continued to work for the paper off and on for seventeen years after we were married.

The way I met my husband was really quite funny. I never had a formal introduction to him. The newspaper office was in the building next to where the Longbranch was (now the Lavender and Lace). They were going to move to a building near the Beaumont. The editor said, "Marjorie, go out on the street and see if you can find a couple of able-bodied men to help us get this Linotype moved." I went out on the street and saw Bill Mills, who I knew, coming down the street with this tall fellow. So I hollered to Bill and asked, "Can you fellows come over and help us move the Linotype?" They said sure, and did.

A couple of weeks later the Ouray girls' basketball team was to play a practice game with the Ridgway girls. My future husband was engaged, at that time, to the Ridgway girls' team coach. During the game, Norma Schwend, the Ouray coach, wanted to substitute me for one of her students. Norma and the Ridgway coach had quite a fight over it. Finally, Norma said, "Margie is going to play." The Ridgway coach said, "Alright, if she plays, I'm going to guard her." Well, here she was, five foot ten or twelve and me, five foot two and 117 pounds. She guarded me alright. Every time I'd get the ball and go to make a basket she'd give me the hip. She did that four or five times. Finally, as I was going to the basket, she gave me the hip and staggered me, and I lit in some fellow's lap on the sidelines. I'm Irish. I came up fighting. She was running away from me but I caught her and tripped her and knocked her down. I had my fist up in the air and was going to slam her one when the referee threw me out of the game. My future husband asked his partner, Billy Mills, "Who is that?" "Oh," he said, "That's a new gal here in town, her name is Marjorie Williams."

Along about Thanksgiving time, five of us girls went to a dance, stag. In those days they gave you dance programs and the fellows would put their names in your program so you'd have to dance with them even if they couldn't dance worth a hoot. If you went stag, you could dance with whomever you wanted. At the dance, my future husband — they called him Shorty; he was six feet three — asked me for a dance. We danced several dances and he asked for a date home. I told him, "I turned down several dates, we girls are stagging it." He said, "Well, I brought a girl here, too, but we'll ditch them if you'll let me walk you home. So we ditched them and he walked me home and we just fell in love. We were married six months after that on the 6th of May, 1929.

We dated a lot during those six months; we went to shows or basketball games, we'd go to Montrose to the theater or games. Whatever entertainment there was.

About that time, my parents moved to Alamosa to operate a boardinghouse. While they were gone, my husband and I eloped. I don't know why, I guess we just didn't want anybody to know. I had promised my mother that I would clean the house in which they lived; and, after that was done, my husband and I moved into the little house right behind the Presbyterian Church. It was called the Honeymoon House because a lot of people had spent their honeymoons there. We stayed there for about a year and then my husband was transferred to Colona. Before we were married, my husband had worked for the railroad and for the county highway department. In 1928 he took a job with the state highway department.

Before I was married, the Fox Movie people wanted to come to Ouray to take pictures of the outdoor pool in the wintertime, in March, I think. They were trying to get girls to go in there and swim so they could make the movie. My mother said, "My girls are not going down there and catch their death of pneumonia. I won't have it!" My sister and I sneaked off, down to the City Hall, and got into our bathing suits and caps. They wrapped us in blankets and transported us down to the pool. So we went swimming and were in the Fox Movietone pictures. Shortly after that, my mother and dad moved to a little place in New Mexico. They went to a movie down there and as they were sitting there this Fox Movietone thing came on. Dad said to Mother, "Annie, that's the Ouray pool. "Why," she said, "It is, isn't it." Pretty soon this gal came out on the diving board and took a nice dive into the pool. My dad said, "My God, that was Marjorie." They went clear to New Mexico before they ever found out that I'd gone to the pool.

I remember Second Street well. Lilly Morrell ran one of the cribs. When she or her girls came up town, they never spoke to anyone. They were very ladylike and never tried to press themselves onto anyone. Lilly had a

Marge posing for the movies.

registered bulldog that had pups. My brother, Sherman Williams, was a paper boy and had that route on Second Street. He just loved those little puppies. One day Lilly said, "Sherman, I'm going to give you one of those puppies." So he got a registered bulldog. When my husband and I got married, Sherman gave that bulldog to us for a wedding present.

We lived in Colona for about two years. It was while we were there that Addie was born. It was a very, very mild place to live. I never spent such a lonely two years in my life. There were hardly any people to visit with.

At that time a lot of bums used to come through here and knock on doors, looking for handouts. One day a tramp came to the door and asked me for food. Addie was just a little girl and I told him to get out. I started to pull the screen door this way and he pulled it that way. We still had that little bulldog so I said, "Take him, Buster." Boy, that dog went out there and took him by the seat of the pants and he took right out of there.

After we moved back to Ouray, when Addie was about three, I went back to work. This was during the Depression and we were having a hard time getting along. I used to do anything I could to help out. My parents had moved back from Alamosa, so Mom took care of Addie for me and I worked at the Beaumont as a waitress. I worked off and on whenever Mabel Creel needed someone. The Beaumont had 53 rooms, if I remember; no bathrooms though, just pitchers in the rooms. It was a popular place. Rich people used to come there to dine.

They tipped well. I couldn't have worked there if it hadn't been for the tips.

After that I went back to work on the *Herald*. I worked there off and on again for a number of years. One year, after I had been there for quite a long time, the Spencer family wanted to lease the paper to me. I leased it for one year and ran the paper. Beverly Spencer, who was a wonderful photographer, stayed on and ran the job printing part. The first week that I had it, a young kid was found in his bathroom, hung. He had Boy Scout paraphernalia in there. They never did know whether he got tangled up in that or what happened. That was a difficult story to write.

I wrote a column for the paper, "What's Cookin'?" It had a little bit of everything. If I could get permission from people, I'd tell jokes on them. I had fun doing that.

I ran the paper for one year but lost weight. It was too much for me. My husband said I couldn't renew the lease. I can't remember how many subscribers we had, but I made money on it. The paper was usually four pages and came out on Fridays. We printed on a big press; I had to stand on a box to feed the sheets of newsprint into the press.

We ran specials every once in a while. I know we ran a special when that big accident happened up at the Genessee Mine. The driver was bringing a load of miners down to town and lost control of the bus and went over the embankment at the Lookout. It was right at 5:00 p.m. Beverly Spencer said, "Margie, I've got to get up there

with the camera. We had an old Oldsmobile then so he and I started up there. My husband was just getting off work so we stopped and picked him up. Leo Flor was the undertaker and he asked my husband to handle the ambulance. They needed all available people to handle the injured. I brought a man back to the hospital in the car. I remember him saying all the way down, "Oh, drive carefully, please drive carefully." When I got to the hospital the nurse said to me, "Marjorie, you're needed here, come and help." So I helped bathe them, they had mine muck all over them. I went to bathe a little boy who had a broken hand with the bone sticking out of his thumb. The doctor came in and just shook his head. He died almost while I was bathing him. I didn't panic at the time all this was happening; but after my husband took me home, I just shook like a leaf.

My husband and I went to a lot of dances. I'd go right now if I could. Of course, I don't like the music. I tried to watch the music awards last night on TV. They call it music, but all it is is just a bunch of noise. We used to have waltzes and fox-trots at the dances at the Opera House. They had a big dance floor upstairs.

We used to bowl a lot and I worked on many, many fundraising committees. I solicited for Red Cross and it got so when people saw me coming with a pencil and paper, they wouldn't answer the door.

One time the school band, of which Addie was a member, had a chance to go to Price, Utah for some kind of meet. I was a band mother, and at the meeting the women said, "We'll never get enough money to send those kids to Price." I told them, "If you promise me that I'll never have to serve another sandwich or another doughnut, I'll get the money." They said I was crazy. I told them I liked to go to dances and have fun, but every time I go I've got to spend the whole time serving people. I said, "I get tired of it." I went down to the bank and saw Mr. Kullerstrand, the president, who was a good friend. I said, "Kully, I'm in a bind, I need some help." He told me to come back after the bank was closed and he'd see what he could do. He suggested that we hit up the parents of kids in the band who wanted to go badly. He said, "Hit them up first because they might donate twenty or twenty five dollars." That's what we did, and, by golly, we raised enough money to hire a special bus to take those kids to Price, and I didn't have to serve any more doughnuts and coffee.

During the war I worked as chief clerk for the OPA. I had many girls working in the price department but they didn't like it and quit. Finally I got a hold of Mary Fedel and she worked for me until they closed the office in Ouray. We took citizens' applications for tires, gas, sugar, coffee, and all those things. Then the Board would meet on it and if they were eligible, they got what they requested. If not, they wouldn't.

The main office was in Denver and they used to ask for humorous stories that happened. I sent one story to Denver that was published all over the country. A stockman had made an application for tires for his stock trailer that he used to transport a bull from one ranch to another. His application came before G. A. Franz, Jr., the Ouray mining man, and Frank J. Bush, superintendent of Camp Bird, Limited, who comprised the gasoline and tire panel. They discussed the application and decided to approve it. Then Bush remembered he had applied for a tire and the panel had ruled against him. He exploded, "By Gad, I'm not in favor of this application and here's the reason. I think I'm on par with the bull and if I have to walk to work, I see no reason why the bull shouldn't do the same." But when the votes were counted the bull got the tire. Conclusion: more essential work.

Everything was rationed but, you know, in my opinion that was the worst thing you could do. When you tell people they can't have something, they're going to get it one way or the other. People that got gas didn't use it. They would give it to somebody else and trade stamps. I think they used more commodities than if they had not rationed things.

In 1950 we moved to Ridgway. My husband had worked on the Million Dollar Highway for 28 years. He had been caught in slides but was always able to dig himself out. He always carried shovels with him. Finally his health broke; it was no wonder, going under those slides. It was nerve-wracking. He got up at 3:00 in the morning to open the road so the Idarado miners could get to work. I don't think he ever went to a dance in the winter without having to come home and change clothes and go plow the highway. When there was an opening down here, he applied for it and got it; and we moved to Ridgway.

When he worked on the highway, he decided to keep

a diary to keep track of the weather and what time the slides ran. I've been doing that since 1937. You'd be surprised how one year was about the same as the one before for the timing of the slides.

I was still working for the *Herald* when we moved to Ridgway and I decided that I wouldn't keep driving back and forth to Ouray for little jobs like that. After I quit, Norma Schwend, whose husband owned and operated the plumbing store in Ouray, called and said she and Gene had not had a vacation for many years and wondered if I would take care of the office for them while they took a two-week vacation. I told her I didn't know anything about plumbing supplies, but she said I could just take orders and they would fill them when they got back.

While I was there, Phil Icke came to see me and said his secretary was going to run for County Treasurer. He asked if I would consider working in his law office while she electioneered. I said I would and his secretary got elected so it turned out to be a six-year job. It got to the point that people would come in at 4:30 or 5:00 and want a quick contract or a simple will drawn and I had to stay and do that. I wasn't fair to my husband who worked hard all day and carried a lunch. He needed a hot meal at night so I told them I was going to quit. They didn't take me seriously; but, finally, about the middle of August, 1956, I told them I was giving two-week's notice and then that's it. Mr. Icke's partner, Mr. Carroll, went over to the bank and talked to Harry Lowe to ask if he knew anybody they could hire to replace me. He said he didn't but called me that day and asked me to stop by the bank after work. I thought he wanted me to bring over some files on the collection accounts we handled for them, but he said, "No files, I just want to talk to you." When I got there he asked if I was really going to quit Icke and Carroll and I told him I surely was. He wanted to know the reasons, so I told him. Then he asked, "Well, how would you like to come and work for us?" I said, "My Lord, Harry, I don't know anything about banking." He told me they would teach me, so I went to work. It was kind of a challenge to me. I worked at the bank for eighteen or nineteen years.

I had only been at the bank about six weeks when my husband got a chance to go to the Elks National Convention. When he had been Exalted Ruler, he was working so he had never been able to go to the convention. This time he was an alternate, and when the current Exalted Ruler got tied up in a court case, he had the chance to go. I didn't ask for time off because I had been there such a short time, but when Harry Lowe heard about it he called me in and said, "Marge, this is the chance of a lifetime, we're going to let you go." I was such a country girl, I didn't know what to expect. We left Montrose on the train and when we got to Denver, the Lodge had a big smorgasbord. We got back on the train, and everyplace we went, they kept adding another car. The train kept getting bigger and bigger. We had some time off when we got to Chicago so we went to a ball game at the Cubs Park.

When we went through Chicago, my eyes were as big as saucers. But when we got to New York and went through Harlem, golly, I didn't know what to think; the filth and everything. We went through Wall Street. I couldn't imagine the tall buildings and the narrowness of the streets.

When we got to the hotel, my husband had to go to another hotel to register, so he told me to go to the information booth and find out how to get to Yankee Stadium; we were going to a ball game there. They told me all we had to do was catch the subway beneath the hotel and take the A Train. It would take us right to the park. Then on the way back, catch the A Train again and it would come right back below the hotel.

Bill and Irna Stark from Ouray were along on the trip, and Irna wanted to go shopping at Saks. My land, I thought it was as big as Ridgway. I didn't want to buy any clothes, but when you went into the store, they assigned a girl to take care of your needs. She took us back to this booth so Irna could try on the dresses that she had selected. I just sat in this little alcove and waited for her. When she had picked out the things she wanted, she called the girl, and as we were walking out, someone reached out of an alcove and grabbed my purse. Fortunately, I was able to hang onto it because I had all the travelers checks and a good amount of cash in it. When we got back to the hotel, I told my husband he had to carry part of this; and I just ditched the rest of it in the suitcase and stayed in the room a lot of the time. This was the first time I had seen TV, so I just laid on the bed and watched TV.

It was a wonderful trip for me. They took us around Manhattan Island; we saw Grant's Tomb and the Statue of Liberty. It was wonderful, but I've seen it and I wouldn't want to go back.

In 1953, while I was still working for Phil Icke, some people in Ridgway called me and asked if I would run for town clerk. I thought it over and decided I would. It paid $25 a month, you know. That year there were 53 votes cast and I got 52 of them. I always wondered who didn't like me. I went to all the meetings and did all the bookwork here in my home. This little den of mine was the town hall. We met in a little room back of the fire station, but people came here to the house for ordinances and stuff.

I enjoyed the work, but it finally got to be too difficult. I think I quit in 1974. There were two factions in town and keeping the minutes got too difficult. The town had an ordinance about cattle, goats, and horses in town. Some people thought they shouldn't meddle in other people's business, so cattle and horses ran loose in town. That's why I put the fence up around my house. One of the ranchers used to have an old, red bobtailed bull in the field across from the house that would come into the yard. I could always chase him out. One day a black bull came in, and when I went to chase him out he took after me. That's when I decided to put up the fence.

In 1957 there was an explosion at the County Shop here in Ridgway. Something happened to set off some dynamite in the shop. When the explosion went off, it just turned the pictures on the wall in the house, it was that close. Addie and Don, who lived next door, ran down toward the shop, but, when they saw how bad it was, they started to run away. A board came flying through the air and hit Addie on the head.

A man working for the power company had gone up a pole to check the meter and was killed when the dynamite exploded. The fire chief was badly injured, too. They took up a collection for him and raised $5,951.13. That was a lot of money in those days.

I retired from the bank and the town clerk job at about the same time. I thought what a joy this is going to be not to have to get up at 5:00 in the morning and take a shower and get dressed. In the wintertime I won't have to run out into the garage and warm up the car and then slide up that road to work. After they started seeding the clouds, the roads were just like grease. I ran off the road into the ditch several times. Finally, I went down to Gay Johnsons and had them put winter tires on all four wheels. I got along pretty well after that. If you can drive in Ouray, you can drive anyplace, because it's all uphill or downhill.

After I retired, it was just great for two or three months. Of course, I woke up at the same time every morning. After having worked for so many years, I couldn't sleep in in the morning. I still can't. But I'd look out and see those great big snowflakes falling and think, this is heaven. After about three months the walls started closing in on me. I thought I've got to get a hobby or I'll go crazy. Addie said, "Mother, you had a colorful life and have seen and done so many interesting things, why don't you write a book?" So I did. I kept diaries for many years here in Ouray but hadn't done so in Lake City. I started trying to recall all the interesting things in Lake City and all that happened after I came to Ouray. Then I'd think of something else in Lake City and add that. It's kind of rambling.

It's done, about 220 pages, single-spaced. I thought of getting it published, but I'm not an author. And I couldn't get it published because I name names: doctors, lawyers, prominent people who have descendants. Sometimes I put things in there that weren't pleasant. They could sue me for libel, so I decided that it would just stay in the family. Addie said I just want my grandchildren and great grandchildren to see what an ornery old grandmother they had.

I went back to Lake City a year ago. My great grandfather fought in the Civil War and the government issued some of those old veterans stones for their graves. My grandfather was one of those so I went over to the dedication of that. My husband's family, brothers and sisters, are all buried out here in the Dallas Cemetery. His brother, Earl, who hadn't seen the family for seventeen years, came back to visit one year. We got to see him, then he suddenly died. I think that man came home to die.

With all due respect to Ouray, I really like living here in Ridgway better. It's more open, we don't get as much snow and we get an hour's more sunshine a day. I love Ouray, but I really enjoy living here.

Mary Fedel

MINER'S WIFE

Mary was reluctant to be interviewed but finally consented with some encouragement from Mary Ann Dismant who typed many of the transcripts. It soon became evident that Mary had volumes of stories to tell about growing up in Ouray. Mary's husband, Frank, died at age 94 a couple of years ago. Since that time Mary has spent her winters away from Ouray but returns every summer to spend time in her home and with the four generations of her family that still live here.

My parents brought me to this country from Tyrol, Austria in 1906. We first lived in Ogden, Utah. In 1910 my mother, who was a widow, remarried a man who was in mining and we moved to Ouray. At that time the town was so full that it was hard to find a house, so we had to move in with Tuffy Flor's mother. She gave us two rooms to live in until we could find a house. My stepfather had a son and, of course, my mother had me. I had an older brother who had been left behind in the old country. He came over here after World War I. My

"Frank...was a timberer and that was it. He either timbered or he didn't work. He would never work where there was machines or drilling of any kind. He would never go in where there was all that dry dust. That was why he lived 94 years."

mother had nothing when she came to America. She had always planned to come over here and work for a little while and then go back. That changed when she met Mr. Moscon and married. Our first house was a little shack that was later torn down. When we lived here, there was a hot water stream running beside the road down at the ball park. My stepbrother and I would go down there barefoot and catch frogs. We would sell them to the restaurants; we'd get a nickel apiece for frog legs.

My dad went to work at the Bright Diamond Mine up at the Blowout and worked there for four or five years. He used to stay up at the Bright Diamond all week and come home on weekends. A lot of the miners worked seven days a week; they didn't have to take Sundays off, but my dad liked to come home.

Then he went into partnership with Henry Zanella's dad selling ice to the town. We didn't have fancy refrigerators then, we had iceboxes. They made ice down at Piedmont and would get two train carloads each winter.

That would do the whole town for the summer. They had to go down and cut the ice themselves. In the summer he would deliver ice all over town. He had a truck that sat way up high on solid rubber wheels. He was so proud of that old thing. I used to think it was quite a thrill to ride on that truck.

They also built a brick building to make pop and ice cream. The walls are still standing on Oak Street right across from the Washateria. They made ice cream in quarts and half gallons and packed ice around the old-fashioned containers. They made any kind of pop you can think of; real good pop, not like the junk they make today. They had a counter where Dad would bottle the pop and Mr. Zanella would cap it with one of those old-fashioned hand cappers. It would take forever and a day. They used to recycle the bottles. My mother and I used to go and help them. They had three tubs where they heated the water by coal to wash and sterilize the bottles. They did everything by hand. They worked hard but did real well. They sold out around the time of the Depression. He didn't live long after that. He had worked too long in the hard rock and got pneumonia from which he never did recover.

I was ten when we moved here. I had gone to the first four years of school in Ogden, Utah. When we arrived in Ogden I started in the first grade right away. They kept me one week and then told my cousin, who had sent us the money to come to this country, that this little girl has got to learn to talk a little bit. We don't have time to teach her. There were 38 kids in my class and they couldn't be bothered. It wasn't like today, you know. My cousin told them that they would take me where I'd get help, so they took me to the Sacred Heart Catholic School. I was there for six months, and I could speak English as well as I do now. I stayed there the whole four years we lived in Ogden, even though we had to pay for me to go to school.

When I came to Ouray, they put me back in the fourth grade. The school was right where it is now. Of course, the building is new. There were 37 or 38 kids in the school with one teacher. I think there were six other kids in my class. The teacher was Mr. Henn, Roger and Bernice's father. He was a good teacher but very strict. They were a lot stricter than they are now. I only got to go to the eighth grade. I never had a chance to go to high school. I had to work and help out.

My parents and another family had bought a rooming house while I was still in school. They called it the Belvedere; it was where the Coachlight is now. It had 27 rooms for miners. It had been rented by Tuffy Flor. In 1916 Mrs. Flor said they were going to buy the Western Hotel so I had to quit school to help my parents run the Belvedere when we moved in. My mother took in railroaders, too. Those railroaders were the nicest guys. We had five different crews coming in every night. I did the cooking with my mother's help. My sisters were just growing up at that time. We cooked two meals for the boarders, breakfast and supper. My mother sold the Belvedere in 1951 and moved in with my husband and me.

As kids, we made our own fun; we never had anyone

make it for us. We used to coast on sleds on the hills and we used to ice skate on the flume. Some of the boys made a big pond at the bottom of Cascade flume. Our folks would give us wienies so we would roast hot dogs by the pond. We had the best time doing nothing. We hiked a lot; under Cascade or up to the Spud Patch. But at 8:00 p.m. all of us had to be in. No kids were on the streets after 8:00. It wasn't a city ordinance or anything; it was our parents.

When I was in school there was a bunch of girls that were always together, about four or five of us. Our parents used to give us 10 cents to go to the movies; 5 cents for the movie and 5 cents for popcorn. One Sunday we decided that we would walk down to the Bachelor Switch where the train stopped. The train stopped there to drop off groceries, milk, and other things for the families that lived there. We walked from town down there, paid a nickel, and rode the train into Ouray. Boy, you should have seen us. We thought we were something, getting off the train in town. That was our treat instead of going to the show. That bunch, we saved our pennies.

At Halloween, my father would say to my stepbrother and me, "All right, kids, go ahead and go out to have a good time, but if I find out that you have done anything that destroys property, it will be your last time." Parents were stricter than they are now. One year my friend, Norma Schwend, and I got in with a bunch of boys for some reason. I don't know how we got mixed up with that crowd. Usually the girls traveled together and at Halloween would just take a chair and put it on the sidewalk or mark up some windows. That year we went to the Beaumont where they had nine clothes lines and the boys clipped every one of those lines; not at the end, but right in the middle and destroyed them. Mr. Creel, the owner of the Beaumont found out, and, by gosh, he came up with my name and Norma's. He came over to the bottling works and said to my dad, "Well, Fred, I guess you'll have to help pay for those clothes lines. Your girl was in with that bunch." My dad came home and asked, "Did you have fun on Halloween?" "Yes," I said, "We had pretty much fun, but I didn't like it too well, there were too many roughnecks." I'll never forget that, that's exactly what I told him. He said, "Yes, and you right among them." "Yes, but," I said, "I don't know how we got in with them." He asked if I had anything to do with those clothes lines. I told him that I stood on the sidewalk and watched and got scared but poor Norma got into it with those boys that did it. "Well," he said, "what are you going to do about paying for the clothes line?" I said, I never cut those lines." He said, "It doesn't make any difference."

The next year he wouldn't let me go out on Halloween, and, I remember, it cost me the whole sum of a dollar and a half to pay for those lines. I got the money by doing little chores for this person or that, getting their mail or something. We were good rustlers for money because we had to be, we didn't have any spare money. I don't think youngsters today have the memories I've got. Some were bad but most of them were sure glorious. I grew up at a good, clean time.

When I was in school, I worked for 2 1/2 years for John P. Roberts in the house next to the Courthouse. I took care of his two little girls and waited on tables. They were wealthy people and built a greenhouse. After they left here, they went into the floral business in Englewood. Judge Icke lived in that house later and grew beautiful flowers for the whole town. Later, I worked for the Story family for two years until I got out of school. Mr. Story built most of the big buildings in town. I took care of a youngster there and waited on tables for them. I got a whole sum of $18.00 a month. That was a lot then. After I left school I worked for my folks at the hotel until I got married. I left school in 1916; that was when the country went dry.

I met my husband, Frank, in Ouray. He had come to this area to mine. He had been in and out of town for two years before I really got to know him. He was working at the Mountain Top Mine when the flu epidemic hit in 1918. They closed all the mines down because it spread so fast. He got sick so he came to my folk's place to get a room because he heard we had steam heat. When he started getting serious, we were in the same house all of the time. We couldn't really date much because we couldn't go out anywhere on the street. We were quarantined, more or less. Mrs. Flor had all the miners from the Camp Bird and the Atlas and they were in there to stay. All the people at the St. Elmo were quarantined, too. My folks weren't quarantined because they had all those railroaders and we didn't have anybody that was sick.

It was a bad time. A lot of people died. My mother and I went around and took care of quite a few people and never got sick. We took care of one family of five that had two other relatives living with them, only four of them survived. They would die in no time, the fever was so high. It was horrible. There was only one doctor in town and there was no medicine to treat the flu.

Dr. Bates was the town doctor. He never got the flu, he was a tough guy. I liked him; a lot of people didn't, but he was all right. He was a good doctor. He was a cowboy; said he wanted to die with his boots on, and he pretty nearly did, too. He was quite a character.

They had a hard time getting places to bury all the people who died from the flu. They had to enlarge the cemetery. Up on the east side of the cemetery, that's where all the flu victims are buried.

Frank and I were married in January, 1919, when I was 18. We moved in with my folks. Shortly after we were married, Frank couldn't get a job around Ouray so he said we should move to Telluride. He had worked for five years at the Smuggler before he came to Ouray. He had a cousin living over there and we moved in with him. I took care of the cousin's three kids; his wife had divorced him. We couldn't find a house at the time. Telluride was like Ouray; everything was filled up. Frank got a job timbering. He was a timberer and that was it. He either timbered or he didn't work. He would never work where there was machines or drilling of any kind. He would never go in where there was all that dry dust. That was why he lived 94 years. Those old miners were lucky to reach the age of 50.

Three weeks after he started on the job, when we thought we were going to get a company house to move into up at the mine, the boss told Frank that he wanted him to work in a new area where they had just given someone a big contract. Frank went in there and found that it was just like going into a smokehouse. He told the boss he wouldn't work there. The boss told him he had to go in; they needed him, but Frank said, no, and went in and drew his time, and we moved back to Ouray. My folks were glad because they needed help. They had all those railroaders to take care of.

When we came back to Ouray, Frank went to work at the Mountain Top Mine, up in Governors Basin above the Revenue. The mines were going pretty well around here then. We stayed with my folks for quite awhile.

In the late twenties we bought a hotel called the Mountain View. It stood where San Miguel Power office is now. We had our first two sons, Al and Francis at that time. The hotel had 27 rooms in two stories. I had 16 permanent boarders so the place was always full. I never had a finer bunch of roughnecks than those miners. I'll stick up for a miner as long as I live. My husband was a miner, my dad was a miner, and so was my brother, John. I've never been around a finer bunch of people than I had in that house. They knew a lady at that time. They respected me far more than some of the other places I worked. I did the cooking and raised my family. I lost a baby between Francis and Dick and then Norm was born. We raised four sons while we ran the hotel. Final-ly I got sick from working so hard, so we had to sell out.

We were fortunate. We sold it to a nice young couple from Durango, those poor people. They gave us a down payment and we held all the papers and everything. They went to Durango to get all their belongings and furniture and were gone five days when the hotel burned down. They hadn't owned it for more than a month or so when it burned. We got our money out of it since we were holding the insurance, but we felt pretty bad because they were nice kids. They tore it down. We lived with my mother for a while and then bought a house up on the hill.

During the Depression my husband got a lease at the Tomboy in Telluride. He and his brother and two other fellows went over there to work. They took our son, Al, who was a freshman in high school, along to work with them during the summer. They panned gold at the Tomboy dump. They did pretty well; it did us for a whole year. They put up a little stamp mill and had a little crusher and tables where they got a little gold at the end of each day. One of the fellows built a wheel that ran from the water coming from the mine. Telluride was starting to build up a little at the time, and the water that came from the mine went down into the river in Telluride. They had to use cyanide to catch the gold, and my husband was afraid they would contaminate the water supply for the town, so they pulled out. He had the lease for five years, but he never went back.

During the Depression, in about 1932, the town was in bad shape. Frank was out of work for about 2 1/2 years

Stage in front of the Beaumont Hotel.

but we were getting by at the hotel. Mr. Zanett got Mr. Franz to come to town and they started the Pony Mine. Frank had worked on the Wedge for some leasers, so Mr. Zanett knew that Frank knew mining pretty well and knew that area and asked him to come out and run the mine. That's how Frank was with Mr. Franz for so many years. Mr. Franz came from St. Louis and was connected with some lawyers there who put up the money for the mine. When Mr. Franz died, Frank and another fellow took the lease and worked it for five years. He did well out there. That's what put us on our feet.

During the Depression my son, Francis, who was in high school, worked as a busboy at the Beaumont. The trains and buses were coming in and the place was always full. That was an elegant hotel in those days. He told me that they needed help down there; so, since times were hard, I went down and asked Mr. Creel for a job. I told him since I had a family I could only work certain hours. He said that would be fine, but I would have to start by washing dishes. I washed dishes on the afternoon shift for a month. Then I started baking pies and went from there to cooking.

The cook, Mickey, a colored lady, had been there for seven years. She got a job offer from Sadie West to cook at a restaurant on Main Street for $150 a month. The Beaumont was only paying her $100 a month. She spoke to Mr. Creel and asked him for a $50 a month raise. He said he couldn't pay it, and she told him he could. They went round and round. Finally she said she was quitting. He said, "The heck, you say, you wouldn't leave me, you've been here seven years." Her answer was, "You think I won't, you better come up with the money or I'll quit." She did quit and he had no one to cook breakfast in the morning. He pleaded with me to take over the cooking for the hotel. After talking it over with Frank, who said he could get along, I agreed to do the morning cooking for a few days until Mr. Creel could find a replacement. Mr. Creel thought I would stick it out so he never looked for a new cook. I got along all right since I had a Swedish girl working with me in the kitchen who was awfully good help. I stayed there until Thanksgiving and then gave him my notice. He had a big party coming from Montrose for Thanksgiving dinner and he asked me to stay until that was done, and then he promised to get a new cook. I worked there about six months. There aren't many places I haven't worked in Ouray.

When times were hard we got along fine. We never had to go to the government for anything. That's one thing my husband was proud of. A minister living next to us kept telling Frank that since he had such a big family he should go down and get some help. All Frank said was, "I will not." They were paving the highway at the time and every morning he would go down and ask for a job. They asked him if he was on relief, and when he told them no they said, "Sorry." The people on relief got preference for the jobs.

They brought in a lot of government work to Ouray during the Depression. My brother-in-law, he had married my younger sister, and a friend went around and built CCC camps where men worked during the Depression. They built one at Crested Butte and one at Dillon. They made enough money to eat on. Times were tough.

I worked at a lot of jobs during the Depression. I did housework for people and I worked at the hospital. The hospital was full all of the time then. When I came to Ouray the hospital was run by nuns, the Sisters of the Church. A couple of years after we got here, I was thirteen or fourteen, I think, I got an awful sore throat. I was so sick that my mother called in the doctor, Dr. Sickenberger. He told mother that I would have to have my tonsils out. I'll never forget; I had my tonsils out in this hospital. During the Depression, when times were tough and everything closed, the Sisters sold the hospital. When the Idarado started up they took over the hospital and brought in Dr. Spangler. He was just an elegant person and a wonderful family doctor.

I remember the first car we had. My father and my husband bought it together. It was a Willis Knight. It was a nice car at the time. Imagine buying a new car for a thousand dollars. My mother got sick at that time, and the doctor told my dad that she had better go somewhere and get away from all that work, so my dad took the car and drove her to Glenwood Springs. Frank went to Denver and bought a brand new Dodge for $1200. When my dad came home he fell in love with that car so Frank told him to drive it anytime. Finally my dad went to Denver and got himself a Dodge.

When Al was just a little squirt, less than thirteen, his dad taught him to drive. We had an open Ford that belonged to the mine where Frank was working. Whenever we needed something in Montrose we'd put two pillows on the seat and Al and I would drive to Montrose. A round trip would take us half a day because the roads weren't very good. We were afraid to go into the middle of town since Al was so little, so we'd park way out on the edge of town; they called it Mexican town. Then we walked seven blocks uptown, did our shopping, and came home.

We did a lot of shopping in Montrose at that time even though there were stores in Ouray. We needed a big volume since we had boarders. We went to the farms and bought a sack of potatoes or a sack of onions. We had to buy it in a lot, not ten pounds at a time.

I always wanted to learn to drive but never did. Frank took me to the ball park one time, but he had a little jeep that kept dying on me. He said I couldn't remember anything. He didn't have patience with me. You know it's no good to have your own people teach you. I fooled him one time. I backed that Dodge out one time and went clear to Ridgway. That scared him to death when I didn't get home. My mother got to worrying, so he came looking for me in the truck. I met him by the old mill north of town. The look he gave me; I could have gone off the road. He was so mad at me. After that, that ended it.

In the forties Frank leased and mined at the Pony for five years and five years at the Highland Chief up above the Revenue. Then he came to Ouray and worked as the janitor at the school for eleven years. He didn't like that much; mining was in his blood. He finally retired in about 1951.

During the second world war, when Al and Francis were in the service, I worked for the OPA for Marge Israel. I had a good time working with her. We were in charge of ration coupons and had to go into the stores to make sure that they were not overpricing people. Initially my job was to check on the stores, but I hated that since all the people knew me since I was a kid, and they were trying so hard to be fair. I couldn't turn them in if their prices were a little high. So Marge and I traded jobs. She checked the stores and I handled the ration coupons. People used to get so mad at me. They thought the government was cheating them when they couldn't get any more gas or tires or more of what they wanted.

Once when a man from Denver came to check on our office he found that Marge and I had traded jobs, and he said that since I was supposed to be the price clerk and wasn't doing that I might lose my job. The local OPA Board, which was unpaid, told him that if he fired me he would have to get a whole new board, and he would have a hard time doing that since no one wanted to be on that board and take all the grief. I never heard another thing about it. I stayed where I was, and she stayed where she was. I got the job when Marge came to me and told me that the lady that worked with her was quitting. She said I was entitled to the job since I had two boys in the service. I told her I only had an eighth grade education and didn't think I was qualified. She told me to just come on to work. I was glad she did because I could use the money. She was a good friend. I worked there for about two years until they closed the office after the war. After that I worked in the Post Office for twenty-four years, retiring in 1973.

When my folks ran the Belvedere, we were right down next to Second Street where the Gold Belt and all that was. That was a red hot district, I'll tell you. But you know, those ladies knew their place. They never went up town. They were there and they were respected for what they were; no trouble, nothing.

There was a livery stable behind the Western Hotel, one down on Second Street by the river run by Johnny Donald, a big freighter, and another one on Main Street next to the flume. The miners had horses; they didn't have cars. They rode horses back and forth to the mines. They'd get a job and rent a horse for $2.00 and away they'd go. I remember when the livery stable behind the Western burned down. It was an awfully big fire because of all that hay. It burned for hours.

Frank helped put in the pool when the town put it in. Mr. Franz donated all the pipe to get the hot water down to the pool. He was a wonderful man for this town. The people in town bought bonds to help finance the pool. My mother put in $500 and Frank put in $500. All the work was done by hand; even the pool was dug out by hand, all hard work. I used to go swim there often.

Frank and I were never much for dances. We used to play cards a lot, and we used to get together with the Flors often. They had a big family, and we had a big family. We'd get together and sing, and, oh golly, it was grand. You know people don't do that any more. Frank was active in the Elks, so we went there a lot. We never took trips. I think once, after we'd been married 35 years, we took a trip to Denver to see my sister. It seems like we spent all our time working.

Would you believe in 67 years together Frank and I were never apart. Only, I'll tell you, that poor soul had various illnesses, first one thing then another. It seemed like every two or three years he landed down in the hospital. This last one didn't last long; he passed away peacefully. It's hard to be in this house without him. Sixty-seven years, never been apart, is something you know. I've had more rest and freedom since Frank is gone than I ever had in my whole life because my life was so full of this and that. That's how times were then. 'Tisn't like now, people look forward to a little vacation. We didn't know what a vacation was. We worked all the time.

After my husband died, I went to see my son who lives in Utah. I had only been there once before in the fifteen years he owned that house. Another son, who lives in Denver, said to me after Frank died that since I had a birthday coming, he was buying me a ticket to go to Pennsylvania to see my great granddaughters who live there. Imagine! Clear back there. The last time I was back East was when I got off the boat. I want to tell you, I went to swim in the Atlantic where I came off the boat. I swam at Camp Maine in New Jersey that summer. I did more traveling in the last two or three years, since Frank is gone, than I did in my whole lifetime. We never went anywhere, you know. I used to like to go but Frank, he wanted to stay home, so home we stayed.

I even started walking a lot. Mary Hollingsworth, a friend, and I got together and walked every day. We'd go to the Box Canyon or across the river. I still walk; if I didn't I wouldn't be as healthy as I am.

MARVIN GREGORY

BUTCHER

Marvin is a talkative man who has been in Ouray since the mid-thirties. He, like Ouray, has changed with the times. He went from being a butcher to being a carpenter. He lives on Oak Street in a house with a beautiful view of the Amphitheater. Marvin is well known around town and recently has been working at the museum.

I was born in north-central Kansas and lived there until I was twelve years old. My dad was a wheat farmer. A series of disasters wiped him out; three years in a row, crops were bad. One year there was a drought; another year the market was off. He finally collected all his animals and machinery and had an auction. It didn't bring much, but enough to buy tickets to western Colorado. In Kansas, he knew nothing about raising fruit, but eventually he pruned apple trees when he moved to Hotchkiss. He worked as a laborer for the rest of his life, taking care of the high school as custodian until he died.

". . . gold mining was out of favor during the war. They couldn't get supplies to mine unless they were producing something considered necessary to the war effort. Gold didn't qualify. I guess you couldn't make bullets out of it."

After I grew up, I left Hotchkiss and went to work in Cedaredge as a butcher. The job was alright as jobs go, but I wasn't happy there. I had a nice boss, a fine guy, but he had a 21-year-old son who was impossible to get along with. He was arrogant, egotistical, all in all disagreeable. So I started looking for another job.

Even though this was in the middle of the Depression, I had never been out of a job. I had some good friends among the salesmen who came by the market to take meat orders. When I wanted another job, I let them know and they looked around for me. One day in 1936 I got a letter from Everett Smith, part owner of Smith's Mercantile, where Duckett's is now. He was in the market for a new butcher and wrote to ask if I would come to Ouray to see him and talk about a job. He even said he would come to Cedaredge to see me if necessary. I came up to see him on a Sunday and a week later went to work. I guess the salesmen got me a job.

I was already married by the time I moved to Ouray.

The way Ruth and I met and courted was kind of a disaster. I was in the sixth grade when we moved to Hotchkiss and it was the first time I ever went to a town school; that was really something. I had gone to the first five grades in a one-room country school with one teacher for all eight grades. In Hotchkiss there was a different room and teacher for each grade. Ruth was in the sixth grade, too, but didn't make much of an impression on me. Ruth sat way back in the corner of the room, mostly looking at the end of her nose. There was a pretty little girl with blond hair and curls who sat right in front of me that really impressed me. Ruth's father was a practical Missouri man who made her dress warmly in the winter. Girls, in those days, didn't wear pants; they wore skirts, but he made her wear long underwear. You could see the folds of her long underwear under her socks.

It wasn't until about the eighth grade, when Ruth was beginning to look pretty nice, that she made any impression on me. It was kind of funny how that began. Ruth, my brother Gerald, who was two years younger, and a bunch of other kids had been out playing in the barn one afternoon. They came by our house on the way to Ruth's house just as it was beginning to get dark. Gerald got to our house and just dropped off. I thought that wasn't a bit nice since Ruth had to walk on a ways, so I ran and caught up with her and walked her home. There were huge poplar trees along the street. I thought I ought to protect her; you never know what might jump out from behind one of those trees. I felt pretty important. She let me take hold of her hand. That did it.

We only dated spasmodically in high school. I had to give all the other girls a turn. I had a big time and was engaged to a couple of other girls, but it never worked out. In 1930, after we graduated from high school, Ruth went to California to live with her uncle. In 1933 she came back to Hotchkiss. I was already working as a meat cutter, and every day she would walk past the store and, maybe pretty soon, walk back again. She told me later that she had lost a lot of her shyness in California and had to make a lot of trips up and down the street to make sure I'd see her. I ignored her at first but finally decided I wasn't being nice and asked her for a date. I had a car, a 1926 Chevrolet, and took her for a ride. I drove up on the 'dobies, just like you do now in a Jeep, and parked up on top where there was no road, looking east. Pretty soon the moon came up. My God, I never saw it so big. Somehow I kind of lost my mind and thought I might as well make the attempt, so I suggested marriage. She made me wait probably two minutes before giving me an answer. That was the longest two minutes I ever spent.

We didn't have a big wedding, nobody did. It was during the Depression, and we were too poor. We didn't even invite our parents. We wanted it brief and quiet, as small as you could have it and still be legal. My brother went along as my best man, and Ruth had a friend go with her to the minister's house. That was the whole party.

We were married on a Saturday evening at 9:00. I was working in the market at that time, and Saturday nights, in most farm towns, the farmers came in to do their weekend shopping. Closing hour was supposed to be 9:00, but most of them would visit on the street until ten minutes before nine and then head to the market, so it would be 11:00 before we got closed. That night my boss let me off at 8:00 so I could go home and get out the old washtub on the kitchen floor to take a bath.

In those days, a girl in a rural area couldn't get married without a chivaree. In the beginning, friends would wait until you moved into your house and then they'd come with noisemakers of various kinds and whoop and holler. You were supposed to be prepared with candy and treats and invite them in. Then they got to refining it. Your friends would kidnap the bride and, with the collusion of the marshal, lock the groom in the jail, maybe leaving him there overnight. That caused serious trouble sometimes.

I had some friends, Ernest and Helen, who had been close. Ernest used to ask me to go to dances with him since he didn't like to dance. Helen and I did, so I would dance with her and he would talk with the guys. My friends thought I was going to be married, but they couldn't find out when. If they had, my car would not have run. The distributor cap would have been missing or something like that. We borrowed Ernest's car and drove to the minister's house, leaving my car parked right in front of my dad's house where I was still living. The guys watching didn't have anything to go on. After the wedding, we drove back to my house and loaded our packed suitcases, said good-bye to the family and Ernest and Ellen, and took off. We got chivareed after we got

back, which was alright, but I wanted to make our wedding trip. My boss had given me a week off.

We went to Delta that first night, just out of reach of our friends. The next day we fooled around a little in Grand Junction, visiting relatives, and then spent the night in Price, Utah. The next day we drove to Salt Lake City. It was beautiful then. I'd never been in a city that big, so I know I committed a lot of country-kid errors. The cops would just look at me and grin; they never said anything to me. Driving into Salt Lake City, there was nine miles of blacktop. That was the first blacktop I ever saw, going up State Street. I thought it was wonderful. You couldn't hear any rattles in the car or anything.

In those days the only paved roads in western Colorado were the main streets in the towns. The rest of the roads weren't crushed gravel, just screened river gravel. There were round bevels that pop and fly when your car runs over it or corduroy like washboard. The only way to approximate a smooth ride was to drive above 60 so you just skimmed over the tops and missed the dips in between.

The first time I came to Ouray was in 1928 with my aunt and uncle, just to see the city and the mountains. Going back that evening we got on Kelly's Trail which was the old road high up on the hill south of Billy Creek. It was a one-track road with turnouts that looked down on the train tracks. As we drove toward Montrose we overtook the passenger train. My aunt had never seen a narrow-gauge train and thought it was the cutest little thing. We kept pace with it for a long time so she could watch it moving along below us. I think its fastest speed was about 25 miles per hour, but when it was first put in, it was the fastest way to get to Montrose.

The first Christmas we lived in Ouray, we drove over to Hotchkiss to spend the day with my folks. On the way home, driving along Kelly's Trail, it was snowing, and I saw a lot of lights on the road ahead of us. I thought something terrible had happened. When we got there the road was blocked, so we stopped and I walked up to see what was going on. A car had spun out and was crosswise in the road. At that point the road was so narrow that he couldn't back up because he was against the bank, and if he went forward six inches his wheels would be off the edge. A lot of guys were standing around wondering what to do. I suggested that maybe we could get a hold of the bumpers and fenders and just jiggle and bounce it around and get it turned in the right direction. There were enough men standing there so it worked, and we were able to get it lined up in the road and were able to move on. It must have snowed seven or eight inches up there that night. In 1937 they relocated the road down in the river bottom where it is now.

They started paving the highways in the late thirties. No paving was done on the Million Dollar Highway until after World War II. They may have paved as far as the tunnel before 1955 or '56, but it was after that that they paved the road farther up. In the 1960s they had a widening program and repaired the road. When we came to Ouray it was the original Million Dollar Highway, and we were proud of it. I liked to drive it. Every pass in the state was like that one, one track with turnouts. The turnouts were widened places where you could stop to let another car pass. They had been built when the roads were only used by wagons. Most of the time you could see from one turnout to the next, so whichever car was closest to the turnout could stop to let the oncoming car pass. In the old wagon days, there was often an outrider, a man on horseback that went ahead to see what was coming. That way they could avoid having to back up wagon teams. He was also there to assist any wagon driver that was having trouble.

The first summer we were in Ouray, some friends with a pretty good car drove us up to Ironton to show us around. There was still about a block of buildings standing, and here and there you could see a fireplug. The old post office had functioned until 1921, but it was closed then. The last postmaster at Ironton told us that he kept wanting to close the post office but couldn't get any action. Finally he just packed everything in boxes and brought it to the Ouray Post Office and told them, "Do whatever you can with this stuff, I'm closing up." Gillette, the man that made a fortune on Gillette razors, had a little house up there where he spent his summers. He liked to come and play around with his mines. He was never a miner, he just invested in them.

Ouray in the '30s still had a little bit of the old days. There were a lot of old country people, some with European accents. There were a lot of mining people who were different than the farm people I was used to. Prohibition had been repealed for three years. You'd find the miners in the bars on paydays and other nights, too. In fact, you could find as many Christians in there as you could find in church on Sunday. In Cedaredge, where I'd worked for a year when I was 25, most of the customers were of my parent's generation. I could never get them to call me by my first name; it was Mr. Gregory. In Ouray it was Marv or Marvin, right off. In two weeks some of them treated me as if I was one of their kids. I had never been anywhere where you could make friends in so short a time. There were Cousin Jacks, skilled miners from Cornwall, England; Austrians, Italians, and quite a few Swedes.

There was one old family by the name of Wright. Mrs. Wright was a little, short lady, about as broad as she was tall, who could swear like a fireman, but everybody loved her. One night I was driving home slowly, because it was so icy, when I saw Mrs. Wright start across the street. Just when she got past the middle of the street, I saw her fall like a ton of bricks. I was sure she was hurt. I pulled up along side her and rolled down the window to see if I could help her. She jumped to her feet just like a little girl. Her eyesight was failing, and she couldn't see who I was until she got close, so she stuck her head inside the window and, with her hands on her hips, said, "Goddamned slick out here, ain't it?" We had a lot of those people; they were wonderful people.

The first winter or two that I was here the mines still had a lot men living in boardinghouses. The Camp Bird still had a big boardinghouse in operation; so did the Revenue and Mineral Farms mines. They each had 30 or 40 or 50 men living at the mines. They all bought supplies from the market. The four Fellin Brothers had a transfer business and owned the franchise on the Sneffels Road. They did all the freight hauling on that road. In the wintertime the boardinghouses would order a quarter of beef or maybe a whole beef. I'd cut it into a size that they could load on a pack mule and sew it into muslin with a burlap cover.

At that time the county didn't have any plows or dozers heavy enough to go through the snowslides. The road boss, Ed West, had a crew of 15 men; shovelers, who would stop by the market at 7:00 in the morning, when I opened, to buy candles to wax their shovels so snow wouldn't stick to them. Then they would go out and shovel the slides out. It might take two weeks to shovel through the Waterhole or Hayden Slide. In the meantime no trucks could get through, so the Fellin Brothers had a string of 50 pack mules that they used to take meat, canned goods, and whatever else was needed to the boardinghouses. By 1938 they got some equipment so they didn't run the pack strings anymore. The last I remember pack strings operating was about 1940. Lars Pilkaer who owned half interest in the Chief Ouray Mine, was working there, and the only way they could get supplies up there was by pack string. It was always that way.

The Fellin Brothers ran the trucks, too. They hauled concentrate to the smelter in Leadville until it closed down after World War II. Then they hauled to Pueblo and Salt Lake City. Finally, the only place where concentrate could be taken was El Paso, Texas. They had a truck that would haul 20 tons.

When I came, Bill McCullough, Barbara Spencer's father, and his partner, Floyd Withrow, were operating the American Nettie. They had about six miners besides themselves. They would stay up there all week. They hiked the old Horsethief Trail with backpacks. They were different than the little backpacks we have today. They had a wood or tin frame, way down their back, and you could load 50 or 60 pounds of supplies in them. The whole crew would stop at the market on Monday morning, load up, go up the trail, and stay all week. If you had a pair of binoculars, you could pick them out going up the trail once in a while. They would work for two or three months, charging their supplies on a charge account. They would sort out the high grade ore, bring it down the hill on the American Nettie tram to the mill, now called the Silver Shield, and when they had a carload of crude, ship it out. Then they'd come in, pay their bill, buy a new car, and start all over again. They were still mining when World War II got underway, but gold mining was out of favor during the war. They couldn't get supplies to mine with unless they were producing something considered necessary to the war effort. Gold didn't qualify. I guess you couldn't make bullets out of it. They were still making money even though gold was only $35.00 an ounce.

I quit cutting meat in 1942. My boss was an alcoholic who was going blind and having difficulty walking. He was only in his mid 50s. He had two boys of draft age and was fretting that they might have to go to war. I went to work one Monday morning and found him in the cooler, the big one where I hung pork, veal, and hams. He chose to go in there to commit suicide. I stayed on three months and quit. There wasn't anybody to write my paycheck.

I could have bought Smith's half of the corporation, but I was afraid. Carl Lucker, the baker, owned one-half of the stock, and he said I could buy the other half with no money down and pay for it out of the store earnings. Smith had borrowed money on his half of the stock without telling the baker. The war was getting under way more and more and things were kind of tight. There were a lot of unpaid bills, and you had to ration sugar and things like that. It worried me, and I refused the opportunity. Old Gus Nickel had been a meat cutter there years before, and they talked him into taking over the store. He came out all right and made money when he sold the store to Duckett.

When I was working in the market, we had a refrigeration plant. I was told it was the first refrigeration plant installed in western Colorado, in 1916. The compressor was big; it stood taller than I do, and used ammonia. The compressor had a big flywheel driven by a five-horsepower motor. The valves in the cylinder head made a sound like a pig grunting. If you were standing beside it when it started up, it would make you jump. Iron pipes carried the compressed ammonia into the coils on the inside of the cooler. It was still in use when I left the market. The coolers had originally been iceboxes. The iceman would come in and put in several blocks of ice to keep things cold.

There was an icehouse here in town, and they put up ice down at Piedmont. There was a place called Hohl's Grove where the bridge crosses the river at Piedmont. The owner had diverted the river into some ponds where the ice would freeze in the winter. In the summertime they would use it for picnic grounds. They would even put little boats on the ponds, little canoes, but the ponds were there to make ice. The railroad came right through the area, and they would load the ice on flatcars and bring it to Ouray and store it in the icehouse. They had enough ice to supply all the markets and the people that wanted it in the summertime. When we moved here the icehouse was still in use; mechanical refrigerators were just becoming household items.

The icehouse caught fire and burned the first year I lived here. Boy, it was a fire. It smoked for days and days. They used sawdust as an insulator to keep the ice. You could store ice in there one year and it would still be there the next year if you didn't use it. If you insulated it enough, it didn't melt. After the fire the sawdust smoldered for a good many days. After the fire I think most people got refrigerators. I don't remember the iceman delivering ice after that. In Hotchkiss, as kids, we used to follow the ice wagon. The iceman would drag a block of ice onto the tailgate, chip it with an ice pick so it would break into the right size, and take a block into the houses and put it in the icebox. The kids would pick up the chips and put them into their mouths. We followed the iceman all over town.

During the Depression, when I came here, there were five grocery stores and two meat markets. You couldn't let your competition get the jump on you. On Sundays I was expected to visit all the restaurants to make sure they had enough hamburger and supplies to get through the day. If you didn't, your competition might take over their business. Often customers would know that you would be downtown at the restaurants, so they would catch you and say there was something they forgot the day before, always some excuse. I'd usually get stuck at the store until noon or after on Sunday. And, too, the refrigerator was not thermostatically controlled. You kept a thermometer in there and had to turn it on and off to keep it at the right temperature. There were brine tanks in the refrigerator that would hold for about 24 hours if you cooled them down to a low temperature as long as you didn't open the door. Every Sunday I checked the thermometer and ran the cooling compressor if it needed to be colder.

When I came to Ouray, there were some pretty good cooks in the restaurants. Mr. and Mrs. Creel ran a pretty high-class operation at the Beaumont. The dining room was something, and they thought it looked real classy to have a black cook. They always had one if they could get one. Mickey Caldwell, a mulatto, cooked for them when I first arrived. Later, something happened and she went to work for Sadie West. I got to know her well because I dealt with her for her meat. She was quite a cook. Frank Crane was one heck of a chef, but he was really an itinerant; he moved around quite a bit. He'd hit in the summer when it was busy and Sadie or somebody would always hire him. Then in the fall, when things slacked off a bit, he'd take off. His wife, who was from La Junta, claimed to be a granddaughter of Kit Carson so it was kind of fun to know her.

Charlie Jones, Louis's brother, was a marvelous chef. He'd open up a restaurant, run it for a year or two, then decide to go somewhere else. He opened a restaurant two or three times in Ouray and always made a success of it. He made huge pies and never served less than a quarter of a nine-inch pie. Many people couldn't get around a whole serving. He originated the Village Diner; it was called Jones's Diner then.

One time when Charlie wanted to open a restaurant again, he rented the building where Benjie's rock shop is now. For years that was a restaurant. At that time the building was owned by Mrs. Pricco. She was a sweet, little old lady, but she was a widow and always thought people were ready to take advantage of her because she was a widow. When Charlie got the building, the floor was in kind of bad shape. He knew that she wouldn't spend any money to bring the building up to standard, so, at his own expense, he put in a tile floor. It really looked nice. One day Mrs. Pricco came by and looked in the window and saw the floor. She was pleased. She went in and asked, since it looked so nice, didn't Charlie think it was worth a little more rent?

In the 30's there were seven or eight bull elk around Ouray. The Amphitheater was a preserve at that time.

The Elks Lodge had brought some bulls in here to build up the herd since it was nearly depleted. Those elk discovered the green grass on the vacant lots where the Twin Peaks and Box Canyon Motels are now. There were springs along that land. The elk would come into town, right in our backyards. They came right up to my back door. Some people would feed them and that almost brought on a civil war. Some people didn't want them walking in their backyards; they might break down the shrubbery. Others didn't think it was all that serious, and, anyway, the elk attracted a lot of attention. The oldest bull, we called him Solomon, would come into town and the other bulls would follow him. The cows and bulls moved about separately, except during mating season, so the cows usually stayed up on the hillside. But those bulls would walk right down Main Street in the middle of the day if they felt like it.

One day when I was working for Julius Sonza in his market, I was stocking a case at about 7:00 A.M., when I heard something at the front of the store. I thought a kid going to school had thrown a rock or something. I glanced up and there was Solomon with his nose against the glass, looking in and hitting the glass with his antlers.

A fellow named Harry, who was a bookkeeper and the county treasurer, didn't want the elk in his garden, afraid they'd damage his raspberries. He didn't know too much practical stuff, but he did know there were electric fences. He got some wire and strung it around the perimeter of his property, grounded it on one end, and plugged the other end into a 110-volt outlet. He got up

Wild Elk on the Steps of B.P.O. Elks
No. 492, Ouray, Colo.

Charter members of the Elks Club.

119

one morning and he had a dead elk in the yard. He was kind of troubled. It could have been a person. All you need for an electric fence is a six-volt battery.

One day there was a lot of excitement in town. Everyone in town had clothes lines attached to pulleys just outside their back door. You could step out on the back porch, hang the clothes on the line, and pull the rope on the pulley to run the clothes out into the yard. If you put on a big load, the line would sag down toward the ground. One day an elk came tearing down the street with a clothes line dangling from his antlers. There was lingerie and I don't know what all on that line. I don't know if they recovered all that stuff, but he sure made off with it.

Bill Walker, who had been a marshal, a shotgun rider on the Fellin stage, and a guard in the gold room at the Camp Bird, always liked the elk. He'd put out apples for the elk, and they got so that when they'd see him bring out the apples they would run down to him. Old Solomon would put his nose in the bucket to get an apple. One day Dan Carey, an old man who was a little afraid of the elk, was taking his coal bucket out to the coal house next to the alley to get some coal for his stove. Solomon was around the house and saw him with the bucket and came right after him. Dan thought Solomon was going to charge him so he ran in the coal house and shut the door. Solomon kept him prisoner in there for about an hour. Mrs. Carey thought he had gone to town and Solomon just thought he had some apples.

In 1956 or '57 the Wildlife Department opened the area to hunting. The boundaries were within about 200 yards of the school. We tried to get them to change the boundaries but had no luck. That year somebody shot and killed Solomon. I think they had some pretty tough chewing even though he was partially apple fed.

I wasn't here when the flood of 1929 hit Ouray. I had visited the year before with my uncle and aunt and had seen the pool. Five streams join the Uncompaghre in the townsite: Oak Creek, Canyon Creek, Portland Creek, Cascade Creek, and Skyrocket Creek; and every one of them hit here. They say the storm took a circular path and dumped water on every one. They said that hill of gravel just below the pool was built up in 30 minutes and the pool was completely filled with gravel. The next year the townspeople shoveled the gravel out of the pool into trucks and hauled it away. It was all done by hand; there were no front-end loaders then. The bathhouse was rebuilt with materials that came from a house at the Treasury Tunnel.

Mr. Clay, the power plant operator, had a house close to the river. Mrs. Clay, as all of the women did at that time, did a lot of canning and kept her canned goods in a little cellar under the house. She got into the cellar through a trap door in the floor. During the flood the cellar, which was below river level, filled up to the top. She told me that for months afterward when she wanted some fruit or something she just lifted the trap door, paddled the water, and just waited for the right can to float by.

In 1937 we were living in a house on the south end of

Second Street. At that time they were lowering and widening the switchbacks on the highway just above town. When they were going to blast on the highway they blew a whistle, and the mothers in that area had to gather their children and go to what is now Baker's Manor. We'd wait there until they blasted, and then went home again. We had to leave the doors and windows in the house open so the concussion would not damage the house. Every time we went home, we'd find plaster on the table or the phone off the wall, or something.

We had a girl staying with us and going to school. One day when Ruth got home, she found a large rock had come through the roof, landed in the middle of the girl's bed, broken the slats underneath, and damaged the floor. The next day, when the whistle blew all clear and she went home, she found the house next door demolished. That was Albert Schneider's mother's house. Fortunately, the insurance was ready to pay for the damage right away. Unfortunately, Mrs. Schneider bought the house we were living in so we had to move.

In 1942 the Rice Lumber yard burned. There was a planing mill where the Victorian Inn is now located. The fire siren went off at precisely 12:00 so everyone thought it was just the noon siren. It took a little while for people to respond but they finally knew something else was going on because the siren just kept blowing. It didn't make any difference because the fire went so fast there was no controlling it. Everything burned except the little office; the mill and the lumber shed burned all the way to the ground. Barrels of tar exploded and blazing tar paper landed on the hills around here, starting little fires. The ranger who lived here at the time was also a scout leader, so he got the boy scouts out all over the mountain putting out fires.

The house next to me caught fire and burned to the ground. I went home and tried to use the garden hose to wet down the west side of my house with a garden hose to keep it from catching fire from the heat. It got too hot for me to stay there and I had to give up. Finally, they sent some equipment up from the fire to wet down the houses that were still standing. Our part of town got its water from the Oak Creek Reservoir, and they pulled it down so much that there was just enough water to put a trickle on my house and the house just above me. Two houses just behind us were destroyed by the fire. They said that blazing tar paper landed all the way up at the old Erickson Dairy, north and west of town.

In 1942, when I left the market, I joined up with a painter and worked with him that summer and the next winter, hanging paper and doing interior decorating. One day I was hanging paper and Kullerstrand at the bank called me. He always seemed to know where I was. He said, "Marvin, when you get a chance, come down. I want to see you." He had a blunt way about him. I thought I was really in trouble, I must have written too many checks. I headed back to his office where he was sitting at the window. He said, "When you get through over there I want you to bring your tools and tear this wall out of here and put the door over there." He just laid it out that way, never even gave me a drawing. I had never even framed a wall before. When it came to the wiring I thought he would hire an electrician, but he said, "You can do it." I didn't know how, but I remodeled the whole back end. Through the years I did a lot of projects there. I remodeled the top floor and put the elevator in. My crew and I built the shaft and then a technician came to put in the compressor for the hydraulic elevator. I think Kully got a tax break for putting in the elevator, upgrading his building.

I had a crew of six or seven men in the summer and brought it down to just two in the winter, unless I had a building to finish. I didn't do that often because you had to hire ten guys to shovel snow out of the building, and you couldn't make any money.

In those days, during the war, you couldn't get good lumber. It was all green with sap dripping out of it. It wasn't planed to size, just sawed. There was a lot of variation in it, but that was all you could get. You couldn't buy trusses, there was no factory making trusses, so you had to cut your rafters and lay them out, too. I had to learn how to do that, so I bought technical books and magazines. A man who had been an architect in China for years had a set of architectural engineers' reference books which he gave me.

There were two old-timers who took me under their wing and taught me a lot. One was Ed Henning, a sharp man. He showed me how to lay out a graph of roof rafters with a steel square. Then you could just take your rule and pick the length of every rafter and cut it. Axel Erickson, an old Swede who was Ramona Radcliff's grandfather, had helped build those fancy houses up at the Camp Bird. He was near the generation of my grandfather, and I was 31 or 32. He'd call me up and say, "Marvin, some people want me to do some work on their roof, and I don't feel like climbing up there. If you'll come and help me for a day, I'll trade a day." That was good for me because when I had him, he'd show me things. I learned a lot from him.

I had a steel square book. You might not believe it, but you can use a steel square as a calculator. You can lay out a circle or ellipse with a steel square. You can do just amazing things. I never learned it all, but it's all in the book.

I worked in construction until I retired, about 35 years. For a while I had a big crew and took house contracts, but it got too complicated. I was supposed to pay income tax for the crew and that made too much bookwork. I don't like bookwork. I was too small an operator to afford an accountant and a little too big to get along without one. I was in the middle and that was a bad situation, so I quit taking contracts. Then I specialized doing concrete and masonry. I worked with one or two other men as partners, so they paid their own income tax.

I had to learn how to plaster on wood lath. I had to learn that because when I started, we didn't have dry wall. I had to learn how to mix plaster and how to mix mortar with lime. When masonry cement came in, I didn't use it at first because it was too expensive, but finally had to because the dealers didn't like to handle lime. The lime came in paper sacks, and, during the rainy season, humidity would get in the paper sacks in the warehouse and rupture the sacks. That would put lime all over the place and the dealers didn't like it. They make lime by burning limestone in a kiln and adding water. It gets hotter than the dickens. You have to watch it and cool it out by adding a little water and stirring it or it will get flaky and not good to use.

I built the Wiesbaden, the Alpine, most of the Cottage Court, about half of the Antlers, and helped build the Box Canyon. I built the house that Howard Williams lives in and several foundations for Ray Scoggins when he started operating here. Later, I commuted to Montrose and laid bricks.

Sometimes I got frustrated because I was doing a lot of little jobs that the big contractors didn't want to bother with. Those often tied me up so I couldn't take some of the bigger jobs where you could make more money.

The City Hall fire was in January 1950. A lot of people have theories about what started the fire, but I think mine is as good as anyone's. Some people thought it was arson, but I think it was started from a cigarette in the trash. The old council room was where the library is now. It was used as a courtroom, too. There was a gallery where you could sit at council meetings, and the council always sat on the other side of the rail. I served on the council before the building burned.

The Rotary Club used to have dinners in the council room, and the Woman's Club would cater them. There was a little kitchen just off the council room back under the stairs going up to the library. There was always a big cardboard box under the stairs where the trash was dumped when they policed the tables after the dinner. I was out of town that night, but the reports were that the fire started about 11:00 o'clock, after the Rotary Club had held its meeting. The fire started in the stairway, went up the stairs, and spread from there. I'm sure that someone dumped an ashtray with a still smoldering cigarette into the trash and that's how the fire started.

I was living in Montrose at that time but wanted to get back to Ouray so the kids would have some place to run, so I moved back in time to help rebuild City Hall. I did almost all of the stuccoing and plastering on the outside. The stucco I put on there in 1950 is still there. Since there wasn't much insurance, much of the work was done by volunteer labor. I couldn't volunteer totally, but I took the job at the regular rate and kicked back half of my wages. I plastered the big room upstairs and the bell tower. They put the old bell up there, but it had fallen all the way through to the basement in the fire and had a big crack in it; it has what I call a sick tone.

The upstairs room was to be finished later; they didn't have the money. Ralph Kullerstrand was about as community-minded as anybody I know. That winter he called me and told me to come over, he wanted to talk to me. He said, "That room upstairs ought to be finished. Go up and make an estimate for plastering the walls." I figured it up and took it to him, and he said, "Well, get your stuff up there and do it." He put up the money to do it. Next spring or winter he called me again and told me not to tell anyone who was behind it but to get the price on laying a new hardwood floor upstairs. I got the estimate and the job. My brother, who was working for me at the time, and I did the job with volunteer help from some of the guys. Even Kully came up and nailed a little flooring.

One day when the bank was closed, three or four guys from the bank came up to help. They weren't carpenters, and it's hard to drive nails in hardwood if you don't know how to do it. Kully wanted to try a nailing machine, one of the earliest attempts at a machine nailer, and it didn't work well. My brother and I soon got disgusted with that and gave up on it. We started in one corner, hand driving the nails to draw the lip over the tongue, and while they were fooling with the machine we just about finished the floor.

Another winter, in '52 or '53, I put up the ceiling tile. Again Kully paid for that. There was a lot of donated money for rebuilding City Hall, but Kully probably donated more than anybody.

The reason the building had to be plastered and stuccoed was that we couldn't get the brick that had been used before. We could get a yellow hard brick but not the red mud brick that had been used on the original building. I think that old brick was made right here down by the swimming pool. I'm almost certain that the Beaumont was built with that brick, too. It was finished and open in July 1887, and the first train didn't come into town until December 1887. The rutty old road was so rough you could barely get wagons over it. There would have been stories about hauling in the bricks if that was the case, and there was nothing recorded in the newspapers or anywhere else.

I know the courthouse was built with those bricks. Frank Carney had the masonry contract on the courthouse, and he owned the brick yard where he made bricks. At other times he spent his time as lieutenant governor of state; twice, I think.

After I retired from the construction business, I worked as the City and County Building Inspector for several years. Since then I've devoted most of my time to historical research and writing and housekeeping.

My first magazine article was published in 1959 in *True West* and I've contributed a good many articles to the newspaper.

P. David Smith and I have written two books. The first was "Mountain Mysteries" and the second, "The Million Dollar Highway". Each of us would write a chapter and then exchange them so we could critique and edit the other's work. It's kind of a strange system, but it worked well for us.

In the past five or six years, I've worked as a volunteer at the Museum. I was Chairman of the Steering Committee when we organized the Historical Society but have never held an office in the Society since. I like it better that way. I'm free to do research and act as a consultant but don't get bogged down in the day-to-day affairs of administering the Museum.

THE COW CREEK LADIES

The next three women all lived on small ranches in the Cow Creek area, east of Ridgway. Almost all of the small ranches in Cow Creek have been incorporated into large ranches owned, for the most part, by absentee landlords.

RANCH WIFE

Edith lives in Ridgway near the post office. She talked about life on Cow Creek. Perhaps the best remembered thing from this interview is the graphic discussion of how to slaughter a pig. In the original transcript, the typist describes my voice becoming weaker; that was only the tip of the iceberg in terms of my feelings.

I was born in 1903 in an old cabin four miles east of Ridgway on what is now the Walchle place. My maiden name was Perotti. My parents and two older brothers came to Colorado from Italy in 1888. My younger brother, Albert, was born here. They came with a bunch of people who had heard about the gold mines around Ouray. My father worked in the mines for awhile and

"We used to truck the pigs to Denver to sell them... It would take a day and part of a night to get to Denver in the thirties. Denver wasn't nearly as big as it is now. You could almost find your way around without too much trouble."

then homesteaded the place where I was born. Later, he homesteaded five other places. It was all open country at that time.

I went through eight grades at the Cow Creek School; all eight grades were in one room. In nice weather we walked across the fields to school, about three miles. In the winter we rode horseback. There was a little shed for the horses at the school. We loosened the cinches on the saddle and tied the horses in the shed. Then at four o'clock we'd come out, get our horses, and ride home. We would just as soon walk as fool around with the horses, so we walked as often as we could.

We always had to do our chores before we went to school in the morning. We helped feed the cattle and the calves and cleaned out the barns. In the evening after school, we came in and got a slice of bread, and then went out and rounded up the stock to put them in the barn. My dad kept about ten milk cows. The one that I milked had jumped a ditch and thrown her hip out.

She was leaning over. I milked her because I could get down and milk her easier than the bigger kids. After milking we brought the milk in, separated it, and then went out and fed the calves and the pigs.

My mother churned butter and made cheese. Boy, was she a cheese maker. After running the milk through the separator to get the cream to make butter, she would take the skimmed milk and put it in big galvanized tubs in the milk house to sour. In the summertime it would sour in two or three days; in the wintertime it took a little longer. In the wintertime she saved one or two cups of whey from the cheese and put it in the tubs of fresh milk to make it sour faster. After the milk soured, she put a tablet of rennet in the milk and stirred it until it hardened like cottage cheese. Then she strained it into little coarse cloth bags and put it into a round colander until it quit draining. When it was in the colander, she pressed it down to shape it into discs about nine inches across and a couple of inches thick. Each colander would make two rounds of cheese. After the cheese quit draining in the colander, she hung the bags out on a line for two or three days until it dried and set. Then she would take this white cheese out of the bags and it would be ready to go to market.

Once a week we would take the butter, cheese, and eggs — we had lots of chickens — to Ouray to peddle. There were a lot of families in Ouray at that time, so we had regular orders to fill. That trip to Ouray took the bigger share of the day. It took about two hours to drive a team with a wagon or buggy to town. We didn't hurry. The roads at that time were just narrow, dirt roads. After we filled the orders we visited with different people, picked up a few groceries, and headed back down the road.

When I was in school, we didn't have much homework. We had reading, arithmetic, and spelling. That was what you had to learn to do. We didn't have things like they have now. In the evenings, if you had a few spare minutes, you worked on your spelling or arithmetic. We didn't have television or phonographs or a lot of stuff like that to contend with.

There were usually ten to fifteen kids at the Cow Creek School. We played a lot of baseball; that was the biggest game. We sometimes played hide-and-seek or pump-pump-pull-away, too. They did have swings for us to swing on.

We never had any entertainment at school except at Christmas time. They had their Christmas programs, and that was the size of it; that's all they had. Gifts at Christmas were small, just what people could afford. They didn't go out and get anything elaborate. It was just very plain.

We did have a lot of dances. They were box socials. That's where the women fix up a box — most generally a shoe box — of sandwiches and cake or whatever for two people. They would decorate the box, and then take them to the social where they would be auctioned off to the men. They would sell for all the way from fifty cents to maybe two or three dollars. If some of the men would know a certain lady's box, they'd bid a little higher, just to try to outdo each other. After the bidding the man who bought the box would look at the name, then go hunt up the lady and sit down and eat their lunch. When everybody was through the music would start. You danced the first dance with the partner you ate with. They had a violin and, maybe, a piano or organ. Once in a while, somebody would play a mouth harp. After the first dance you would change partners. A lot of the times you would be dancing and someone else would come up and tap the fellow on the back and take the girl and dance with her. You might not get halfway around before someone else would come and take you for another few steps. There was always a big crowd. The dances were always full.

We had dances once a week. It didn't cost much, whatever you wanted to give. You could donate a quarter, or fifty cents, or a dollar to give to the fellow that was playing. One week they'd have the dance at the Cow Creek Schoolhouse. Then the next week they'd move it down to Mayfield or Alkali. The Alkali School was down by the old Ethridge place. The Mayfield School was down near where Wes Ashley lives, where Cow Creek joins the Uncompahgre.

Sometimes we would go to dances on horseback and sometimes we would ride in a buggy. Often groups from the neighborhood would get together and go. The dances would start at eight thirty or nine and, a lot of the times, it would be daylight before the dances would break up. It would be kind of sleepy riding home after the dances. When you got home it would be broad daylight, and you'd have to start out with your chores.

I met my husband at the dances. He also worked for my brothers a lot. We were married in April the year I was eighteen at the courthouse in Ouray. Just my husband and I and my brother and his wife attended the wedding. We moved into the house, just across from the home place, where Mrs. Matasovic, who owns the OXO Ranch, lives now. It's not the same house; it has been rebuilt. Our ranch was the last one up the Cow Creek Road; The OXO owns that now, too. We had about 600 acres and raised hay, oats, and wheat.

The next year we moved down near the town of Old Dallas. That's going to be covered by the new lake. We lived there for 50 years. The train ran right at the edge of our property. Passenger trains came through twice a day and freights whenever they needed them. We raised hay and cattle and had two or three milk cows. We raised quite a few pigs. My husband bought a little car, a one-seat affair, the year before we got married. After we were married, he bought a truck; a Chevrolet, I think. We used to truck the pigs to Denver to sell them. It would take a year to fatten the pigs to get them ready for market. Then we would take 25 or 30 of them to Denver. It would take a day and part of a night to get to Denver in the thirties. Denver wasn't nearly as big as it is now. You could almost find your way around without too much trouble. We would take the pigs to the stockyards where they would weigh them and give you your money; then we would head back home.

We went to Ridgway about once a week to buy

Stock train on the Dallas Divide.

groceries. The old building across the highway from the laundromat was the creamery where we sold milk and butter. There were two grocery stores in town, pretty nice stores. You used to be able to go in with a five-dollar bill and buy a lot of groceries. There was a drugstore in the building where the teepee factory is now. You can still see the barber pole where the ice cream store is now. The depot building has been moved from its original location but is still standing. There was a livery stable and a shoe store. The building that houses the hardware store used to be a drug store and the bank was next door where the ice cream shop is now.

Most of the ranchers brought their cattle to the stockyards in Ridgway to sell them, but we generally trucked ours to Montrose.

We butchered our own pigs for our use. We had a big iron pot, bigger than a bathtub, that we would set up on rocks and build a fire under it to heat water. When the water was almost boiling we'd bring a pig up, hold it down, and cut its throat. When it stopped bleeding, we had a hoist to lift the pig into the water. We'd dip the pig into the water two or three times to make sure they were soaked well. Then we would lay them on the table and use scraper knives (about four inches long and one-and-a-half inches wide) to scrape the hair off them. When they were scraped clean, we rolled them over and opened them up and took the entrails out of them; we saved the heart and liver. Then we hung them up to cool. Then we cut them up.

In the winter we often let them hang if they would freeze. If we wanted to cure them, we put the meat in barrels of salt water brine for two or three weeks. We used about five pounds of salt per pig to cure it. After it was cured, we hung the meat in a bag in an earth cellar. The meat would stay good for as long as you needed it.

We butchered cattle, too. We skinned the cow and hung it in a place we fixed up with fine window screen. After the meat aged, we cut it up and put it in quart jars. We had a big tank, about one-and-one-half by two feet, with shelves in it. You filled it with water and put the jars in, then just kept the water boiling until the meat was cooked. You just had to watch the water to keep it boiling on the wood stove. It took anywhere from three to five hours. We used to save some of the meat by letting it hang out and freeze. When you wanted fresh meat, you would just go out and cut off a slice.

My husband went hunting every fall. You didn't have to go far to get deer. There were plenty right out in the field. Of course, that was no fun. You had to rig up your pack outfit and horses and go to the hills. We usually went out for a couple of days on our hunting trips.

I remember hunting bear when I still lived at home. My brothers had bear traps that they set up towards Courthouse. That was lots of fun. One time they had a cub in the trap. It was a lot of fun getting him out of there. They had to tie him — both front legs and both hind legs — and put a muzzle on his nose. Then they loaded him on a wagon and brought him down to my brother's place. They kept him tied on a chain until he tamed down a bit, then they gave him to the City Park in Denver.

They had to shoot the big bears. They were trying to get rid of them because they were getting into people's stock and killing cattle.

You could eat the meat, but I wouldn't really crave it. It's real tough and coarse, not fine meat. I wouldn't want to have many meals of it, although the taste isn't bad.

My husband had a coal mine up Billy Creek just under the Cimarrons. We still own it, but I imagine it is all caved in now. It's been years since I was up there. Occasionally, I used to go up to the mine to help load coal. I didn't mind going into the mine, although you couldn't see anything; it was just black. We would load coal in the car and then a horse would pull it out to where it could be dumped down a chute to the outside. They loaded the trucks from that pile at the bottom of the chute. My husband and a hired man usually went back and forth to the mine every day, but if they were too busy they could stay up there overnight.

Many people drove up to the mine to haul their own coal, but most of the time my husband delivered coal to Ouray, Ridgway, Telluride — just different places around here. In the summer he used a truck to haul coal but in the winter he had to haul with horses and a sled. We had a four-horse team of big Belgians. If the snow wasn't too deep, he would hook a two-horse team to the truck and pull it out to where he could drive the truck. When the snow got too deep, he hooked all four horses to the sled. The sled was as big as a truck bed and had double runners, two on each side. The runners were made of wood with wide steel on the bottom. There were three steel rods running between the runners to hold them in place.

It took an hour to drive the truck to the mine and longer if he had to drive the horses. We sold the coal for three dollars a ton, delivered. Toward the end we were getting five dollars a ton. That was a lot of work for three dollars. After my husband died, my son, Lester, had coal shipped down here by train from Paonia which he would deliver to our customers. After the trains stopped, he trucked coal from Paonia for a couple of years, but that got to be too much of a struggle, so he gave it up.

In the summer if there wasn't too much going on at the ranch I would go up to the mine and stay for a couple of days, but most of the time I did the farming at this end while he was in the coal business up there. We had twenty-five or thirty head of cattle and three or four milk cows that I had to milk twice a day. We were raising hay, so I had to irrigate the fields. I churned a little butter, but I never made cheese like my mother did.

We didn't have electricity at the ranch for many years, so we made our own icebox. It was a big box about four feet high and two feet on each side with shelves inside. You put ice inside and covered the outside with gunny sacks that you kept wet. If you set it in the shade, it kept things cool for a long time. When the ice melted, you put another little chunk in. It would stay in pretty good shape for forty-eight hours.

We got our water from a spring in the cottonwoods

next to the river. That was one of my chores for most of my life, carrying buckets of cold water from that spring. We didn't have running water in the house until we got electricity at the ranch. That made things a lot easier. We built a pump house at the spring and could pump water up to the house. Before that, it was pack it uphill.

We bathed in one of those little round galvanized tubs, about twelve or fourteen inches deep. We would pack our water up and heat it in one of those big boilers on the stove. We never had a real bath tub until we got electricity in; then we splurged.

Living on a ranch was a full-time job, but we made fun out of all of it. The best times were going fishing. We'd load the kids up and take off and camp overnight on a weekend. The hardest part was shoveling ditches. We did that for a long time, until we got tractors to do it with. That was always hard work for me. I never did take too kindly to that.

CLARA ISRAEL

RANCH WIFE

Clara lives in a log home in Ridgway that she shares with her daughter. She talked of living on Cow Creek and a variety of things. One that stands out was how someone was always staying with them. When asked if she didn't get tired of always having people in the house, she responded, as did most of the people interviewed when asked a question that did not make sense to them, "That's the way things were. We didn't know anything different."

My mother and dad came to Ouray from Wisconsin in the 1880s. My Dad had been born in England. I never did know why they moved to Ouray. I suppose, it was go west, young man, go west. I was the youngest in the family, and I never asked any questions. I just took it for granted that he'd always lived here. When I got older and wanted to ask questions, it was too late. When dad got here, he did whatever he could. He tried to get into mining, helping with drilling or something. He didn't stay too long at that. Then he worked in the brick yard. He told me that he helped quarry the bricks that are

"The Depression lasted until the late thirties. Of course they had a war to get out of it. I always figured that's why they got into the war."

in the courthouse. My oldest brother was born in Ouray in 1888. Then Dad moved to Montrose County and farmed in that area. All the other kids but me were born in Montrose County.

Finally, Dad bought the family ranch near Colona. The ranch was right where the road goes past the Colona store. When they put in the road they took out the house. I was born in Colona in 1909. Dad delivered me. He never talked about it, but there was no doctor there at the time.

I grew up in Colona and went to school there from first grade through high school. The whole school was in one building. The high school had one room, the primary grades had one room, intermediate grades had a room, and the seventh and eight grade had one room. I enjoyed school; I guess because I just enjoyed learning.

Besides, when I wasn't in school, I was at home working. We all had chores. I guess my first chore was getting out of bed. When I was in school I had to leave home at 7:00. When I got home, I had to help milk after I got the cows in. In the winter, as soon as I got home,

I had to start carrying wood and water and coal. In the summertime, as soon as school was out, I had to herd cows on foot until about 11:00 or 11:30. Then I would pick strawberries until the strawberry season was over; then the currants would come in and we'd pick currants. Later, we had a few raspberries. My sister and I had to help our dad with whatever he was doing; shocking hay or stacking hay. The boys were all gone by that time, so we were kept busy, and we did the housework in between. You live on a ranch; you all work. The ranch wasn't big. Dad raised a little hay and a few potatoes.

We had a big house. There was a living room, a big kitchen, a big pantry, and a bedroom downstairs and bedrooms upstairs. The walls were papered with oilcloth. We heated with wood stoves and coal stoves. They smoked. We washed the walls twice a year. We had a well for water that was 25-30 yards from the house. You hauled the water in and you hauled it out. We didn't have electricity. We studied by a coal oil lamp. If we wanted hot water, we heated it on the stove. We took our baths in the wash tub. In the wintertime we put the tub in front of the cook stove and put the oven door down and took our baths. It didn't take long.

When I was a kid, Colona had a grocery store, a dry goods store, a hardware, a doctor's office, a pool hall, and a post office. They all disappeared while I was growing up. Dad got a car when I was about five years old. When he wanted to go to Colona to get groceries, he'd take the car. If he just went to get the mail, he took a horse.

I rode a horse to school part of the time. There was a barn at school where kids put their horses during the day. The horses were pretty well-behaved. If one was a little bit ornery, they threw it out. Some of the kids came a long way to school; some even came off Log Hill. Some of them walked; some of them rode horses; and some of them lived right in Colona. Some of my older sisters had gone to grade school at the Mayfield School, where the Spud Hill Ranch is now, but, when I went to school, we had moved to the house in Colona. One of my older sisters was the teacher when I was in the sixth and seventh grades.

I guess I always knew my husband, Lester, when I was growing up. He was from Ridgway, and two of my brothers worked for his dad at one time or another. We would meet at dances and then started dating. He asked me to marry him, and I said yes and we got married. That was all there was to it. We were married in 1928 at the Christian Church in Montrose. Lester's sister and her husband had been married there in February, and we got married in March.

We moved to a ranch out on Cow Creek, about six miles from the highway where the bridge crosses Cow Creek. I lived there for 56 years. We had 250 acres plus summer pasture and raised hay and cattle. We had a few milk cows, and I raised a few chickens. We worked everything with horses. When we were first married, our only transportation was saddle horses. I didn't think that was so neat. We lived seven miles from town. We didn't get to Ridgway too often. In the summertime, if we had to get a lot of groceries, we took the wagon to town, and in the wintertime we used the sled. That was quite a long haul.

In the wintertime Lester used to haul ice and coal. We had an icehouse, so he would take a sled with a four-horse team over to the pond near Piedmont and saw blocks of ice to haul home. He had a pretty good-sized sled box, so the ice blocks were heavy. They were as wide and deep as a table top and about a foot thick. When he got home, he packed the blocks in sawdust and stored them in the icehouse. That was a full day's job. He left early in the morning and it would be getting dark before he got home. He used the same sled to haul coal from the mines up on the Cimarrons. I never went along on these trips. I was busy at home doing my housework. Then I was out doing the chores, feeding the cows, whatever had to be done. I did all our washing over a board; you had to carry in all your water and carry it all out. Then you had to get wood and coal. I usually had two others beside Lester to cook for, and sometimes three or four others.

It seemed like people just flocked to our house. There always seemed to be some young man who worked for someone else in the summer and then was out of a job in the winter. He would stay with us in the winter and work for his board and room. My brother-in-law lived with us for awhile. I knew that he would live with us because Lester told me before we got married that he would make his home with us. Their mother had just passed away. Part of the time my daddy-in-law lived with us and occasionally my sister-in-law. There was always somebody.

In the summertime, as soon as we could, we moved the cows up on the hill to pasture and started to irrigate to raise hay. Then in the fall, we brought them back down and fed them all winter.

A ranch in Cow Creek.

Lester decided that we had to rotate crops, so we started raising grain. I thought it was one of the worst moves he ever made, but he said we had to have grain to feed the stock. Every other farm was doing the same thing, so we helped each other with the thrashing. First, we mowed the grain, then we had a binder that bound the shocks that had to be stacked. Then they would bring in the thrashing machine. It was an old steam engine that you had to feed coal and water. That was when all the ranches got together. The men worked in the fields and the ladies helped each other get the meals. We had good unity. Everybody helped everybody.

We did the same thing when we put up hay. We moved the hay and raked it and then used a team of horses to push the buck rake to put the hay on the stacker. Lester used to help put up hay all over the valley around Ridgway.

They used to plow the roads out to Cow Creek with a four-horse snowplow. It worked pretty well, at least in the center of the road. They never came as far as our place, so if the snow got too deep, that was when we dug out the saddle horses. Sometimes in the winter, we couldn't get the car out, so we went to Ridgway by horseback. We usually went to town about once a week, whenever the cream was ready to ship. The creamery in Ridgway would buy our extra cream. You bring the cream in and they would test it and give you your check, then you would wash your can and go home. We kept from five to eight milk cows so it would take about a week to fill up a five-gallon can of cream. We always

had all we needed, and we always had our own butter. Sometimes, we had a little bit more than that. It depended on how long the cows were milked, which ones were fresh. Some of them had richer cream than others. I had a dasher churn for the butter. It went up and down for hours. When we got electricity in the late thirties, I got a mixer to churn with. That was easy.

Lester got our first car in 1928. I never did drive it. It had a different pedal for each of the three gears: reverse, low, and high.

The Depression hit the Ridgway area in 1932. There was no work; there was no money; and the little bank in Ridgway went broke. We used to sell five gallons of cream for a dollar and a half. That had to buy all our groceries. Of course, I did have a garden, and we had our eggs and milk. We lived on what we had. People had to sell their cows to pay their taxes. I think at one time beef was selling for seven cents a pound. What you had you stretched.

On our days off from ranching, we rode in the hills to check the cows. We'd check them to see how they were, check the pastures to see if there was a fence down, and check the water holes. Sometimes, we had to move them to higher pastures. We used to brand the new calves on the hill. If we found a new calf we built a fire, heated the branding iron, caught the calf, and put our brand on him. One person could do that if you could hog-tie the calf, but it was easier if you had two people: one to rope and one to brand. I wouldn't do any of it. They tried to get me to vaccinate, but I wouldn't do that either.

Our brand was a quarter-circle with an H beside it. It went on the side of the cow. We cut in the ear marks, too. Ours was just a slit in the ear. Each rancher had a different brand and a different ear mark. All that would make for a long day but it was a day off from our usual work.

In the fall all the ranchers would get together to round up the cattle on the reserve and bring them down to the ranches. You worked. You didn't leave stragglers. You had to watch to be sure they headed out the right way. If you had somebody that knew what they were doing, it was pretty easy because they knew where the trails took off and where the cows could lose themselves. If it was a nice day; it was great. If it wasn't, if it was wet and cold and muddy, you froze. It didn't make any difference what the day was, when the time came you worked. You always had to get the cows off the reserve by a certain day. Your permit specified a certain number of cattle for a certain number of days. They used to have rangers that checked on your cows.

The Depression lasted until the late thirties. Of course, they had to have a war to get out of it. I always figured that's why they got into the war. During the war everything was rationed: sugar, coffee, tires, and gasoline. They rationed gas so you didn't wear out your tires. If you needed a pair of rubber boots to do your irrigating, you had to have stamps. So many stamps were issued, and if you didn't have the stamps, you didn't buy the boots. We got along fine because we were used to it. People who weren't used to doing without had trouble, I suppose. I learned not to use sugar in my coffee, and I didn't make as many cakes; things like that. We couldn't can much fruit; that was difficult without sugar, although some people used honey. The ration on coffee was difficult, I don't think any of us got as much as we wanted. It was similar in World War I. They wouldn't let us buy white flour, only rye or whole wheat. To this day I don't care for it; I was so sick and tired of that dark bread. And mother was a wonderful baker, too.

After World War II, we got more machinery on the ranch. Lester had a tractor by then, but the work went on pretty much the same as before. We did build a new house. The foundation on the old house was going out from under it and there was no way to replace it. The new house had a kitchen and a utility room and a full basement with a furnace room. We finally had to build on another bedroom to accommodate all the people that were always staying with us. It was a nice house, but I really liked that old house.

Our daughter, Charlene, went to school at the Cow Creek School, which was a couple of miles from the ranch. My sister-in-law taught there for awhile. There were a lot of Israels around here.

I started going to dances in 1921. There was always a dance at one of the schools in the area on Saturday night. They'd move the desks back and have the dance right in the middle of the school. One time the dance would be at the Cow Creek School, the next week at Mayfield or Dallas School, or someplace else. There would be a violin and a banjo or a guitar. There was usually somebody that could chord on the organ. They would dance waltzes, the two-step, and the fox-trot, and then they'd have a circle dance. In Ridgway they had dances at the Sherbino or at the Mentone, the hotel that burned down. Sometimes they had dances at two places and people would go back and forth between them.

I remember going through Ridgway a few times when I was a child. I had a sister that lived in Telluride, but I didn't know anybody there. When I moved to Cow Creek, Ridgway had three grocery stores, a butcher shop, a bank, a dry goods store, a hardware store, a theater, and a drug store where they sold candy and had a fountain. The druggist was registered and filled prescriptions. We had a doctor there, too. There was a barbershop, an art store, and several filling stations. There was a garage where the Little Chef is now. There used to be a Catholic Church in town, but that burned down.

Cow Creek used to be a community unto itself, much like the town of Dallas. At one time there were just the ranches and the school. You used to meet your neighbors in the middle of the road and visit. Then we built the community hall in 1936 and had a meeting place. It doesn't seem that long ago. Three fellows went up and cut the timber in the wintertime, and two others hauled it out with horses and sleds. A carpenter here in Ridgway told them how to go about building a stockade-type building. They started the building in the wintertime, and we had our first dance that spring. A lot of the men in the area went out and helped with the construction whenever they could get away.

They paid for that building by giving dances at a dollar a couple. We had a kitchen and served suppers, initially for twenty-five cents. Later they went up to thirty-five cents and finally to fifty cents. You got a sandwich, a salad, some pickles, and potato chips. The dances were held once a week. The orchestras came from Ridgway or Colona. There was even one that came from Gunnison. At that time you got change in silver dollars. At the first dance, Lester had his pockets so full of silver dollars that he was about to split his pants and coat. There were so many people at the first dance that there was hardly room to dance and there wasn't room to park the cars.

We had a square dance club that met once a week. There was room for five or six sets on that floor. I got tired of square dancing. They're all right, but they get old. I got tired of cooking for the dances, too. Groups of us took turns cooking the suppers for the dances. I think there were about five or six groups that cooked those suppers. Finally, the dances just kind of quit.

Everyone out there was really close and I think I'm the only one left.

138

SYBIL STEALY

RANCH WIFE

Sybil lives in Montrose now. She talked about ranch life and going to the mountains to move cattle. Moving cattle — or at least going to the mountains — was one of her favorite activities.

I was born at home near Parachute, Colorado in 1911. My father was a farmer so we lived at various different places around Parachute as I was growing up. I went to a two-room country school on Battlement Mesa for my first three years. The lower four grades were in one room and the upper four grades in the other room. Even though they did all that building on Battlement Mesa during the oil shale boom, that old school is still standing. Later we moved near Rifle and I lived there until I went to beauty school in Grand Junction.

I met my husband, Vaughn, through his uncle who worked for a neighbor of ours. Vaughn would come over to visit his uncle, and we just started dating. Vaughn was ranching near Ridgway and it was hard for him to get

"You never know what you are going to get for your cattle when you sell them. You just take them to market and take what they give you. What you get for what you sell is in no comparison to what you have to pay for what you buy."

away. We didn't get together all that often, but he came as often as he could. When I went to school in Grand Junction, he was able to come more often. We got married on December the 10th, 1940.

Vaughn was born at his grandmother's house out on Cow Creek. That house is now part of the Sleeping Indian Ranch. His parents lived on the upper end of Cow Creek in the house that is now the Owl Creek Ranch, owned by the Mitchells. They moved to a house farther down Cow Creek in about 1928. That's the place we moved to when we got married. Vaughn passed away in 1981. I stayed at the ranch until the summer of 1982 when I moved to Montrose.

Vaughn went to the old Cow Creek School. He and his brother rode horseback five miles from their home to the school every day. He went through four years of high school in three years in Ridgway, riding horseback every day except for one winter. That winter he stayed with a family by the name of Carmichael who ran the store in Ridgway. Vaughn worked in the store after school and on Saturday, then he would go home on Sunday. In all those three years, he was never tardy or absent. He used to leave home about seven, cut across Dry Creek, and get to school about eight. I imagine those kids made those horses travel along pretty good.

Ranching is a hard life but a good life. My husband and I always worked together. I was always an outdoor-type person; I loved to be outside. I tried to arrange my work so if he wanted to fix fence we just took off and fixed fence. We raised hay and ran cattle, so we did a lot of riding. I always did love to ride, so I didn't mind that.

We ran about 250 head of cattle. We'd work all summer putting up hay; then we'd work all winter feeding that hay to the cattle. Until about 1962 we put our hay up loose and fed with a team. After that we bought machinery and baled the hay. We mowed with a team, raked with a team, and ran the buck rake with a team. Then we took the hay in, put it on the stacker, pulled the loads up, and put it on the stack. There were usually two men on top stacking the hay.

In the wintertime we'd pull a sled out to the stack with a team. Then we would climb up on the stack, throw the loose hay onto the sled, and pull the sled out into the field and scatter the hay for the cattle. The sled had both front and back runners made out of wood and covered with strips of iron to make it slide on the snow. It was always cold feeding in the winter, but it was fun.

Later after we got machinery, we pulled a wagon loaded with bales with a tractor. I drove the tractor and my husband threw the hay off for the cattle. When we fed loose hay, we used to start about 9 o'clock in the morning and it would be afternoon when we got done. It didn't take over three hours to feed with bales.

We calved in the spring. It would be kind of rough when you had your baby calves. You'd be up nights and in all kind of weather trying to keep them alive. We had a little pasture down below the house where we could lock all the cows that were going to calve. That way you didn't have too much territory to cover to check on them. We checked the older cows late in the evening and again first thing in the morning. You had to check the first calf heifers more often. We kept them in the corral. We checked them at 10 o'clock just before we went to bed; then one of us had to get up about 2 o'clock to check them again; then we checked them early in the morning. If everything was alright, you could go back to bed, hopefully to sleep. If one of them was having trouble, I'd go back and get Vaughn, and we would both be up for the rest of the night. If there was something wrong that we couldn't take care of, we would have to call the vet out in the middle of the night.

If the calf was too big, or if it was a breech birth, you sometimes had to help with the birth. We used a pulling chain, sort of like a choke chain on a dog. You reached in and got hold of one foot, or two feet if you could, looped the chain around it and just pulled to help the cow deliver the calf. If the veterinarian had to come, he sometimes did a caesarean section. Most of the cows heal up real fast and seem to get along real well.

Most of the calves did alright, even when it was cold. We did have sheds filled with straw down at the barn where we calved the heifers. The old cows that calved out in the timber pretty much took care of their own calves. Still, it was kind of an iffy proposition. You'd lose some in spite of all you could do. Some of them might get pneumonia, some of them might get scours, and, maybe, some of them just wouldn't be right when they were born. You just take your chances, that's all; save as many of them as you can. We did have medication to treat scours, which is calf diarrhea. That helped, but you still sometimes would lose one.

Calving season usually lasted about two months. You go along pretty well and have a lot of calves, then they start to dwindle off. You would always have a few that calved later, so you would be getting calves even after you took the cows to summer pasture. You'd get that all over with, then the next spring you'd start and do the same thing all over again.

Before we took the cows to summer pasture, we had to brand. All the neighbors out in Cow Creek would get together to brand. We would brand at one place one day and someplace else the next day. It was a fun time because all the ladies got together to fix dinner. The lady where the branding was taking place usually prepared the meat and potatoes, and the other women would bring salads, desserts, and whatever. We just had a big day of it.

The branding usually went on for a week. The men would work all morning, come in for lunch, then finish up in an hour or two in the afternoon. Once in a while, they would brand at two places in the same day, but usually they just worked at one place in a day.

When we branded at our place, I had to help corral the cattle in the morning, then I had dinner to prepare. When they branded at someone else's place, I would go over fairly early in the morning to help get everything ready. Then there was always the cleaning up afterward, the dishes to wash and everything. We just visited and had a good time. I always kind of looked forward to branding time.

If calves were born after branding time, Vaughn and I had to brand the unbranded ones before we took them up to summer pasture.

We were always happy when the time came, and we could gather the cattle and take them to the mountain. We kept the cattle in pastures above the house in the spring; then about the first of July, we moved them up to summer pasture on our reserve. We had grazing rights up in Red Creek, Cow Creek, and Courthouse Creek; all those creeks to the south of the ranch. We trailed them on horseback. You just start them out and follow them until they get there. Sometimes they go where you want them to go and sometimes they don't, but we always managed to get them there.

In the summer, between irrigating and taking care of things around the ranch, we would get our horses and go for a ride to move the cattle from one place to another. You couldn't leave cattle in one place until they rubbed the grass into the ground. Everybody tried to save the grass as much as they could.

The biggest problem we had on our summer range was larkspur. We didn't have as much problem as the ranchers who ran cattle on Horsefly where they had little larkspur. We had giant larkspur that would grow as tall as a man on horseback. If cattle got into patches of larkspur and nothing disturbed them, they might eat it and live. If something disturbed them and they started running they'd just drop dead. It seemed to cause bleeding problems that affected their lungs. We lost quite a few that way. It was discouraging to go out and find two or three animals lying there dead. There was nothing you could do, you just left them up there in that rough country.

When we rode the high country, it would be an all day trip. We'd leave early in the morning and not get back until late in the evening, sometimes after dark. We'd take a lunch: sandwiches, some kind of fruit, an apple or something, cookies, and a candy bar. We usually moved the cows quite a ways. We would turn one bunch up Cow Creek and just let them graze on the hillsides. The next time we would gather them and take them clear out on top towards the head of Red Creek. That was quite a trip up all those switchbacks on that crooked trail. Then we'd have to ride all the way home.

We usually moved each bunch four or five times a year. They often drifted around themselves. They know where they want to go and what they want to do. Sometimes they would just go off by themselves. Then you would have a job finding them when you wanted to move them to new grass. Once, years ago before Vaughn and I were married, he lost a bull that he never did find. He rode and rode but never could locate that animal. That didn't happen often. Usually they would just get in a place and stay there. You'd have to go get them out or they would probably just stay there and starve to death.

We usually saw bear every time we went out riding. Sometimes I thought we saw them up too close if they had cubs. Bears can move as fast as any animal I ever saw, really cover the country. The bear never bothered the cattle. They'll eat a dead one but we never knew a bear to kill a cow. Too much other stuff to eat, I suppose.

The neighbors all helped one another with their operations. It seemed like they just worked together. I think that's becoming a lost art. It doesn't seem like people now days are as neighborly and help one another as much as they used to. I remember during the war years, you couldn't get help, so three or four of the neighbors banded together to put the hay up. The hay at the lower altitudes would be ready first, so they started there and just worked up.

We usually started haying about the middle of July. If the weather was good, you could get finished in about two weeks. If you ran into rainy weather, that would slow you down so you might not get done until the end of August. Most of the ranchers would be done haying by Labor Day, although some years it might take them into late September if the weather was bad.

We had about 160 acres in hay. On the days that Vaughn couldn't hay, he would ride to see about the cattle.

Sometimes I would go along, but often I had to stay and catch up with my work. I did what every housewife does: cooking, washing, ironing, and, of course, I raised a garden. I canned vegetables from the garden and all kinds of fruits: cherries, pears, peaches, and apples. We had apple trees, but we had to get pears and peaches from the lower country. We had quite a few red raspberries. Those berries used to come on just about the time haying started. I'd have to get up real early in the morning and go out and pick the raspberries before we could go to the hayfield.

Years ago we didn't bring the cattle down from the mountain until the middle of October. When they built roads in there, we always tried to get our cattle down to the ranch before hunting season. The roads brought the hunters in. During the fall roundup, we always picked up a few strays. We just brought them down to the ranch and called the owner to tell him we had a cow or two and a few calves that belonged to him. We knew all the people that were running cattle up there.

In the fall we would cull our herd. You always had a cow that was getting old or some that hadn't had a calf. These would go to market along with the steer calves and the heifers you didn't keep. We always kept some of the heifers for replacement cows. We usually sold somewhere between 50 and 75 calves each year. In later years we trucked the cattle to La Junta to the sale. Before that we never sold calves in the fall. We kept them until they were yearlings.

At that time the railroad still came to Ridgway. They shipped the cattle by railroad car from there to Kansas City. We used to trail the cattle from the ranch to Ridgway. That was fun, even though you used to almost freeze to death when you started out early in the morning. We didn't have much trouble getting them to the highway, but sometimes you would have quite a time getting them across the highway. The highway was oiled, and they didn't like that oil. After you got them across the highway, there was a gate that you drove them through and then down the hill and across the river to the stockyards.

After you got the cattle into the stockyards, you ran them from one corral to another through the cutting lanes, so the brand inspector could inspect them to be sure that you didn't have one that didn't belong to you. Our brand was Open-A-Bar-Two-Slashes. Of course, every cow had an earmark, too. Ours was an underbit in the left ear. An underbit was just a V cut out of the ear. Other people did different things to the ears. Some of them cut off the top of the ears or cut notches in different places. All that is done when you brand in the spring. The brand inspector had a book that told him all the brands belonging to different people. If you found one that didn't belong to you, the brand inspector cut that cow out and notified the people that it belonged to so they could pick it up.

You never know what you are going to get for your cattle when you sell them. You just take them to market and take what they give you. That's why it's getting so hard for the cattlemen and the sheepmen anymore. What

The town of Dallas.

you get for what you sell is in no comparison to what you have to pay for what you buy. The price of a piece of machinery is going up, but the price you're getting for your critters isn't. In fact, the price has gone down in the past six or seven years. The price fluctuates. It's up; it's down. Years ago you could hardly give a cow away. The trouble now is what you have to buy. If you go to where they sell machinery and ask them how much a tractor costs, they tell you. If you want it, you pay that price. If you take a cow to market you don't tell them what you want for that cow, you take what they give you. But that is what you raise them for, that's your living, so you have to sell. You can't keep them all.

We used to keep about six bulls for our herd. We used to buy them from people in the bull business. You have to be a pretty good judge of cattle to pick out a bull that you think is going to produce good calves. You just pick it out, pay for it, and take it home and hope that it doesn't die of poison, or break a leg, or something in the next year.

Years ago Vaughn used to butcher our own beef. We didn't have refrigeration, so we had to can most of the meat. It takes quite a while to can a cow. Later when we had a deep freeze, we took the cow down to one of the slaughterhouses in Delta or Cedaredge where they butcher them, cut them up, and wrap them ready for the freezer. We didn't get electricity out in Cow Creek until 1942; and I didn't get an electric range until years later, so I did all my cooking and canning on a coal range.

Vaughn never was much of a hunter. He killed a few deer but never did kill an elk. We did like to fish, though. We went fishing every time we got a chance. When we were first married we had to go on horseback; that was the only way to get there. We would ride as far up Cow Creek as we could go and then take our fishing equipment and walk up the canyon on foot. We would fish all the way up to Difficulty Creek and then fish coming back. We would also go over to the West Fork of the Cimarron to fish. There weren't any roads, so not many people got in there. There was good fishing in those days.

We used to visit back and forth with our neighbors quite a bit, especially in the wintertime. We'd go to one of the neighbors for dinner and then play cards for awhile. We used to go to the dances at Cow Creek, too. When we were first married, they had a dance every Saturday night. We joined a square dance club and went to Montrose and lot of other places to go square dancing in the wintertime.

They borrowed money from the bank to build the Cow Creek Dance Hall, so they gave dances to pay for it. Those dances were rousing affairs. They always had a big crowd. They never sold drinks in the dance hall, but people had liquor in their cars in the parking lot. Some of them would get pretty inebriated. There would be a fight or two now and again, but, on the whole, they didn't have too much trouble.

We always had an orchestra from Montrose or someplace. We would dance waltzes, fox-trots, schottisches, and polkas. Every once in a while they'd throw in a square dance. We always had a circle waltz. In a circle waltz you would be dancing with some partner and someone would holler "circle," and you would get back in a circle, holding hands with a man on each side. Then you would change partners and dance with someone else. It was a lot of fun.

The dances started at nine o'clock and lasted until two in the morning. Sometimes people would want to take up a collection to keep the orchestra playing longer, but that didn't happen often. People were worn out and ready to go home by two o'clock.

In the wintertime we used to go sleigh riding a lot. Somebody would tie a bobsled to the back of a pickup, and four or five of us would pile in, and we go out sleighriding on the roads around here. They didn't keep the roads plowed like they do now. We'd get dumped off every once in a while. Sometimes I thought we were all crazy. After we were done, we would go to somebody's house for hot chocolate.

When you live on a ranch, it's a full-time job. You couldn't take time off to do much traveling. In the later years, when we had a hired man, we took off on several trips to different places. One year we went to Phoenix with another couple. Another time we went clear down to Nogales. One year we went with my brother and his wife to Clovis, New Mexico. My brother was born near Clovis and had never been back there.

We went to one place that I didn't care too much about; that was Yellowstone. Some parts of it I really enjoyed, but that bubbling mud, I could do without that. I don't want any more of it. I enjoyed seeing the moose, elk, and deer. We didn't get to see any bear.

Once we went to Corvallis, Oregon. I don't know if I would want to live there, but I really enjoyed Oregon. We went to San Diego to see a niece and nephew that lived there. We did a lot of fun things; there's so much to see around San Diego. We went to the zoo, the Wild Animal Park, and to Sea World. We drove to Anaheim one evening and took in Disneyland the next day. If I had to live in California, I'd want to live in San Diego. But, now I don't expect to live out in California.

T. J. WAND

RANCH HAND

T.J. came to Ouray late; he was not born here and did not move here until the sixties. His perspective provides a picture of what ranching was like after modernization — after the tractor, after the horse was no longer the power for farm machinery and transportation. T.J. has now moved to Montrose; a freak twist found him to be allergic to hay and meant an end to ranch life.

My wife, Clara, and I moved to Ridgway in 1960. At that time I was living in Oregon working for a mining company. I wanted to get away from that job because it kept me indoors too much of the time. When Harry Combs, who had just bought the Sleeping Indian Ranch, called and offered me the job of managing the ranch here, we moved back to Colorado.

I was born in Paonia, Colorado in 1919 and went all the way through school there. I lived there until I went into the Marines in January 1942. Clara, who was born in Naturita but raised in Paonia, and I were married in

"We lived out in Pleasant Valley on one of Marie Scott's properties. She was quite an old gal, one of the shrewdest business persons that you could ever run into. . . I don't think that she would out and out cheat you, but she would outsmart you."

San Diego in November 1942. Shortly after that I was shipped to the South Pacific with the 3rd Marine Division. There were several times over the next few years when I didn't think I was going to get through. We made three landings: Bougainville, Guam, and Iwo Jima. I don't know how anybody lived through the first 72 hours on Iwo Jima.

After the war we moved back to Paonia and I went to work for the Farmer brothers. These two men from Paonia had first started a construction company and then gone into the uranium mining business. I worked for them here in Colorado, and then from 1954 or '55 to 1960, I worked in one of their mines in Oregon.

I met Harry Combs through the Farmer brothers. We became friends and I used to stay in their home in Denver when I went to the stock show. That's what led to the offer to manage his ranch.

After Harry Combs bought the ranch, he renamed it the Sleeping Indian after that peak you can see south of the main house. He built a landing strip out there, right in the middle of the hayfield. I couldn't see that. I was more interested in the stock part of it. That was my job, taking care of the livestock. I did everything on the ranch, all the riding. We had grazing permits up Cow Creek and on the east side of the Cimarron, so I got plenty of opportunity to ride.

The people out on Cow Creek at that time were quite clannish, kind of like old hillbillies in Kentucky. Maybe not to that extent but you weren't accepted until they were ready for you. Fortunately, Ray Worley, who had sold the ranch to Harry Combs, took me under his wing and got me acquainted with all the people out there. I got first-hand knowledge about who had trouble with whom and what I was up against. It made it a lot easier because the people were quite standoffish.

Ray Worley was a character. He had no mischief in his eye; he was pretty serious. He was a trader; I mean he'd do anything to beat you out of a nickel, yet he'd be the first guy to come around if you were in trouble.

At one time Worley had a pack of dogs that he used to hunt mountain lions on the west fork of the Cimarron. Whenever anyone would see fresh tracks, they'd get hold of Ray and he would take his horses and dogs out after them. If the tracks were fresh, the dogs would tree the lion and he would shoot it. He was an old guy, but he got quite a few. People always wanted Ray to write up his experiences of hunting mountain lions. We almost got him to do it once. Ray was driving his tractor on the highway and someone ran into him and broke his leg. Doc Bates had him in the hospital in Ouray, so he

had time to write about hunting, but no one could talk him into doing it.

I was up on Worley's place one time chasing cattle and ran into an old still. I know it was a still because my horse damn near jumped into it. I don't know if he made whiskey or not, but if he didn't, he was one of the few that didn't. I went back several times after that but never could find that still again.

I worked for Combs for two years; then Harry leased the ranch and cattle to Ed McNewton, so I went to work for Mrs. Carroll Hotchkiss. The Hotchkiss family ranch is the only original ownership still out on Cow Creek. I worked for her six years, then Bob Six got hold of me, and I went to work for him. If I knew then what I know now, I wouldn't have done that.

Nobody got along well with Bob Six. He was not a congenial type. He was smooth; he would have made a hell of a politician. But if you crossed him, he had the money to take care of you.

Six, who was President of Continental Airlines, and his wife, Audrey Meadows, built a great big mansion on the hill on the Lazy 6 Ranch. I was unfortunate enough to be the ranch manager when the house caught on fire. To this day I don't know what caused the fire. They think a sump pump in the basement pulled all the water out and let sewer gas back up. When the motor on the walk-in freezer started, it may have ignited the gas. Ben Israel, who owned the last place up on Cow Creek, now called the Owl Creek Ranch and owned by the Mitchells, called me about 4:00 A.M. He asked if I had looked out the window lately. When I looked up at the big house, it was just a mass of flames. I thought maybe we could get into the house to save Six's tremendous gun collection, bronze statues, and things like that, but there was nothing you could do. You just had to stand there and watch it burn.

When we came to Ridgway it wasn't much, just a sleepy little cow town. There was a post office, a store, a filling station, a liquor store, and a drug store. The Sunset and the Little Chef were both here. Milt Mitchell had the Mercantile, but it has been rebuilt after the explosion at the county shop. They had dynamite stored in the shop and, when the building caught on fire, the dynamite blew up. A power company employee apparently was trying to cut off the power when the building blew up and was killed. They had quite a lawsuit over that.

The narrow gauge still came into town then because they had the stockyards down there, just about where the new city hall is located. The first two or three years I worked here, all the ranchers out on Cow Creek used to get together and drive their cattle to the stockyards for shipment to Denver or Kansas City. We would start separating the calves and the cattle we were going to ship about 8:00 A.M. Then we would take off on horseback for town. It was six or seven miles to Ridgway, so it took us about four hours. We had a few good horse races chasing those calves because you never knew where they were going to go. We never lost any of them though. It was definitely western. We would come off the highway, drop down off the top of the hill, ford the river,

and push them into the loading pens. We always did this in November when it was cold, so somebody always had a bottle or two. The cold never bothered us. We had a lot of fun. We usually ended up in the Little Chef for a late lunch at 2:00 or 3:00 P.M. and had a few more.

All those ranches out on Cow Creek have changed hands a number of times. Vaughn and Sybil Stealy, two of the finest people we ever knew, lived on what is now the Chimney Peak Ranch. It was owned by a fellow named John Morris. His son Emery bought it from his mother for $12,000 after his father died. He sold the ranch to some people named Flanagan. They sold it to Archie Baker. Baker sold it to Dean Johnson, the current owner, for something in excess of a quarter of a million dollars. That all took place over the course of ten to twelve years. Combs, I think, paid only about $100,000 for the original part of the Sleeping Indian Ranch. The man who bought the ranch from him also bought the Ethridge Ranch and paid $6 or $10 million or something like that for the whole works. Now that's only hearsay, but it was a lot of money, and all that land increased in value a great deal in a short period of time.

After I left Six, I went to work for a friend of Clara's family who was raising Charolais cattle out in Redvale. I knew better than to go to work for him, and that's putting it mildly, but I did. He was a very domineering type. I stayed with him for not quite three years and then came back to Ridgway to work for Bruce Phillips.

We lived out in Pleasant Valley on one of Marie Scott's properties. She was quite an old gal, one of the shrewdest business persons that you could ever run into. She had one goal, and you had better not be in her way. I don't think that she would out and out cheat you, but she would outsmart you. Just look at what she acquired. She did it all on her own; she didn't have any help. One thing about Marie, she would always do what she said she was going to do. If she said she would be some place at a certain time, she'd be there. If she was going to do a job, build a fence or something, it would get done. There was no procrastination.

The thing I remember about Marie more than anything else is that she contracted having fences built, and if they weren't built to her specifications, you did it over. Her corner posts were set four feet in the ground and her line posts three feet. Somebody contracted to build fence for her on Specie Mesa. It was pretty hard digging so they cut the posts off. She always used eight-foot posts, so she knew how deep they were dug in. Well, they cut off the bottoms of these posts and threw them away, but she found these pieces. She made them go back and do the whole thing over again. She paid for it, and she always had her own way of doing things.

During all the years I worked on ranches around here, the ranchers would get together in the spring to help each other with the branding. We used to do it the old-fashioned way. We'd rope each calf, wrestle it down, hold it, and brand it. We would brand 150 to 200 at a time, and you could get kicked around a good bit wrestling that many calves. Now they use a branding table. It's a lot easier on the calves and a lot easier on the help.

Bronc riding at the Ridgway Rodeo.

150

Now you just drive the calves into a chute next to the table, squeeze them tight, and tip the table over so the calf is on its side. Of course you have to do it right. A couple of years ago, I was helping brand out at Gene Adam's place and a calf didn't go into the chute; it just jumped over the rail. I never thought a thing about it and just grabbed him as he went by. He was tougher than I was and I ended up flat on my back with the calf on top of me.

It's been a good life, and I enjoyed it. Now I can't work any more. I've got bronchitis and emphysema awfully bad, and I just cannot work fast. With the cold and the low atmospheric pressure, I just can't do it anymore.

LOUIS JONES

MINER

Louis is a short, stocky man with a fringe of white hair on his head and a merry twinkle in his eyes. He lives by himself but has numerous children and stepchildren in the area. Reluctantly, he will leave town to visit them occasionally. He says he's retired, but, even after a recent heart attack, you can still find him down at Rice Lumber, helping his friend Ray Scoggins.

I was born in Lyon, France in 1908. My dad had been in Ouray twice before he ever married my mother. He had made a stake up at the Camp Bird and then returned to France. After he came back to France, my brother Charlie, another boy who died, and I were born. My dad went back to Ouray and sent for us to come to the United States when I was three. He met us at Ellis Island just like all the old-timers did. We lived in New York for a short time, then moved to Mt. Carmel, Pennsylvania where my dad worked in a coal mine. Later he came back to Ouray to work in the mines, leaving us in Pennsylvania.

"When I first started in the mines, I worked single jacking. You hit a drill steel with a mallet, turning the steel each time you hit it . . . You do that for eight hours, and you think your wrist is going to break."

We stayed there until my mother died. Dad came back to make arrangements to bring us to Ouray when he had enough money. My brother and I finally came to Ouray on June the 21st, 1921. We were adopted by a friend of my dad's on the 21st of July, 1921. That's how I got the name Jones.

As soon as we were adopted, my father went to California where he worked as a blacksmith in the mines. That September, when I was thirteen, I ran away from here and went to California where my dad was working. I rode the freights. I came back to Ouray in about December that year. If I stayed in any one place for any period of time, I always had to go to school, but every spring I'd take off. I made 28 trips to California while I was growing up.

I didn't have much schooling after I came to Ouray, just a little bit here and there. Once when I was in California, I tried to tell them that I was about ready to graduate, so they put me in the eighth grade, but that didn't work, so they put me back in the seventh grade. Then I ran away and came back here to Ouray and never did go back to school; so I really quit school in the sixth grade when I was seventeen years old.

We had four grocery stores and a bakery. I used to deliver bread for the baker and I delivered papers for Frank and Albert when I was a kid.

The pool hall, Chambers's place, is where the Apteka is now. The kids in town always went in there to play pool. There was a card playing place, Billy Beaver's, on what is now the vacant lot next to the post office. They didn't let any of us kids in there. The women in town were pretty straight-laced; they didn't want the kids mixing with the card players.

I had started working when I was thirteen, washing dishes in a restaurant. Then when I was seventeen, I started to go down to the Navajo Dam to get a job when they were building that, but I got snowed-in in Silverton and stayed there.

I started working as a dishwasher at the old Mayflower Mine. That's where my brother, Charlie, learned to cook. Later, I worked in the mine. Earlier when they were mining at the Mayflower they used the single jack and the double jack. Then the machines came in; the first ones were dry. That's why a lot of the men are dead now. When I started working as a machine helper, running drilling machines, we had water with the machines. That settled the dust.

In the morning we'd go into the change room and change our clothes and wait for the ore train to take us in. Then we'd go in and work. It was work, too; wet and cold and miserable. The temperature in the mine stayed about the same year-round, about 50 degrees. You had to wear a coat all the time.

Later, I worked in a place called the Forty-four Raise. A bunch of Swedes were driving that raise. They ran it forty-four hundred feet up into the Shenandoah. I was running the hoist. That was a pretty good job. All I did all day was sit there and wait for signals and send them material. I had some one else to load the hoist. I just ran it up and down, up and down. That got old.

When I worked in Silverton, I lived at the mine. We had everything we wanted there. The commissary had a pool table and card tables where there were games going on all the time. At the Sunnyside Mine, you never went outside at all in the winter. Everything was either underground or under sheds. You went from one building to another under sheds.

We had good food, better than the restaurants serve now. The French Bakery ordered food for the mine and stocked up enough to last all winter. The food was sent to the mine on trams and they would usually fill up the mine pantry once a year.

When I was single, I just stayed at the mine. After I got married I would try to come down to town once a month. I'd take a tram down to Eureka then take a train into town. The trains were still running in those days. That train was really something. If you wanted to go to Ouray, you would take the train from Eureka to Silverton and spend the night in Silverton. The next day you would ride down to Durango and spend the night there.

Then you'd go to Telluride and spend the night there. On the next day you'd ride to Ridgway and hope you got there before the train went through for Ouray. It took four days to go around. Now you can do it in couple of hours.

It was nice living at the mine. Everybody got along well. You never had fights, even in card games. You knew better, because if you did, you got kicked out and sent down the hill. So everybody was pleasant.

When you worked in a mine, you rode the ore train in and then were hoisted either up or down to the level you worked on. When you got to the working level, you could walk in if it wasn't too far, but most of the time there was a motor to take you in.

While I was in Silverton I met my first wife. We planned to get married but were snowed in for ninety days. Finally, she slipped away from school and we ran down to Aztec and got married. We had two girls that we started to raise in Silverton.

Most of the mines in this area had shut down long before the Depression. The only one running was the Mayflower in Silverton. As I understand it, the mines were running out of ore. They weren't getting enough to pay the stockholders. During the Depression, the mines had to raise wages, too. If you remember, when you went on relief, the government paid you a dollar and ten cents an hour. Miners were getting three dollars a day at that time.

When the Depression first hit in Silverton, everything was working. You could quit a job three times in a day and not lose an hour's work. It was that good. In 1929 most of the money that was opening up all the old mines was English money. When the crash occurred, they all pulled their horns in and quit. I was working up at Eureka at the time, driving a tunnel through the mountain toward the Sunnyside Mine. I didn't even know they were going to close. We knew the banks had closed and all that, but we were still working. One day in 1929, I went down to the post office to pick up a new suit I had ordered. It was a C.O.D. package for 65 bucks, so I went down to the office and asked them if I could draw a check to pay for the suit. The owner, Martin, said, "God, I'm sorry, Jones, but we don't have the money," I asked how are we going to get our money and he said, "You ain't." I went back up and told the cook about it and he told me not to worry, we'd get our money. I asked him if he would loan me the money, and he said, "Sure, Sure." He was the banker for a lot of us and lost everything. He never got a cent of it back. That was when it really hit.

We moved back to Ouray in 1935. I went to work for Condotti and Kullerstrand, the banker, in the Barstow Tunnel up at the Idarado. It wasn't called the Idarado then. The mine was later sold to a group that came from the Sunshine Mine in Couer d'Alene, Idaho. That's how the mine got its name. They ran it for quite awhile until the war broke out. I heard the government put in four million dollars to carve a tunnel to the Black Bear. They needed the ore. That's what made the Idarado. It ran for a long time until it got too deep; too expensive. But someday mining will all come back to Ironton. You watch and see. The last job I had at the Idarado was when I was carpentering. They called me up to build core boxes. Those were the boxes they put the drilling cores in. I must have made five or six hundred of those boxes. They drilled that country up, down, and every direction. Some of those cores were awful rich. I also built an assay office for them. They had me tear out the assay office at the Barstow and build one at the Idarado. I saw their plans, fifty-year plans. I saw the map, the future of what the Idarado was going to look like. Everything went down into Ironton Park. That's the logical place to look for gold and they still own all that.

In the winter of 1936, I went to Arizona to work as a timber man in the mines. It was nice; the mines were hot. The temperature in the mines was eighty or ninety. You stripped to work in those mines. I timbered there until one day when I had left a birch standing with a nail in it. The efficiency manager came over and said, "Hey, Jones, is that yours?" "Well," I said, "I'm going to knock it over." He said, "It's too late; you've got thirty days coming." So I quit and came back to Ouray.

When I left I had a wife and three kids. When I got back I had nobody. They had left. I had been sending money every two weeks and I didn't even know they had left.

I worked a couple of winters at the Revenue Mine. I also worked at the Beaver Belfast up at the end of Ironton Park, where all that colored water is coming out. Later I worked at the Mineral Farm Mine and at a manganese mine at Box Canyon.

Then I went bumming around in Nevada, working in the gold field. I'd work a month or so in one place then move on to the next place. Miners are like that. We used to call them ten-day miners, and I wasn't even a ten-day.

When I came back to Ouray, Bud Franz hired me to work at the Bachelor. I went up there that night, and I was working with a little Italian guy. We called him Jimmy the Wop. He worked on one side of the car, mucking, and I worked on the other side. He chewed snuff and ate garlic and liked to drink wine. He was drunk that night, and every time he'd throw a shovel over into the car, he'd blow spit. I was on the other side of the car and I'd get it all in the face. I got so damn sick, I went out. This was the first shift I worked. Bud came over and asked what was the matter and I said, "I'm sick, I'm sick." He told me that I had to go back in and finish the work, but I said, "No, I'm not going back in; I'll come back tomorrow." He told me, "If you don't go back in you needn't come back. You'll never work in this camp again." I never did work for that guy again.

People were having a hard time during the Depression in Ouray. The only work that was going on, as I remember it, was the county. The county overseer was a veteran from the first war, and if you weren't a veteran you couldn't get a job. I know, because I asked him.

When I first started in the mines, I worked single jacking. You hit a drill steel with a mallet, turning the steel each time you hit it. Each time you turn it, it goes in a little. You do that for eight hours, and you think your wrist is going to break. After you drilled in about a foot, you put half a stick of powder in and blow loose the rock. The old miners used to double jack; one man holds and turns the steel and the other man swings the sledge. I never did any double jacking.

When the drilling machines came in, you could drill holes five of six feet deep. You could take a lot more face out then. They tried to break at least six feet every shear.

After the rock was broken loose, you pushed a car up to the face and loaded it by hand, mucking. They gave you a dollar a car at that time. If you could load seventeen cars you got seventeen dollars between you and your partner. That wasn't much, but it was better than three dollars a day. Now they have mucking machines to do that job.

When I went to work in Silverton, the mining machine men got three and a quarter and the nipper three dollars. That was a day, not an hour. Of course, you could buy a loaf of bread for a dime then.

In the mine you would drive a tunnel and then, here and there, build a little raise and hollow it out. Sometimes they would build chutes to get the ore down to the next level; sometimes they would just build another raise under the drift where all the ore was and drop it down. On the main level, they always had chutes built of wood with metal gates. You'd fill the chute, then the motor would bring the tram cars under the chute, and you would open the gate and fill the cars. Sometimes a chute could hold enough to fill 20 or 30 cars.

When you were working on a tunnel below the main level, you used round buckets to hoist the ore up to the tram cars. When I worked in the copper mines in Arizona, they used bigger buckets than what you see around here: ten, thirty, fifty, even one hundred tons. There were six thousand men working at that mine, and we used to ride down in buckets, sixty-six men to a bucket. They dropped us down 5500 feet. It felt as if your feet would leave the floor.

At the Mayflower in Silverton in the early days, they used to tram the ore from the mine to the mill. We used to ride the tram buckets up to the mine, three men to a bucket. It was a loop. They would load a bucket with ore up at the mine, and as it came down to the mill, it would pull the empty buckets up. One winter when I rode the tram it got down to 45 degrees below and never got above 22 below for two weeks straight. That was cold. When I was first living in Ouray, you could hear the tram at Bachelor here in town when it was running.

All the mines had their own mill. The ore was crushed and then run through an agitator. The agitator brought the ore up to a table that vibrated and let all the metal fall down into a big tank. Then it went onto a belt and into a launderer that's made of wood. After that it went to the dryer, a big wheel with a carpet on it. Heat is blown through and the ore dries and drops off. It is separated into different types: lead, silver, gold. All the mines had base metals as well as gold and silver.

I worked in the mines until the war broke out. They said you couldn't quit a job; if you quit they'd draft you. I was 37 then and I didn't like to be tied down, so I quit.

I was out of work for I don't know how long. I worked part time for Frank Rice at the lumber yard unloading timber for the mines. He used to pay me to unload coal, too; ten cents a ton. I was glad to get it.

There was an old carpenter around here named Axel Erikson who owned a place up on the mesa above the Bachelor Switch. He came into the lumberyard one day while I was talking to Frank Rice and said, "Louis, did you ever put any roofs on?" I said, "Hell, I don't know, why?" He said, "I've got the old Poor Farm down the valley. Why don't you go down there and put a roof on it for me?" I went down and put a new roof on it, which is still there, and that's how I got started doing carpentry.

When I got through with the roof, he had me calcimine the inside. That building used to have the finest wood you ever saw. Teak wood, different colors, and I had to go all over it with calcimine. The county owned it then; it was the Poor Farm where they had two or three old people. It was open for quite a few years, but they finally discontinued it after everybody died.

Later the Webers bought the place and I did quite a bit of remodeling for them. They sold it to an Italian outfit, the De Julios who lived there for awhile. Now it has been empty for twenty years or more.

I bought the house I live in now in 1940, paid $400.00 for it. I paid it off $15.00 a month. At that time you could buy any house in town for $500.00. Times have changed, I turned down $100,000 for this corner. I don't want to sell it. I may have to some day if they keep going up with the taxes.

I remarried in 1941. My second wife had three kids, and we had one more together. My second wife was a Mormon, a jack Mormon. When the kids were all little, she was a good Mormon, but after they grew up, she didn't want to be bothered with it any more. We used to have services here; the Mormons never had a church here in town, so they took turns meeting in people's houses. A Mormon man moved to town and found out that she was a Mormon. He'd call up and my wife would tell me she didn't want to talk to him. I'd say, "No, my wife says she's not interested. He'd call and call. Finally, I got insulting on the phone one day. That got him. The funny part is, when my wife died, he preached the sermon. When he was preaching at the funeral, he was looking right at me.

It seems as if there were more people in Ouray in the twenties and thirties. All the houses were always full. Of course, they've built more since. They didn't really start building in town until Ray Scoggins came here about twenty-five years ago.

There were lots of bars in town and two or three different restaurants. My brother ran restaurants in several places in town. In fact, he was the last one to run the restaurant in the Beaumont. That was a beautiful place. He ran a restaurant at the Columbus which was a saloon where the Silver Nugget is now. I put the floor in there and never got paid for it. The floor is still there. In fact, I was working there the day my dad died in California. My wife called and told me that a woman had called saying she was my stepmother. I hadn't heard from her

The girls at the Temple of Music.

in I don't know how many years. I called back and she said my dad had died and wondered what I wanted to do. I said, "I don't care what you do." I had no money to go out there. My brother was in Phoenix at the time and said he'd help her out if she needed money, but he couldn't go because he was tied up. We didn't care for our father after what he did to us.

One thing I won't talk about is the girls on the line. They were always good to me. I've met them in other towns, and they took me in like I was their son. They were never allowed uptown, but they were better behaved than some of the straight-laced ones. A lot of the girls lived here in town. The place where I was raised had six, the Temple of Music had four or five, the Bon Ton had two or three, and the cribs all had them. They were in Silverton and Telluride, too.

When I was bumming around, I was working out of Winslow, Arizona one time. I was walking along the road when a big, black car with a big, black chauffeur pulled up and someone called out, "Get in here. What are you doing around here?" It was one of the girls that used to be here, Hazel. Big Hazel. God, she was nice. She took me in and I worked for my keep. She had a place just outside of Winslow. Winslow was a railroad siding. It was just like mining. Wherever there were railroads, there were girls. Wherever I would go, if I would see one of the girls that had been in Ouray or Silverton or Telluride, I'd go in and say hi. They all knew me. They'd ask, "Are you doing all right? You need any money? You eating? You have a place to sleep?" There weren't many people who would do that for you.

When I was a kid, I used to run errands for the girls. I would run uptown to get things for them. They paid us a dollar. It's the only time you saw any money. They always paid well. When they had hard times, we would just forget it. We could tell. I think the last one here was Lilly, Lilly Morrell. She died.

There used to be some real characters living in Ouray, but some of them have relatives living here now. I want to skip them.

ADOLPH JORDAN

MULE SKINNER

Adolph has obviously been living alone for quite awhile. His house is a one-room cabin at the old American Nettie Mill where he is caretaker. He has a large dog which is relatively friendly. The room contains elements of a living room, kitchen, bedroom, bathroom (portapotty), and most importantly, shop for mining equipment. Adolph is not one to spend time worrying about such niceties as dusting, vacuuming, and cleaning.

The kitchen consists of numerous extension cords leading to a toaster, frying pan, etc. There is no oven or range. There is a large wood stove and it is obviously most convenient to split wood for the stove right next to it, in the kitchen and living room, where the two easy chairs face the stove.

Adolph was reluctant to be interviewed, but, once started, he told stories constantly, almost as if to make sure they wouldn't be lost.

I was born in Missouri in 1909 but moved to South Dakota when I was two-and-one-half years old. My

> *"I've been covered up seven times in snowslides... You had to ride under them; there was no way around them, and the slides had the right-of-way."*

father bought a ranch next to the Cheyenne River Sioux Indian Reservation. I lost my father in 1918 in the flu epidemic. My brothers and I were left with two ranches, 500 head of cattle, 3,600 sheep, and we didn't know how many horses. We raised and shipped horses to Chicago and Kansas City where they had big auctions.

When I was about 15 or 16 my brother and I traded for a bunch of Indian ponies on the Cheyenne River and rodded them all the way to southern Missouri. We drove them about 750 miles. We started out in the winter with only about fifty cents apiece in our pockets. Only one horse in the bunch was broken, and I tied a pack on him. We didn't have a pack saddle. We just rolled up a few groceries in each end of a bedroll and tied it onto him bareback and turned him loose. Then we jumped onto two green horses and took off with that bunch of horses. We broke a new horse every day and got through with 27 head of horses. They were all broke when we got to Missouri, and we sold them all.

I stayed in Missouri for a while, working the harvest

and living with my grandparents. My grandfather and his brothers owned farms adjoining those of the James family. I'm related to Jessie and Frank James. Jessie and Frank weren't bad people. They were forced into the situation they were in. When they put the railroad in, they killed Jessie and Frank's father and several other farmers to get their land. Old man James was a preacher. Jessie and Frank were preachers, too. They could preach a pretty good sermon.

Jessie and Frank held up a bank in Sheridan about six miles north of where my grandfather lived. That night they rode back to my grandfather's place and he put them up in the barn. They slept with their horses, and the next morning my grandfather took them breakfast. After they ate, they rode out of there. They rode awfully good horses. They didn't stay on the road; they rode in the open and jumped fences.

When I got a little older, 17 and 18, I followed the harvest for two years. I started in Salina, Kansas and ended up in the Dakotas. I worked for three or four months of the harvest pitching bundles and driving teams. They'd cut the wheat with binders and shocked the grain. Then we pitched the bundles onto the hay rack and drove to the threshing machine where you pitched the bundles into the machine. That's the way they threshed the grain.

In 1927, when I was 18, I came out to this country. I punched cows and broke horses on the ranches out of Ridgway. I worked some in the La Sal Mountains, too. I was a pretty good cow puncher.

In 1929 I got married and moved up on Horsefly, where I farmed for five years. I raised grain and milked cows. We sold cream in Ridgway. All three of my children were born up there.

We raised everything we needed. We could feed our family on less than one hundred dollars a year. All you needed was a little salt and sugar. We took our wheat to the flour mill and had it ground so we had our flour for the winter. We raised our vegetables and put carrots, potatoes, and everything we needed in the root cellar. We also canned a lot of stuff, swiss chard and everything; we'd have five or six hundred quarts of stuff canned to put in the cellar. Whenever we needed something we'd open up a can of stuff that we had. We had everything we wanted.

I killed lots of jack rabbits. We had rabbit pie and all kinds of rabbit. They're good eating when they're fat. A jack rabbit is not too good if he's poor, but these rabbits were fat. They'd come down off Horsefly Peak, sometimes two or three hundred of them in a line and go straight to a grain stack. They could eat a grain stack down in a week, so we had to get rid of them. These rabbits were big; they were crossed with some other kind of rabbit, might of been a snowshoe. Now a lot of people don't believe this but it's the absolute truth. We killed two jack rabbits up there that weighed over one hundred pounds. I've got a picture of one down at my boy's place that was about four feet long and fat.

In the spring I'd go down around Ridgway and help the ranchers brand, dehorn, and castrate their calves. In the fall I'd take a team down and help put up hay.

It was nice on Horsefly in the summer, but it was pretty

snowy in the winter. One winter one of the neighbors had a guy from Virginia working for him. In the fall when it started to snow, he wrote home and said, "We got six inches of the beautiful last night." In the winter, each time it snowed he'd write that we got a foot and a half or two feet of "the beautiful" last night. By spring he wrote, "We got about three feet of the damn stuff last night." He got tired of the snow, but that's the way it goes.

We had a lot of fun up there. We'd go to old schoolhouse or to somebody's house and have dances or card parties. In the spring the sun would settle the snow and it would crust. You could drive a team and sled and go over the crust like ocean waves. You could go anywhere you wanted, driving over the tops of the fences. But you had to be back before ten in the morning, or it began to thaw and the horses would break through. So we had our parties at night. We'd leave about ten or eleven at night and be back in time to milk the cows in the morning. Everybody had to bundle up in the sleds to keep warm, so we'd bring the quilts and stuff in and roll the kids up in them and let them go to sleep wherever you could find a place. We'd all have a big time. We had a lot of fun, more fun than now and it didn't cost you nothin'.

The dances were great. Sometimes you wouldn't have anything but a jew's harp. Sometimes somebody would play a banjo or a fiddle. There was an old organ at the schoolhouse. Everybody brought something to eat. The women baked pies or cobblers or cakes and brought it to the dance.

In 1934 my oldest boy was about ready to go to school, and, since they were closing the school up on Horsefly, we decided to move to Ouray. There weren't many kids left up on Horsefly, so they quit having school up there. I didn't want them to fight the winter snow going to school either.

When I first came here in 1927, everything was handled with horses and mules. Everything was freighted out of the mountains with wagons, two-horse, four-horse, and six-horse teams, hauling the ore off the hills and supplies up to the mines. The small outfits packed the ore out and the supplies in on burros and mules. In the mornings there were quite a few horses and mules going up the street at six o'clock. You could hear the bells ringing, the mule skinners cussing, and the chains jangling. In the evening it would be the same when they came back in.

In 1934 I bought the mail contract for the Camp Bird and the Barstow mines from Dave Boring. I bought his horses and pack outfit and got the lease on the livery stable on Main Street that Howard Linscott uses now. I was pretty handy with horses and mules, so when I got this opportunity it fit right in with me. I was a pretty good packer when I was young, but I learned more from the old packers here. I had horses downstairs and upstairs both. In the winter I didn't keep too many; eight or ten mules and six or eight or ten saddle horses. In the summertime I'd have thirty to sixty head. I did all my own shoeing and broke all the horses. I never had an accident all the time I was packing. Not one.

We packed mail up to the Camp Bird and the Upper Camp Bird, then went back across the old logging road to the Revenue where the old Sneffels Post Office was. We didn't use the post office much; we usually went straight to the boardinghouse at the Revenue. We also took groceries in with the mail and brought laundry out. The miners would send their laundry down to their families to get it washed.

I also rented horses to the miners. They'd ride them up the hill, then do up the reins and turn them loose. I kept grain in the box down at the stable so the horses would come back by themselves. I'd unsaddle them and feed them grain when they got back.

I hauled ore with a four-horse team, I didn't drive my six-horse team much but drove it some. My horses were pretty light. I had some heavy horses when I first came up here, but Johnny Donald had the big freight outfit. He was killed here in the barn, then the Fellins bought it. They freighted with horses and mules. They had two fifteen mule strings packing down from the Upper Camp Bird to the Lower Camp Bird.

There was a platform down there where they unloaded the sacks. They had a fifty-ton mill at the Camp Bird where they concentrated the ore. Then it would be brought down by six-horse teams to the railroad in town where it would be shipped to the smelter. The railroad kept a fire in the stove in the covered car they shipped the concentrate in. In the winter the sacks were wet and would be frozen by the time they got to town. They were hard to handle. I imagine the sacks would be thawed by the time they got to the smelter and be easier to unload.

I hauled some ore, but mostly I packed ore for the prospectors when they did their assessment work. When they got a little ore, I packed it out for them on mules. A mule would wear out a pair of shoes in ten days, because it would just be sliding on rocks as it came down from the mines.

I packed coal in to the American Nettie every year. I put a gunnysack of coal on each side of a mule. I packed all the tin that went on that big boardinghouse, too. One time I went up there with 22 head loaded in one string. Sometimes the mules give you a hard time, but they get used to it. You have to work them in. They're just like a team. The first time you hook them up, they don't know anything. You train them by using them. You put the harness or saddle on them and use them. I used to break lots of horses and mules. Usually you hook them up with something that's already broken; that's the easiest way. But if you hook two green ones together, you've got a little problem or two. If you don't know much, you'll have a lot of trouble. If you know how, it doesn't take too long. Work them until they get a little tired a few times; that does the job. It usually takes a year before a horse or a mule will do everything you want them to do, so he's absolutely dependable.

For two years I went up to the Wanakah every three weeks and packed out a car load of ore. I'd take my saddle horse and five or six mules up to the mine, and then take the mules 1,000 feet underground to pack out the ore. I'd come out of the mine and take it about a quarter of a mile to the tram house and unload it. The next day they would load the sacks in a jig-back tram and tram it down the mountain to a chute.

A jig-back tram is one where the loaded bucket pulls the empty bucket back up the hill. They would unload the sacks into a chute and slide the ore down into a gondola car that the narrow-gauge train had pushed in. The train would take the crude ore to the smelter. They put about 25 tons on those gondola cars, so I made quite a few trips with those pack mules.

I had to go back to Kansas City to the hospital one time. While I was there, I walked into a pool hall where a guy in there was telling the fellows he had just come back from "Coloradi". He said, "You ought to see them burros, how they go straight up the sides of the mountain. They'll pack fifteen, sixteen hundred pounds. "I was standing there with my big hat and cowboy boots on, and when he looked around and saw me I asked, "How much did you say those burros packed?" He said, "Maybe we did have those burros loaded a bit too heavy."

I've had burros that would pack more than their own weight but 100 or 150 pounds is about what they pack. A mule will pack 200 pounds pretty well, most of the time. If you have a short pack trip, sometimes you can load them heavier.

You can get a mule or a work horse to pull a heavier load than they can carry. You put the heavy stuff on a strong boat and slide it or in a wagon and haul it. They just have to pull and stretch and then get their feet under them and pull again.

When we hauled with horse teams we'd haul five tons on the wagons in the summertime and about seven and a half tons on sleds in the winter. It was easier to pull the sleds. Those wagons were awfully heavy, they weighed five or six tons empty. There were no springs on those wagons, so it took a lot of blacksmith work to keep them up. You had to strap yourself into the spring seat of the wagons. When those wagon wheels hit a rock and went over it, you'd drop down and go this way and that. If you were holding six lines to the horses, you couldn't hang on. On a six-horse team, you had one rein for each horse that stopped and started him and turned him right or left. That way, you can make each horse do different things. When you are going up those switchbacks the outside wheelhorse has to pull the whole load, sometimes as much as 30 feet. If all the horses pull at the same time, the back wheels of the wagon will go over the side. The horses that worked those big wagons weighed over a ton, maybe 2,300 or 2,400 pounds. You put a little horse in there, he can't do it. He ain't got the weight. And you don't work the wheeler; only when you need them. The wheelers were the horses next to the wagon. The pointers were the middle two horses, and the leaders were the two front horses.

They used to buy a lot of those big, old draft studs — stallions, from the east. They were cranky. When you were driving them up the mountain and stopped to water them, you had to unhook the outside tugs on the wheelers so they could turn and get a drink from the trough. Sometimes one of those studs would grab the other one by the neck, and they'd take the whole wagon over the hill. Kill them all. You could still see wheels from those wagons down in the creek a couple of years ago.

In the wintertime, driving the sleds, your hands would freeze. It was pretty painful trying to hang onto those heavy lines. You had to be pretty stout. Coming downhill in the winter, we put rough locks on the sleds. They were great big chains that we put under the back runners, then we had dogs on each side of the runners. They were big fingers that stick down into the snow when you put the brakes on. Once a track was made in the snow, it iced up and you stayed in the track all winter; but you had to have the chains under there or you couldn't hold the sled back. Those sleds were wide track, so there was room for the horses to walk inside the track, but the leaders and the pointers had to work all over. You had to keep them strung out.

In the spring of the year, we had to get up and leave town at twelve or one o'clock at night. 'Cause when the sun hit that snow, it would melt, and the horses couldn't stay up. We had to get up there while it was still froze and get off of there before it would melt. So we'd leave here about twelve or one or two. We'd set our time with the weather, of course. Sometimes we could leave at four o'clock and make it; sometimes we would have to leave at twelve or one o'clock. And we'd saddle up and load the mules and go on up and deliver our packages and mail and get down off of there before it thawed out.

I've been covered up seven times in snowslides. I was covered three times in the Waterhole Slide. You had to

Wagon train on Camp Bird Road.

166

ride under them; there was no way around them, and the slides had the right-of-way. In the spring you hear a boom up there. That's when the cone breaks off. In the winter you can't hear anything; it just comes. Millions of tons of snow will come down, and it will break off chunks of trees as big around as you can reach around. It takes a lot of power to do that. The old-timers all told us if you are caught in a slide, close your eyes and hold your nose and hope that your ears are covered, cause it will blow in. That snow will find a vacuum and put it right in. That's what kills people; they drown. They breathe that fine snow and it kills them. A lot of people have been killed.

When I was covered, my horse dug me out sometimes. I had an old dog that dug me out once. One time my horse dug in and the bridle bit pulled the hide off my face. A horse has the best nose of any animal; they can smell you. I wasn't in but a foot under the snow, but it packed so hard it would hold up a horse. You can't even move, but he dug in and broke the crust. Once the hard crust is broken, you can usually wiggle yourself free.

I've had mules knocked down by slides many times, but they usually get up on their own. They're stronger, you know. One time I was bringing some machinery down from the old U.S. Mill with a string of four mules. A slide about three or four feet thick and a hundred yards wide came down, and that thing knocked three of those mules' feet out from under them. They rode on top of that slide down about a hundred yards. They was abouncing up and down; it looked like they were going up ten feet sometimes. It had skinned up their legs a little bit, but if they had gotten under it, the slide would have ground them up and killed them. But it threw them up in the air, and they lit on top of the snow. The lead rope was broken free. We always kept rotten pig tails on the pack saddles so if something did happen, they'd break pretty easily. I went down, got the mules on their feet, straightened up the pack saddles, and led them up. They didn't hardly make a dent in the snow where the slide had run. It was packed that hard. Yeah, them snowslides, they will do some freakish things.

One time I lost some mules in a wet spring slide in the Towers Slide, on a trail that goes to the Upper Camp Bird. It was stormy. You could have got killed anytime up there; it could have come again. I shoveled for 36 hours straight to get those two mules out. That'll separate the men from the boys. I shoveled and tromped the snow in front of them and moved them a little bit and then shoveled and tromped some more until I got them on the trail. Not another soul come up the trail that whole time; but I made it, saved my mules.

I packed the first load of medicine and supplies into the Camp Bird when the slide that took out the boardinghouse killed the people up there. The whole basin above the mine, about three miles of it, ran that time. Mrs. Israel, the cook, was killed when she went to the door to watch the slide. When it came by the suction just pulled her out and killed her. Another fellow was killed when the slide knocked him into the spring where he was taking tailings samples for the mill and drowned him. The snow pushed Ethan Roberts up against the old cook stove and burned him pretty bad, but it didn't kill him. It also pinned Ralph Dunn, the superintendent, in the shop for a while. After someone skied down for help, I took the first pack outfit to the mine. I was packing over 60 feet of snow in places where that slide had run.

One time I put two compressors up at the Little Fanny Mine in Silverton. The men running that mine had rolled two compressors off the trail and busted them up pretty good trying to get them up there. They came over to see Charlie Bell; he was running the Camp Bird, and he sent them down to see me. He said if anybody can put them up there, he'll get it up there for you. I went over and looked the job over. In one place the trail was a little over 200 yards long and not more than eighteen inches wide. The compressor had to be on a little wooden sled to get it up there. I took my horses over there and got a couple of good single jackers to put anchors in the rock above the sled, so we could chain the sled up as we pulled it around the cliff. I got it up there and only broke one little copper pipe when a slide rock came down.

I put machinery up at mines in Silverton where we had to string it on a cable. You would hang the machine on a stationary cable with a pulley, and then use a horse to turn a whim, a vertical drum, that wound up a pull cable that pulled the machine to the top. As the horse worked around and around, he had to step over the cable each time. You can get lots of power that way.

In 1937, when they discovered uranium over in the West End, I took fifty or sixty head of burros over there to haul uranium ore. We worked for Jack Simplot for awhile and then staked out a lot of land for ourselves. I packed about 600 tons of uranium out of there. I had mules in the high country but burros over there. Mules sweat too much. Burros were smaller and didn't heat up so much. They protected themselves better. We had to haul water 50 miles for the burros to drink. The burros would haul the ore to a loading platform at the road where trucks would come to haul it away. I stayed there for a couple of years.

While I was still in Ouray, I went into the tourist business. We packed tourists, taking pack trips with saddle horses. We had saddle horses going everywhere. The kids got big enough so they could guide. They knew the trails so they could lead the tourists out. We had quite a string of horses. My horses were always fat; I never had thin horses. They were always in good shape. When they got a little poor or something, I'd turn them out and let them get fat again. I never worked them very long.

And then I had hunting camps. I had the biggest hunting camp on the Western Slope. We took from 30 to 60 hunters every fall. I had cooks, a night cook and a day cook, and a butcher in camp. I put up a tent for butchering and the butcher would cut up all their meat and package it. I packed it in paper so the hunters could take their meat home already wrapped in packages. I had a butcher from Mountain Air, New Mexico. He was a big, long-armed guy who had a special saw made for him. He could cut up an elk and package it in two hours. I always made the hunter that got the elk be there when it was butchered. That way there was never any squabble about it. They could never say he took part of my meat or something. There was never a chance for arguments. I don't like arguments. I still hold the record for having a complete kill in my camp more than any other guide in the state. Everybody got their game. I bought the first guide's license in the state. I ran that guide service for thirty-five or six years.

I've lived here at the old Wanakah Mill since 1971. I'm just the watchman. I had a place just below here and sold out when Warren Gibbs, who owned the mill at the time, asked me to watch it for him. People were stealing a lot of stuff out of it. They haven't stolen anything since I've been here. I dusted a few of them.

I've still got two horses and two mules out here. I still ride them, too. I was out about eight hours the other day.

GLADYS FOURNIER

RANCH WIFE

The Fournier Ranch is about the highest residence, at 8000 feet, on Dallas Divide, west of Ridgway. It is isolated and wind swept. The houses are painted and well kept. Mrs. Fournier lives in a double-wide which is warm, neat, and light on the inside. She is a tough woman who has her opinions and is willing to share them. She was a hard-working ranch wife and knows the value of work.

I was born in 1903 in southeastern Nebraska, near Lincoln. When I was ten or eleven, we moved to Idaho where my dad and uncle homesteaded a place near Soda Springs, not too far from Pocatello. We lived ten or twelve miles from town, and, since they didn't have buses like they have now, I had to stay with people in Soda Springs to go to high school. When my brother, who was three years younger than me, was ready to go to high school, my dad thought it would be easier for us to get a high school education if we moved somewhere closer to town, so we moved

"I met my husband, Eugene, on the road going to school one day. . . We were married in 1923 in the Catholic Church in Ouray. We didn't have any wedding party or honeymoon. We just went to the hayfield."

to the Ridgway area in 1920.

I was a junior when we moved to Ridgway, and I hated going to school here. We had a nice new school in Soda Springs, but the school in Ridgway was a rickety old building. I just didn't like it.

I never got to know the kids at school well. Since we lived out on Highway 62, five or six miles from town, I had to ride horseback to school; so I spent most of the time going and coming to school. I rode bareback and put my horse in a barn next to the school during the day.

I finished school in 1921; our commencement exercises were in the old Sherbino Theater. We never had proms or anything like that. We were lucky to graduate.

We went to the Community Church in Ridgway, the same one that is there now. We never got to many of the functions. We had a little car then, but the roads were so bad that we couldn't get to town often. They used to have bazaars and women's clubs. We don't attend anymore, but I guess they've got a pretty good going church.

My dad had a hay ranch. We had cattle and milk cows; I suppose we had a pig or two. My job on the ranch was anything that came along. I always helped in the hay season.

After high school I went to college in Gunnison in the summer. It wasn't much of a school then. They've done a lot of building since then. It's quite a complex now.

That fall I started teaching in the old schoolhouse out on Dallas Creek. I taught there for three years and had anywhere from three to six or seven kids in school. I taught whatever grade the kids happened to be in.

We had three schools in our district then: one on Dallas Creek, one in Pleasant Valley, and one on Horsefly Mesa where the kids went to summer school. Now Horsefly is all pastureland; no one lives up there any more. Back then, there were a lot of families up there. The De Julios, an Italian family, moved in like a colony and took up all the land. It was tough, but they didn't know any different. When they got tired, they left the country. That's why no one lives up there anymore.

I don't know if I really liked teaching. That's a hard question to answer, because when you're doing something and you don't know anything else, you don't know whether you like it or not. It was alright. It was a way of life.

I met my husband, Eugene, on the road going to school one day. He was coming across the road on horseback, and we just visited all the way to town. We started dating after that and dated for two or three years.

We were married in 1923 in the Catholic Church in Ouray. We didn't have any wedding party or honeymoon. We just went to the hayfield.

We moved into the bunkhouse on Eugene's folks' ranch. It was just one room with a wood floor, a cook stove, and a table. We ate at the other house most of the time. Eugene worked the place for his dad.

Eugene's father, Mr. Fournier, came here from Quebec, I think; he was a French Canadian. He landed in Telluride and mined, then he bought this place, the home place. My husband's folks were married here, and the kids born here, and everything. That's where they made their living with their cows and their horses and their hay.

The ranch back then wasn't as big as it is now. The hay land was all together, but the pastureland has been added since. Most of the buildings have been added to it, too. My husband, my dad, and I added a couple of rooms to the bunkhouse. That gave us some room which we needed since we had three girls and a boy. Now the ranch is about 1,800 acres.

My husband, Eugene, died in 1941 and our son, Gary, runs the ranch now. He's the third generation on this ranch. We moved into the big house in 1977. We used to run about 200 head of cattle, now Gary runs only about half that many. He has to work alone.

Ranch life was a hard life; a fellow worked. Get up in the morning and eat your breakfast and milk your cows and tend to things, get a middle-of-the-day meal and go back to work, supper, and fall into bed dead tired. It was just the same as when you have a job and you go and do it every day; that's what we did. You had to do it because the animals depended on it. You didn't expect the government to hand you anything. But everything's changed now. People lived differently. It isn't the Ouray County that I know anymore. All my old friends are gone. They've died, a lot of them, or they've left. New people have come in and grabbed up all the land. Over there on the Double RL, two of the best friends I ever had owned that, and they died; they had no heirs. Marie Scott and Lillian Harney were the Scott sisters. They were hard-working people, honest. Marie got to be quite a business lady, but Lorraine just loved her friends and her cats and dogs. She was a good friend. I miss her and going up Dallas Creek to that big house. We used to visit a lot; used to have big dinners. We don't do that any more. We've got TVs now.

Eugene got our first car in 1925 or 26. I used to drive it but I don't anymore. I'll tell you what spoiled me for driving is traffic. I wasn't used to traffic. Too many people. Take a narrow mountain road, that wouldn't bother me. Traffic did defeat me. We went to Phoenix a few times and to Denver a few times. We might see a show or two. Denver wasn't as big as it is now, but it looked big to me. I didn't travel much.

A while back, someone asked if I wouldn't like to go back to the good old days. I stopped and thought awhile, and I said no, not now. I said there's only one thing that I wish we'd do: we used to stop and visit, and we don't do that anymore. We used to have nice, big dinners and, for awhile, we had a card party every week. We'd meet at different houses. Somebody would always come by to say hello and visit. They don't do that anymore. As far as Ouray County is concerned, it's an entirely different concept than when we worked, making our living. I couldn't say if it was friendlier then than now, because I don't know the people around here anymore.

We got by during the Depression. We didn't have much to start with; it didn't hurt us like it did some folks. We had to watch everything, but one thing I can say, we never went hungry and we were never cold. That makes a big difference.

We got electricity in here in 1941. That made things easier; we enjoyed that so much. Now when the electricity goes off, we can't live. I don't know whether it's good to depend on that source for everything or not, but that's the way it is. We got a refrigerator then. We never had an icebox. There never was an icehouse around here so we couldn't get ice. We had a root cellar with a spring in it where we would keep our milk and butter and stuff. We didn't depend on refrigeration like we do now. You kind of adjust your living.

We had a garden for our own use. We raised lettuce and carrots, onions, potatoes, peas — if the chipmunks didn't get them. Not corn or tomatoes; the season isn't right for that here. In the haying season, when the vegetables were ripe at the same time, I'd can beans at night. That's no good. You get too tired.

We used to keep milk cows: a Brown Swiss, a couple of Jerseys, and a nice Holstein. We also broke some of our other cows. When we did that, we'd let the calf have half and we'd take half. We milked as high as twelve cows but generally not that many. It would take two of us about an hour to milk, then we'd have to separate, then carry the milk back out to the pig barrel and slop the pigs. It took quite a bit of time. Take the cows out to pasture, and then go and hunt them at night. They didn't have a place next to the barn, so they'd go out to the pasture. We had to go out and look for them on horseback.

We separated the milk every morning and night. We'd save the cream, and when we had three or four gallons, we'd churn butter.

We'd make the butter in a mold, then take it to the store and sell it. Trade it for groceries. Then things progressed and progressed and the health inspectors came in. They wouldn't let you sell butter unless you had these certain kinds of bars. You never see homemade butter now.

After that we stared selling cream to a creamery in Montrose. We kept the cream in a five or ten gallon can that you had to watch carefully and keep stirred. At the creamery they'd take the cream and test it; the more butterfat you had, the bigger your cream check.

It used to take about six people to put up the hay in the summer. All the family helped, but we usually had to hire extra hands. We had to furnish them beds and meals. That was what the bunkhouse was for originally. I never did the cooking for the hired men. Mrs. Fournier did all that; she was a good cook — meat and bread and potatoes. One year we fed men for at least six weeks before we could do any haying. It rained all the time. You had to keep the men around so they'd be there when you needed them. You had to be flexible. You couldn't schedule the weather.

In the summertime a lot of the miners would take their vacations and work on a ranch. They'd get out in the sun and fresh air. Most of the boys we hired were just younger fellows making extra money working. They didn't have cars so they had to stay with us.

We used four or five teams of horses when we were haying. A team on the mower, a team on the rake, one on the buck rake, and one running the stacker. Then we got what we called the doodlebug. You take a motor from a car or truck, work it over, turn the gears upside down, and use that to power the buck rake. You can just buzz around like a bumblebee.

We finally bought a tractor in the '50s. We never did end up in a problem where we had huge pieces of equipment. We didn't have fields like that. A place like this doesn't warrant that.

In the summer we would put our cattle up in the forest to pasture. When we first came here, all this country was open range. In the spring they'd just turn the cattle out. In the fall they'd have gathering time to bring them home. That's the reason they have the brands. Then the government got in and got the reserve; then we commenced to have rules.

At gathering time all the people that ran cattle would go out and put them in a big bunch, then they'd cut out

The Doodlebug.

their own brand. Sometimes it was a lot of work, getting all the cows paired up with their calves.

We calved in the spring. The milk cows kind of run on their own schedule, but we tried to have the beef cattle calve in the spring just like they do now. The men had to go out during calving season and help. It was quite a chore.

Back then the range law said we had to have Hereford bulls. That was the rule. You see, we'd get a forest permit three or four months in the summertime, and you had to have a certain kind of bull or you couldn't go on that land. We had shorthorn cows, but you had to put Hereford bulls with them. That was what the cattle people seemed to think they wanted, and they made the rules. Nowdays they have all kind of cattle and all kinds of bulls and all colors. It doesn't seem to make any difference. It's the size of the calf that counts.

Branding was a gala affair. They'd get a whole bunch of men out. They'd get their fires and their branding irons and go bring in a calf, throw it, and brand it. If it was a bull they'd work it over and make a steer out of it. You would have to have four or five men, sometimes double that number for branding. There wasn't any set number. You had a roper, two men to throw the calf, and one to brand it.

That was fun, and they always had a big dinner for the men. The women at the ranch where the branding was held would always furnish the dinner. The branding usually only took one day unless you had a big ranch like Marie Scott. During branding and during the round-up, that was a big time. That was when people got together.

In the old days, we used to drive our cattle to the big stockyards here in Ridgway. They didn't have sale rings here at home. It would ruin half a day. It depended on how many gates you had to open and how well they traveled. I remember we pretty near got run over on Ridgway Hill one time. The fellow in the car had a little too much to drink and no brakes. That was a poor combination to meet with the cows. Had to kill one.

We used to load the cattle on the train and ship them to Denver. The men would go along with the cattle. They were our cattle until they went over the scales. Then you'd get your check and that was that. It wasn't necessary to go along with the cows, but it was a lot better. You liked to see how the cattle were cared for, if they were fed and watered. There's lots of little tricks. You'd be surprised. You want to see that they're fed and not jammed around and get down in the car and get stomped to death. You just had to watch them if you wanted to come out on top.

The cattle were always consigned to a commission company that would be responsible and handle the sale. They would send you your check, but you liked to bring the money home yourself.

The men would ride over in the caboose; then they'd get a ticket to come home on the passenger train. They'd come home in style with a check on the cushions.

The men would get a room at a hotel, the Kenmark, I think. They'd ride back and forth to the stockyards on the streetcar. I didn't go too many times; twice, I think. Somebody had to stay home and milk the cows, keep the ranch going.

Now we have trucks come in and haul the cattle to the sale barn in Delta. Now you just go Delta, sell them to the sale yard, sit there, and get your check when they're gone.

I think the trucks really put the train out of business, just like cars put the passenger train out of business.

We used to go to the Orvis Hot Springs. We watched it grow and watched it die. They used to have big crowds there. They had a men's side and a women's side. Nice pool. It flourished for three or four years. We were pretty good friends of the Orvis's. Now I hear they're going to try to open it up again.

Labor day and the 4th of July, that's when the whole community would get together. Everybody knew everybody and they'd visit. Catch up on the gossip. A good gathering. Now they get together and just go their separate ways.

The 4th of July was Ouray's day. Families got together and we'd have a picnic dinner. They'd have the water fights, the hand drilling contest, and sometimes have a ball game. Fireworks. My husband was a water fighter from the word go. He won most of the time. His partners changed — my brother one time, George Hotchkiss; oh, there were different ones. They're all dead now.

In the morning, they'd do like they do now; they'd have games for the kids, getting money out of the sawdust, throwing a slipper, carrying eggs, the three-legged race.

Everyone one would try to go because that's the time they'd see each other.

Labor Day was always Ridgway's. There was al the rodeo there. Eugene used to head the barbecue for close to 35 years. They'd take a couple of beef that had been donated, put them on the spit, turn them, and roast them whole. At first it was free. Everybody would get together to eat in the park and have a good time. Then they'd have the rodeo. Then they decided they needed a little money so they charged 50 cents. Now what do they charge, $3.00? The people from Ouray used to come down for the rodeo more than they do now. Of course, I don't know who lives in Ouray anymore.

The rodeo used to be if somebody had a bucking horse, they'd bring it down. It wasn't commercial. It's a controlled rodeo now. People would bring in their ponies and have a race. They had a wild horse race. You were supposed to bring any horses just off the range and hook them up to a wagon and turn them loose on the race course. I don't think they did that too many times.

We used to get together and have the Cattlemen's Banquet, generally in February. It used to be in the Mentone Hotel, in the big dining room there. The hotel was a brick, three-story building. It was nice for then, probably not as ornate as they get them now. It burned down in '36, I think. There were quite a few hotels. They all burned down, I guess.

I don't know if there was much association between Ridgway and Ouray. Ridgway and Ouray are two different things. Ouray was mining and Ridgway was cat-

tle. There wasn't too much in common — common
ground.

There was always a feud between the schools. The
schools were always competing. Their big ball games
were between each other. And they haven't learned a
thing. I think if the old folks would shut up, the kids
would get along alright. It's always that way.

I can tell you one thing; we lived an uneventful life. It
kept us busy taking care of things; that's the way we got
started and, I guess, that's the way we're going to finish.
We used to go around and have picnics in the surrounding
country, so we kind of know what this country is.

DOROTHY DAVIS

WORKING WOMAN

Dorothy is another person who speaks in a quiet manner. Having lived here most of her life, she has a keen memory for what it was like growing up and working in Ouray in the old days. She is retired now, but having worked at the Nugget, a winter gathering spot for the locals, her face is familiar to most people in town.

My family came to Ouray in 1917 when I was eight years old. I remember the trip on the train but, being young, I didn't pay too much attention to the scenery. My uncle met us in Ridgway and rode the train to Ouray with us; he was the one I was looking forward to seeing. When we got to the old depot, there was a jitney, with seats all along the side, that took us to the Beaumont Hotel.

The Beaumont was beautiful. Two curving stairways went from the middle of a large lobby to the second floor. There was a big dining room on the east side of the second floor. Our room was on the west, on the second floor; the second room from the corner on the south. I don't remember too much about that.

"We did the laundry, too... If you hung your clothes out on a moonlight night and they were frozen, that whitened your clothes better than any bleach."

We stayed at the Beaumont for a night or two while my uncle found a house for us to stay in until we went to the mine. We got to Ouray the 25th or 26th of May and stayed in a Victorian house on Fourth Street until sometime in June when the snow cleared off enough that we could go up to the mine.

My uncle had the lease on the Mickey Breen Mine on the Engineer Pass Road and the Monarch Mine just above it. We were going up to live in the big boardinghouse. I remember loading our household goods and trunks and things on packhorses and mules. In those days you had to go up on horseback.

My mother came to the mine to cook, and my father worked around the mine. My father was lame so he couldn't do too much manual labor. Later he became the bookkeeper.

I roamed the hills around the mine; everything was perfectly lovely then. But mainly I followed my uncle around like a little shadow. He took me into the mine often, and he taught me how to sort ore. Now they have modern mucking machines and regular old dumpsters that go into the mine to haul out the ore. In our day they did it the hard way, by the shovel, so it took them a little longer. When the ore came out of the mine in ore cars, you sorted it and put the high grade in canvas bags and threw the rest in the dump. It was mainly silver and lead.

They loaded the canvas bags on mules and mule trains took the ore to town. Sometimes they'd have as many as 15 or 20 mules going down the hill. The mules were probably from the Ashenfelter stables because later on my father was bookkeeper for Ashenfelter. The Ashenfelter barns were down below the Nugget and the offices were across the street.

My uncle didn't have a big enough production to warrant ore wagons. The ore wagons went up to the Revenue and the Camp Bird. They called them the Sixes because they had six horses. Six or eight wagons went out every morning and came back every evening. They only made one trip a day; it's nine miles up to the Camp Bird and a little farther to the Revenue.

When a miner or anyone else wanted to go up to one of the mines, you rented a horse from one of the stables and rode up. When you got there, you looped the reins around the horn of the saddle and turned the horse loose. The horse would come right back to the barn where it belonged. If you didn't loop the reins around the horn, the horse could get its head down and it would graze on the way down and not be anxious to get back to the barn.

We stayed at the mine all that summer and moved back down to Ouray to a rented house in October so I could start school. I went to the old grade school. At that time they had a separate room and a separate teacher for each grade because the high school was in a building next door. Later, because the high school building was in such bad shape, they condemned it and put the high school upstairs in the grade school building. There were only four rooms on the first floor, so each teacher had two grades. They built the new school in the '30s.

Our graduation was held in the Opera House. We had all our affairs up there: dances, graduation, plays. The dances were wonderful. They had a dance every Saturday night. It was great. If you couldn't go to a dance, you were devastated. The dances weren't just for the high school students, everybody went.

They had dances over at the old KP Hall after basketball games, too. The Knights of Pythias Hall was an old, two-story building where the Mountain Bell building is now. I remember the last dance we went to there. The wallpaper and the whole side of the wall was flapping. The building had been condemned; it was a wonder it didn't fall down.

There were a lot of lodges in town: the Knights of Columbus and the Washington Lodge, and there were two ladies' lodges. They all put on dances. If there wasn't a dance going on there was something wrong. They had refreshments: sandwiches and cakes and coffee. The musicians would get drunk; they hid their bottles out. It was really a lot of fun.

In the Opera House there was a stove on each side of the hall. One was for the ladies and one for the men.

It was cold in the wintertime, but that didn't seem to bother anybody. Everybody had to walk to the dances unless you were rich and had a car. The boys would go and get their girls and walk to the dances and then walk home again afterwards. It was great days.

During my last two years of high school, my father had a grocery store where the 1876 is now. It was called the People's Store. He brought in prepackaged bread from Colorado Springs. That was the first time I saw bread sold in a package because we always had a bakery here in town. He did pretty well with it.

While I was growing up, my uncle left the Mickey Breen and went to California and different places. He'd come back every so often and then leave again. When I was finishing high school, he leased the mine up at the Revenue and lived in the boardinghouse. In the summers I would get a horse and ride up there. I loved doing that.

Dining on the balcony of the Beaumont Hotel.

I loved hiking in the mountains. Groups of us went all the time. If you wanted to have a picnic, you took a hike. If you wanted to go out for breakfast, you hiked to where you wanted to cook your breakfast. Four or five of us would go out on a Sunday morning, taking bacon and eggs and an old battered coffee pot, and go out along a stream and have breakfast. It was beautiful. We used to hike up to the Amphitheater, the Mickey Breen, or the Camp Bird to pick raspberries. I think the young people are kind of lazy now. They don't want to do any walking or hiking. They jump in the car to go a block or two. It would do them good to walk.

After high school I started working as a waitress at the St. Elmo Hotel. Both the St. Elmo and the Beaumont had dining rooms. Several of the boarding or rooming houses served food, too. There, everybody just came in and ate what was put on the table. They served the railroad men and salesmen. When I worked at the St. Elmo, people would leisurely drive up from Montrose for Sunday dinner. People didn't eat out then as much as they do now. Only on special occasions.

The dining room in the St. Elmo was upstairs; it was beautiful. It had hardwood floors, tablecloths, and a bay window. They had a Negro cook who had been there for 30 years. She couldn't read or write and she couldn't give you a recipe. She just knew them. She made the most wonderful biscuits.

It was fun working in the dining room, but it was hard work, too. You didn't eat all day long in those dining rooms. They were open in the morning from six to nine, then opened for lunch from eleven to one, and again in the evening from six to nine. When it was time to close those doors were shut and no one else got in. For each meal, breakfast, lunch, and dinner, there were only three entrees — all the same price.

During the time I was growing up, the town had a bakery, four or five grocery stores, four or five stables, a jewelry store, a kind of department store, a tailor shop, and a woman's dress shop. There were two Chinese laundries. One below the Rebekahs and one on Main Street. Another old Chinaman lived next to Minnie Vanoli's and did laundry for the whole Second Street red light district.

Second Street was taboo. The mothers would instruct the girls, don't go down there. Don't speak to the girls. I never snuck down there. Other kids did errands for the girls and got their behinds whipped all the way home. I had a girl friend who thought that she would go down and run an errand because the girls paid pretty good, but her dad caught her. She didn't try it again.

We played a lot of cards in those days: bridge, Monte Carlo, 500, whist — all of them. Older people mixed with the younger people when there were card games or anything; we all went. The men used to gather up at the Elks to play what they call Solo. The man at the bakery tried to teach his daughter the game, but I don't think we caught on well.

We had curfew when I was a child. The bell in the old bell tower on City Hall would ring at ten minutes after 8:00. You better not be caught out after that time or the policeman who patrolled the street, on foot, marched you home and called your parents. It would be a good idea to have it now, but it stopped after the City Hall burned. I was living across the street at the time and we just stood there and watched it burn and cried and cried. Everybody cried, especially when the old bell tower fell. It was a beautiful building, built by Walsh, and had been there a long, long time.

They are trying to restore it now, but it will never be the same because the beautiful library is gone. There was a beautiful, big reading room in the library. Downstairs in City Hall, there was a council room and a court with a place for the jury and the judge. Now the city fathers don't have a place to hold council meetings.

In those days we lived across the river. In those days everybody had coal stoves. In the morning you would look out the window and smoke would be coming out of all the houses, every house was filled. Pretty soon you'd hear the ore wagons going up the hill for their load. It was wonderful.

We had two full-time doctors in town and a hospital where the museum is now. The hospital operated for 80 years. It had been a Catholic hospital, built by the Sisters of Mercy. Later Dr. Bates owned the hospital as well as the Radium Springs with the cave baths, where the Wiesbaden is now.

The museum is much the same as the hospital was then. The operating room was downstairs instead of upstairs but the rest is the same. I worked there just about a year as a cook. The doctor's daughter and I ran the kitchen. I had a boyfriend, and sometimes it was kind of hard getting up early in the morning and getting down to the hospital to serve the trays by 7:00. Sometimes we'd have a lot and sometimes just a few.

We did the laundry, too. We ironed all the sheets and pillowcases on a mangle. We didn't have dryers. We washed the clothes and hung them on the clothesline, winter, summer, or whatever. Young people now wouldn't be able to do what we did, but we didn't know any better. There wasn't anything else to do. But, you know, they smelled awfully good. If you hung your clothes out on a moonlight night and they were frozen, that whitened your clothes better than any bleach.

By the time I was dating, most people had cars. The boys would come over to your house to see you, or maybe you'd go out and cruise around, or they'd take you to a dance. There was a pavilion over at Box Canyon where we danced in the summer.

There were lots of shows; the theater was next to where the Variety Store is now. On Friday nights the kids got in for ten cents and the adults for twenty cents. When my kids were little, they had special shows on Friday nights: westerns and serials. Sometimes we would go together on Sunday nights.

My maiden name was Davidson, then I went to Zanett. My two boys, Dick and Bob, live here now. I married again a second time, but I did away with that.

I met my first husband in about 1932 when I was working in the hospital. His family lived in Ouray. He worked in the mines and for the power company. Later, they had a coal business. He went to Somerset to buy coal. It was shipped to Ouray on the train and they delivered coal to the mines. They had a hardware store, too.

I went with him on his trips. I didn't work while I was married. Afterward, I went back to waiting tables.

Things were tough in Ouray during the Depression. The mines weren't doing much; there were no jobs. They were in a slump. People lost their businesses. Many people were on welfare. They dealt out staples like potatoes, rice, flour, but you had to have stamps to get them.

Before I got married, I had a job taking care of a little baby for a woman that worked in the telephone office. I had one pair of shoes and a long dress to go to dances. I made a print dress and went to the courthouse to get a pair of shoes; they doled out your shoes. That was what I worked in, and that was all I had. I was paid 50 cents a day. That would amount to about five dollars now. If you had 50 cents, you felt pretty well off; a dollar was great. We didn't let it get us down or anything like that because everybody worked together and helped out one another. But you didn't have any money to spend.

If your boyfriend could come up with a dollar, you would go to the dances. You went to a dance to have your fun. In the Opera House, the musicians would be up on the stage. They drank, and they used to work up a pretty good steam. There would be a piano and drums, maybe a saxophone or horn; a trombone or something like that. Once in awhile, an outside band would come in; everybody would go crazy to go to those outside bands.

Once when our boys were little, a colored band came in. We wanted to go to the dance but there weren't any babysitters. So we just took the boys to the dance, put them to sleep, and danced. Everybody took their kids to the dances. It didn't hurt anybody.

In the old days, we mingled with older people. We were invited right along with the older people; we had a lot of fun with them, and they had a lot of fun with us. Now they go by age groups. You don't belong to our age group, so you don't mingle. They think it's awful to do that now. The older people have lots of experience to share, but the young people just ignore you; you're just not there. Half the time they don't even speak to you. I can't understand that. The last Elk's dance I went to was in the late '70s — about the time the young people were taking over. People in their 60's and 70's, dressed in levis and ski boots, were in one corner, and the young people were in the other. I was just lost. I didn't know what to do.

When we were young, we dressed nice to go to a dance, and we had nice music. The young people do it differently now; it's their generation, but I hardly think, from what I've listened to, that any of their music is going to go down the years, 50 and 70 years, and still be enjoyable. They won't be playing it, I don't think.

After my first marriage ended, I waited tables at the Village Diner. Then in the late 50s, there was kind of a slump where there were no jobs; so I went to Grand Junction and stayed most of the 60s, waiting tables. Then Grand Junction was getting kind of bad and this was my home; my boys and my grandchildren were here, so I decided I'd come back. I waited table after I came back. I couldn't stay away from it; it's in the blood; it's the best kind of job there is. If you have any other kind of job, then you have to buy clothes and take care of them and buy your meals and everything. When you waited table, you have your uniform that is washable and one pair of shoes that you wear. You get one or two meals and your tips. You're a lot better off than the girl that works at the office.

I worked about 25 years as a waitress, off and on. I worked for three different owners at the St. Elmo. The meals at the St. Elmo were wonderful. That Negro cook was marvelous. I boarded and roomed right at the hotel. I made twelve dollars a month plus a few tips. My boss wouldn't let me spend my tips. She put a quart jar up on the china closet that sat at the end of the dining room and made me put my tips in there. She said just see how much you make. She and her husband were nice people; I loved both of them.

I didn't like it after they put the eating place downstairs in the St. Elmo. It's dark. Some people like that, but I was used to working upstairs where it was a lot brighter.

Years ago you used to get cleaned up in the afternoon and go downtown and have a cup of coffee, or monkey around in the stores, or go to the grocery store with friends. Gosh, everybody went downtown, that's where you'd meet people. I don't see people doing that any more. You go downtown now and there's nobody around. People used to get together more. I think television ruined that.

In the late '40s and early '50s, we had a beautiful women's chorus in Ouray. It was delightful. It started out as the Treble Clef Club, and then it turned into the Ouray Women's Chorus. There were between 22 and 25 women in the chorus. I think Helen McMahan organized it. She got the women who were in different choirs and who liked to sing and put them all together. There wasn't anybody else that could lead a chorus like she could. It was really nice for a while, but Helen died in 1956. Sometimes real good things don't last very long; only herpes lasts forever. It's just one of those things.

Young people now don't go in for music like they did when I was growing up. Then all the kids in school that were the least bit talented were taking piano lessons or violin or horn lessons. They used to have a wonderful school band here. When I was going to school, we had a band and an orchestra. The band was so good that they went to Utah and Grand Junction every year to march in parades. We were tickled to death that our band was participating. When I was growing up, nearly all the girls were taking piano lessons. My girlfriend and I played duets in different places like the Women's Club and churches. When our kids started taking lessons they just lost interest.

When I was in school, we had 8th grade graduation exercises just like they had in high school. Now, they just swish right on through. It's junior high; it sounds a lot better, but there isn't any difference in it. I think they're teaching differently now. They're pushing the kids more than they did then. That's why so many kids are under pressure. So many kids can't take that pressure, so they do away with themselves because they can't take it. If it isn't the parents, it's the teachers pushing them through.

Now, if you've noticed, they're even into organ transplants, so, in case they die, they can help save a life. I think that is ridiculous. It's just bad for the kids. They should be kids for as long as the can, until they get into high school. They should have a childhood without any of this other stuff. There's plenty of time for organ transplants. Why bring the kids into it. Maybe some of them might be frightened because that means that they might die. They shouldn't be thinking about things like that. They should be enjoying their life as a child.

Even my boys notice how much different their childhood was from their kids' childhood. They had more problems than we had. I don't remember any problems we had — maybe little problems. Like you get stuck on a boy and he doesn't pay any attention to you — you're devastated. During that time, there was more home life. You stayed home in the evening. Your mother and father were there. You did your lessons and your chores and that was it unless there was a party. Your parties were chaperoned; they had them in the homes or at the school. They didn't give their children as much freedom as they do now. We didn't have as much money to spend either. If you had a dime to go to a show, you were happy as a lark. Or you could buy an ice cream cone. Those were the pleasures.

Now, I don't know what the kid's pleasures are because they've got everything. There's nothing for them to look forward to. When we were freshmen and sophomores, we used to have to work for the juniors and seniors. We decorated, we did all the stuff for their proms. We waited tables when they had a banquet; there were no waitresses. We looked forward to being a junior or senior. That meant a pretty dress, and we enjoyed it more. Now they don't. They start right in the seventh or eighth grade; they have boyfriends; they have formals. So what is there to look forward to? Half of them are discontented or bored. I can tell from my own grandkids. They're bored; they don't have anything to do. There's no fun.

I think it's just the way the world is now. The kids are having to be more serious about everything, and they can't take it. After all, I don't think there's a bit of difference between a ten-year-old girl in my day and a ten-year-old girl now. They should have the same dreams, the same feelings, but they're being pushed a little faster than we were.

If we had a problem, the mothers and dads used to know about it. There really weren't any problems; we had no drugs. Prohibition was in so there was no liquor that you could get hold of unless someone made some wine. Most of us were scared to death to do anything anyway because most of the mothers were like mine. They had an eagle eye and you couldn't get by with anything. They knew where you were all the time; if they didn't they went to look for you.

You couldn't even play hookey. My brother did one time and my mother found out about it. I don't know how, but she went until she found him. He and another boy were down the railroad track having a lot of fun together, playing in the water and throwing rocks. She marched him back home and that was the only time he ever played hookey. You just couldn't get by with anything.

DOMINIC PEROTTI

JACK OF ALL TRADES

Going to Dominic's house was a challenge for a variety of reasons. The first was gaining entrance. Dominic is a reclusive man who, at the time, could not see well and spent most of his time by himself. He did not wish to be interviewed and it took several months of meeting him through common friends, talking to him over fences, and gaining his trust before he agreed to the interview.

Dominic has lived in the old town of Portland virtually all of his life. His is obviously the home of a lifetime bachelor who is set and happy in his own ways. The home has been in the family for over sixty years. Dominic uses wood to heat and cook, and cleaning is not a high priority. Quite some time ago there was a fire, and the back part of the house burned. Signs of that still remain. The kitchen, where Dominic lives for the active part of the day, is crowded. Extension cords are strung to various places for light and small appliances.

Dominic's voice sounds gravelly and is forceful as he tells you of his life. He has a hard time understanding why the things that are so familiar to him make no sense to you.

"Portland used to be a fairly large community. There must have been fourteen or fifteen families living here. There was a grocery store and a post office. There was even a dance hall . . . people used to come to the dances from Ouray and Ridgway."

I was born in 1904 on the Sneva place out in Dry Creek, about five or six miles east of Ridgway. My parents farmed that place and my father worked in the mines. In about 1908 or '09, the family moved to Portland. The old house is still down by the highway, but the windows have been broken out and the doors torn off.

I went to school here in Portland. They had a nice schoolhouse here. In fact, I bought it after they closed the school down and later sold it to my brother. There were anywhere from ten to fourteen kids in the school at one time. The kids came to school from as far down toward Ridgway as the cemetery, as far toward Ouray as the old smelter at the Bachelor Switch, and from across the river. The kids all walked to school, it was a fair distance to walk. Jim Tillman, who lived across the river, had three kids, two boys and a girl, and they used to drive a little cart, pulled by an Indian pony, to school.

Portland used to be a fairly large community. There must have been fourteen or fifteen families living here. There was a grocery store and a post office. There was even a dance hall. It was a pretty good-sized building, and people used to come to the dances from Ouray and Ridgway. After Gibbs bought the place, he tore it down; he tore everything out. He was going to burn it down, but they wouldn't let him. We had a lot of fires around here. I think some of them burned their places down for insurance. I know one family had their place insured for two thousand dollars and the house wasn't worth that much when it burned. The only fire department we had came from Ridgway, so not many of the houses were saved.

I played in the dance band at the old dance hall. All the kids that lived here played in the band. We were all a bunch of old Italians. I played the coronet, and we had a flute, a piccolo, slide trombones. We had eight or ten young kids in the band. We used to go up to the Western Hotel to practice. The man that started the band, Tonio Cuaranta, came here from Pueblo in 1916. That's when I joined. He was the bandmaster, and he could play anything. We got paid a little bit for playing and had dances about once a month. It was fun.

Most of the area around Portland was farming. Some of the land was pretty good and some of it was rocky. I helped my dad clear the land for our farm. We had to cut the trees and then get the stumps out. We blasted the big stumps out and pulled the small ones out with a horse team. To blast the stumps, you'd drill a hole in them and fill them with dynamite. It used to blast those stumps to pieces and would leave quite a hole. Then we plowed the roots out when we plowed the whole field. After plowing, we used a scraper to cut down the high spots and level the field. After we got it leveled, we reseeded and put in irrigation ditches. We got the water for irrigation from the Uncompahgre.

As a kid I worked a lot around these farms. In the spring I helped plant spuds. We used to plow a furrow with a team and a hand-held plow. Sometimes you would just hang the reins around your neck and plant the potatoes as you went, and sometimes the kids would follow the plow, dropping spuds in the furrow. After that was done, you would go back with the plow and cover the furrow again.

In the fall we'd harvest the potatoes, digging them out with either a plow or a shaker digger. The shaker digger has a shaker wheel that shakes the dirt off and leaves the spuds pretty clean.

In the summer I helped with the haying. We did all that with horses, too. We'd cut it, rake it, shock it or pile it up, and then throw it on a wagon and haul it away.

I quit school when I was eighteen, when my father died. He was pretty young when he died, only fifty-six. He had worked in the mines too much and got black lung. I was the oldest in the family and had four sisters and three brothers so I had to go to work to bring the money in to keep the family rolling.

I worked mainly on the farm but I did a lot of other jobs, too. Hell, there was always some work. In the wintertime we used to bale hay. Back then the baler didn't tie the bales automatically. You'd pull the baler up to the haystack and one man would get on the stack to throw the hay down to the baler. Another man would feed the baler. He had to use his foot to stuff the hay down into the baler so the plunger could press the hay together. The plunger was run by a team of horses that walked around in a circle. Every time they went around the circle, the plunger would release and come back to catch

The Orvis Plunge.

another leaf of hay. It wasn't so dangerous if you had it timed right. When you had a full bale, another man had to reach in and tie the bale by hand with wire. There were little adjustment wheels under the baler to make the bales lighter or heavier. The plunger would push the completed bale out so you could stack it.

I used to make ice in the wintertime, too. There was an ice pond down at Piedmont. I used to cut ice blocks about one foot by one and a half feet. Each block weighed three or four hundred pounds. Christ, I lifted a lot of them. After the blocks were cut, a horse would pull them across the ice to a platform. The blocks slid pretty easily on the ice. From the platform, you loaded them on a wagon and hauled them away. In the wintertime you used a sled to haul the ice. You could haul one or two tons on the wagon or sled. Most of the people had ice houses where they stored the ice. If you covered it with sawdust, it would last all summer.

Sometimes I worked in the coal mines at Cow Creek or down by Mayfield. There used to be a coal mine this side of Colona, another one at Coal Creek, and I think, one in Billy Creek. But I never worked in the gold mines. My dad told me to stay out of those mines, so I did. We used to buy coal for two dollars a ton at the mines. We hauled some of it to Frank Rice at the lumberyard, but he had most of his coal shipped in by train from Somerset. He sold coal to the miners for five dollars a ton. Frank Rice was an old-timer here. That lumberyard has been here for a hell of a long time; longer than I was.

We had a lot of fruit on the farm. We raised raspberries, red and blue, to sell, and we had plums and apricots. We raised a lot of apples, too. I used to haul apples to Montrose to the cider press. One year I think I made fifteen gallons of cider.

Every Friday we used to make butter with one of those old one-man churns that went up and down. Then on Saturday we'd take the fruit and butter to Ouray to sell.

I bought this house in 1926 and lived with my mother until she died and then with my sister. My sister got married in 1950 and moved to Dove Creek, so I've been a bachelor since then. I never married.

I bought my first car in 1927; it was a 1918 Ford. I paid twenty-five bucks for it in Montrose. I ran it until 1929 and then sold it to some guy in Naturita for ten or fifteen bucks. I've had several trucks. One was made out of an old Dodge touring car that my brother cut down. I also had a little Chevy coach made out of a truck. My brother bought it for forty bucks and brought it up to me. The last truck I bought was an International pickup, red and white. I paid 1200 dollars for it in 1976. I finally sold it in 1979. Since then I've been walking.

We used to drive to Montrose, after we had cars, to shop. It took an hour or an hour and a half then. I guess most people still go to Montrose for groceries; it's a little cheaper up there.

The highway between here and Ouray has changed quite a bit. It used to be nothing but a horse and buggy trail. Then the automobiles and trucks came and they changed it in about '28 or '29. Part of the highway used to run down by the river and they moved it up. North of here, toward Ridgway, the highway used to run higher up on the hill. It used to take us 30 or 35 minutes to get to Ouray by horse and buggy or spring wagon.

Ouray used to have a lot of saloons. There were saloons up below Cascade; the Variety Store used to be a saloon. A man named Clark ran the Owl's Club during the bootleg days. That was just about where the Deli is now. The old Geneva, the Western Hotel, and the Belvedere were all saloons on Second Street. Bonatti's store on Main Street used to be a saloon. Old Minnie Vanoli used to have a saloon up in Ironton, then she moved down to Main Street and ran a saloon on what is now a vacant lot across from the Silver Nugget. Christ, there used to be a bunch of saloons, but there was plenty of miners to keep them all going. They weren't decorated much, they were just places for people to go in and drink a beer and chat with their neighbors and friends.

Right across from the barn on Main Street, there used to be a blacksmith's shop. We used to take our plowshares there to get them sharpened. They used to put the plowshare in the fireplace to heat it up and then put it on the anvil and hammer them out with a hammer. You could get pretty near everything you would want made there. He was a goddamn good blacksmith. They used to shoe horses there, too. He bought his shoes but had to shape them to fit the horse.

We used to go to Ridgway to buy groceries before we had a car, and, of course, everyone went to Ridgway for the fair and rodeo over Labor Day. That was a big time;

we spent two or three days there. They had races and bucking broncs and bucking steers. They even had a bucking Ford down there one year. They had the wheels offset so it was kind of a rough ride; it was quite a buck.

I've had a pretty good life. I liked it then; course, I'm getting old now and I don't give a damn for nothing anymore. I've seen a hell of a lot of things. I see the houses where people I knew are gone. The townsite is almost gone. Old Charlie Haney, he's gone. Old Mike Pecchio used to live down here and he's gone. And old Sam Eldridge who ran the poor farm for thirteen years is gone.

The poor farm was where they kept the old-timers. The county ran it and paid Sam Eldridge and his wife so much a month to feed them and take care of them. There would be four, five, six, or seven there at any one time. I guess it was mainly old miners who couldn't work anymore who lived there. I guess the food and the treatment was okay. Doc Bates took over the poor farm and ran it for a number of years. They used to keep chickens and rabbits down there. When old Gibbs bought the place he tore down the chicken house and the old barn. Now it's empty.

ANDY SODERQUIST

FARMER

The Soderquists live just south of Colona. The family has been there since the late 1800s; most of the old families around Colona have been there that long. Andy says the difference between Ridgway and Colona is the growing season. "Colona has one. Here we can grow just about anything."

Andy is a tall, strong man and has been working all his life at farming. Like many farmers, he is both a philosopher and philosophical. He said, "The chances of being successful in agriculture are about the same as doing well in Las Vegas." He is a good farmer, but, this year (1988) with the drought and then hail, he has had a 50% loss in oats and more in hay. He is resigned to the loss but is worried about whether the ozone layer is disappearing and if farming is on its way out because of environmental pollution.

"I used to drive to Ridgway to pick up Marge, and then we usually went to a dance. If the dances were up here she would stay with my sister all night; then I'd take her home the next day. It would be too far to go in one night..."

My grandfolks homesteaded out on the eastern slope at Julesburg. They had to haul water in barrels twenty miles with a team and wagon. Grandma stayed out there in the wintertime, raising the family. Grandpa came up to Como to cut wood for the charcoal kilns to earn enough money to buy seed for the next year.

Grandpa and his brother dug the first well in that country. His brother and his wife were always close to them; they came into that country at the same time. The well was hand dug and two hundred forty feet deep and four feet wide at the top. Part of it was lined and part of it wasn't. The EPA would have a heart attack now, but they got good water. All the neighbors got water from them, and they made a little extra money digging wells for other people around there.

In 1895, after being droughted out three years in a row, Granddad loaded everything in the wagon and came over here. There wasn't much in the way of roads then, I guess. The road then ran on the other side of the Gunnison River, through Crawford. They had to take the wagon apart and lower it over a cliff at one place on Black Mesa. They had to lead the horses around.

They landed down here north of Montrose and stayed there the first winter, then moved to Colona. The valley was pretty well settled then.

Granddad raised raspberries, strawberries, and all the vegetables such as beans and corn. He took the produce over to Silverton in a wagon to sell it. He would sell some of it in the evening when he arrived and the rest of it the next morning then come home again.

I was born in 1924 in a house about a mile up the road and spent all my life here. My wife, Marge, was born up in Elk Meadows in 1925. Her folks lived on the Walther place at that time. Later, they moved to the Boucher place on Miller Mesa and then, when she was ready to go to school, moved to Ridgway.

I can remember, as a kid, always having hired men living with us on the farm. There was no bunkhouse; Mother had the upstairs fixed for them. They stayed with us for board and room and ate three meals a day with us. It didn't seem strange to us having someone else living in the house. That was just the way of life and you accepted it. I think people were more congenial then. I think people were closer than they are now. You learned to get along with people. Now people all want to go their own way. It's got to be their own way or it ain't right. We didn't have television. We played cards or games or read a book. We read lots of books. My folks played rummy, cribbage, and a lot of pitch. I can't remember how to play it, but they used matches to bet. Some of the people played bridge, but I never did.

I remember when the folks got a radio. It was in 1935 or '37. Before that we used to go up to the grandfolks to listen to old Amos and Andy every night they were on. Everyone sat around quietly and listened to it. If you weren't quiet you couldn't hear it. The radio was full of static. It wasn't that clear, nothing like your reception today. Grandpa always listened to the news and the market report, and that was it. The radio was a little Philco and took, I think, three or four different batteries to run it. It wasn't a plug in, there was nothing to plug into. There was no electricity.

My grandparents didn't get electricity in their house until 1935 when the REA came through here. A couple of the houses in Colona got electricity in 1918. Old Bob Winnerall, who owned the place my folks bought, and a man named Hotchkiss, who lived on the next place, went together and ran a big power line up here to get electricity from Montrose. It cost them $1500.00. That was a lot of money in those days.

Before that we used coal oil lanterns for light. I remember when the folks got the first Coleman light. Boy, that was quite a Christmas present. It was a much better light than the kerosene lamps. They really haven't improved those Coleman lights from what they were then. In fact, we still have one over at the camp that we used for 55 years or better.

I went to all eight grades at the Colona School. There were two teachers with four grades in each room. There were more rooms in the building, but that was all the teachers they could afford at that time. There were four big rooms downstairs and a big library and a gymnasium upstairs. They used to have quite a basketball team when they had a high school down here. They had had a high school here, but they took it out the year I started school, so I went to high school in Ridgway. Marge went to school in Ridgway, from the first grade to the twelfth. That's how we met; the Colona kids came to Ridgway. The school bus was an old square wooden box on the back of a Chevy truck. It held about 25 passengers and the kids got in and out of the back end.

In 1947, they reorganized the districts and the kids from here and from Billy Creek went to Montrose to school. That was where everybody shopped. Prior to that time, the kids from Billy Creek went to Mayfield School. The rest of the kids, from the Mayfield district line south, went to Ridgway. As soon as they start taking the schools out, it doesn't take long for the town to go downhill.

When I was growing up, Colona was quite a town. We had a post office, a grocery store, a Phillips station, a drug store, a lumberyard, a blacksmith shop, and a pool hall. The passenger train stopped at the depot twice a day. It was different then than it is now. Now it's all restaurants catering to the tourist trade. Then it catered to the farmer; that was their bread and butter. The old fellow that laid out the town was a farmer. So it's an old country town that's disappearing and going to the tourists. Built along the highway, that's all it's got going for it. It's too bad, the way the economy is everything; there are a lot of little country towns that are folding up; there's

nothing to keep them anymore. Once they move the schools out, that's the end of them.

Ridgway was a booming town when I went to school there. The railroad was here then. The biggest employer in town was the roundhouse where they repaired all the engines. Ridgway was the headquarters for the Rio Grande Southern. Trains used to go to Ouray on one line and out through Pleasant Valley to Telluride on the other line. The train went straight up the creek, then switched back to go up the hill, and then went right over the top of the Dallas Divide.

The old Main Street was one block north of the highway. It had all kinds of businesses. They had a drug store, two grocery stores, a movie theater, and a car dealership. What I remember most about Ridgway was the sidewalks. Someone had come in and built brand new beautiful cement sidewalks. The kids roller skated all over town. Now I don't think there's a decent sidewalk in Ridgway.

In 1942, after I got out of high school, another kid from Colona and I went to work for the Rio Grande Southern. They had had a train wreck, wrecking a bunch of ore cars coming down this side of the Dallas. They were coming from Telluride and when they came over the top of the divide they lost their brakes. They went down to the first sharp turn, and everybody bailed out and let her fly. Fortunately, nobody was hurt badly. We worked up there one winter cleaning up the wreck, taking ore out of the cars. It was a mess. The cars had come off the track and laid over on their side, and the last one had run right down through the middle of the whole bunch. The cars were filled with lead concentrate that was wet, so it froze in the cold. We had to pick it loose. It was quite a job cleaning it up. The weather got so stormy in February, they had to close it down until spring. They did get the engine out first. It was laying on its side, too, so they had to get it up on its wheels, and then lay track to get it out of there. It ran alright. I think it's out at Knott's Berry Farm in California now.

We rode to work in the Galloping Goose. Talk about rebuilding the Galloping Goose, I rode in that sucker. It was just like riding in a car. The motor was an old Pierce Arrow with a big body built up on it.

After that I worked for my dad on the farm part of the time and helped other people on their farms around Colona. I worked in the Unaweep Canyon one winter feeding stock on a ranch. I worked two different winters in the Cimarron hauling hay and feeding lambs.

After Marge graduated from high school, she went to teletype school in Omaha, Nebraska. That was during the war, so after graduation she was sent to Wright Patterson Air Force Base in Dayton, Ohio to work as a teletype operator. After the war, she came back to Ouray and worked for a year in the treasurer's office at the courthouse in Ouray. Her job was to go back over all the records and pick up all the mining claims that hadn't been paying taxes. If they weren't on the tax roles, they were put up for sale. There were a lot of them at that time.

After we were married, she never worked away from home. She said that eight-hour job was a lot easier. She got off vacation, and had to go to work is what it amounted to. She didn't work on the farm much, it didn't work out. We had two boys thirteen months apart, so she had her hands full. We always had hired men then, so she had somebody besides me to cook for all the time.

We didn't start dating until I got out of high school. We had known each other before because Marge and my sister were good friends. We dated for four years before we were married. Most of our dates were for dances. They were building the Cow Creek Dance Hall about the time we started dating. We would go there one Saturday night, to the Colona School the next Saturday night, then to the Uncompahgre School the next weekend.

We went on a lot of picnics. Nearly every Sunday a bunch of kids would get together for picnics. We didn't have money to do anything else. We went to a show about once a month if I had fifty cents.

When we went to dances, we would fill the car with all the people you could shove in. There were always three or four couples in the car. Nowadays, the kids don't do that; it's just the two of them together. That's why I think they get bored with each other.

I didn't have a car, so I drove my folk's car. One night some drunks ran into the back of us as we were slowing down to turn off at Colona. The back end was all bent in, but no one was hurt badly. It was lucky because there were six or eight of us in the car that night.

I used to drive to Ridgway to pick up Marge, and then we usually went to a dance. If the dances were up here she would stay with my sister all night; then I'd take her home the next day. It would be too far to go in one night. That's called a racket.

We were married on February 16, 1946 in Montrose. We had a double wedding with my sister and her husband. We didn't even need a coat that day. It was an early spring that year. We had all the crops in and the ditches cleaned by the 25th of March. We've never been able to do it since. We moved into a house about a mile up the road from here and stayed there for one year while I worked for my dad on the farm. Then we moved about a mile down the road to a little house right on the county line and lived there for five years. I was farming that place for Henry Jutland.

In 1952 Dad got sick and was going to sell this place, so we bought it and have lived here ever since. This house was built in 1900. I knew the fellow, Frank Price, who hauled all the rock for this place. He got a dollar a day and his tobacco. It took four years to haul all the rock with a team and wagon. They got the rock in a draw just back of here. The house was started in 1900 and finished in 1904. The original mortar is still intact. Little places

Boarding the Galloping Goose.

around the eaves have had to be caulked, but all in all, it's in pretty good shape. The old fellow, Robert Winnerall, who built the house was going to get married while he was building it, but the gal got tired of waiting and married somebody else. He lived as a bachelor until 1936 when he finally got married. My dad bought the place from him then.

The Winnerall family came from England and all the surveying in this county was done by the Winneralls. The parents are buried up in the old Billy Creek Cemetery.

Mr. Winnerall was pretty farsighted when he built this

place. He had a double chimney clear to the basement with a boiler connected to it down there to heat his water. He also had a water system with a windmill and an overhead wooden tank on a big tower. They used that water system for years.

The abstract on this place isn't very thick; it hasn't been sold many times. A lady by the name of Osborn homesteaded the place, and then Preston Hotchkiss got it from her. He sold it to Winnerall, and Dad got it from him.

We have 100 acres here and I lease another 100 acres up the road. That place has never changed hands either. A family by the name of Brower homesteaded it. He died and his wife went ahead and raised the family. Her granddaughter lives on the place now. Most of Colona is like that. The next place down the road has always been in the Hotchkiss family, and the place south of us has been the Comerer's. The place across the river was homesteaded by the Smiths. It's going to start changing though. The younger generation can't stay in agriculture. There's nothing here for them. There's no money in it. They have to have an outside job.

It used to be possible to make a living in agriculture. You don't get rich, but we got along pretty well. To make a farm work, you have to do it yourself. That's the main thing; you can't hire labor. It's hard to farm with hired labor and make it pay. We've never owed. We've always pretty much run it ourselves. That way you cut out a lot of the mistakes you make with hired labor. It takes a few long hours. You leave here pretty early in the morn-ing and get home pretty late at night. In the winter you feed the cattle, feed the calves, and everything. It's a pretty big job. You get in more than eight hours.

Since the kids have been grown, Marge has worked right along with me. She does all the baling now. Now you have equipment to do everything. There's not as much hand labor as there used to be. When my dad first moved here, he had two or three hired men and did everything with horses. Now you can go out after supper and do all you could do in a whole day with a team.

I bought my first tractor, a little John Deere, in 1954. A fellow bought that tractor and couldn't pay for it and went bankrupt. I bought it through bankruptcy. People always ask what it was like farming with horses. I'll tell you. Real quiet. That's what you notice today — the noise. Now for everything you do, you have a motor running: machinery and noise. Then all you had was horses and they didn't make much noise. It was kind of peaceful and quiet compared to today.

When we first moved here, you used to see one car a day going down the highway, now you see a thousand. You see twenty or thirty cars in a bunch now. It didn't used to be like that. At that time we still had bus service. A lot of people took the Rio Grande bus line. Before that they had the passenger train. I can remember the conductor lighting the lights as the train left Colona. They used to ship all the cattle on the train, too. There weren't any trucks, you had to drive them or ship them on the train.

The first year we were married, we didn't have a

refrigerator. I built a screen cooler and covered it with burlap sacks. We ran water over the sacks to keep things cool. We didn't have a washing machine either. Marge went down to my mother's every Monday morning and washed with her. We bought our own when we moved down to this place.

I bought our first refrigerator right after World War II from a fellow, kind of on the black market. You couldn't buy a refrigerator; there weren't any in the country for sale. They hadn't built any; you know, the war was going on. The fellow I was working for, Jutland, had a son who ran a hardware store. He ordered two refrigerators so he could get one for himself. They both came in the same day, so he called me and told me I could have the other one. One was a General Electric and the other was a Frigidaire. He told me I could have my pick, so I took the General Electric. It's been running ever since, better than forty years and never been touched. It's still out on the back porch. I got the best of the deal, the other one didn't last as long.

We didn't even have a car when we first got married. The folks had a pickup, and we used it. We finally got a truck when we had to have something to haul things in. I guess it was five or six years after we were married before we bought a car. It was a '48 Dodge, fluid drive. A neighbor had it and was going to trade it in, but they wouldn't give him anything for it. We bought it for six hundred dollars and drove it for several years. We kept trading and getting a better car when we could afford it. Times have changed a lot since then.

I guess farming is about all I know. Livestock — I run a bunch of cattle. Feed the feed to them, sell a little hay on the side. Pay the bills. We run a cow camp operation. We run the cows over on the Blue Mesa and the yearlings up on the Little Cimarron in the summertime. Then we feed the calves down here from the first of November until the middle of February, and then we sell them. We keep some for our own use and usually keep a few short age calves over for another year. We have several people who buy them to take them to the locker plant to butcher. They pay on the basis of the hot weight. After the calf is slaughtered and dressed and cleaned, they weigh them. That's what they pay on. As the carcass cools, it loses weight because you lose moisture as it cools, about six per cent, I think. When you buy meat in a butcher shop someone has to pick up that loss. Someone has to pay for it.

When I sell calves, I sell them live. The packer will buy a 1200-pound animal that will only dress out 52 to 54 per cent. Out of a 1000 pounds that he buys there is only 520 pounds that he can use. That doubles your price right quick. If he pays sixty cents a pound live weight the price is automatically a dollar six or eight cents a pound for the carcass. In the store you'll pay ninety cents a pound for hamburger and four dollars a pound for choice steak. Of course, the packer can get some salvage from the hide. They sell it to Japan where it's made into shoes and things. But there is quite a bit of waste before it gets down to the consumer.

It's hard to make a living as a rancher. You've got to

be a scientist, an agronomist, veterinarian. You've got to be a jack-of-all-trades to make it work. You've got to be able to do everything. You have to do your own doctoring and you have to take care of your soil. You learn that by trial and error, I guess. We've leveled our fields to make it easier to irrigate. In some fields I've put in gated pipe for irrigation, but I still do a lot of open-ditch irrigating. Sometimes it takes an hour or an hour and a half to get the water running in the ditch properly.

We started leveling the fields about fifteen or twenty years ago, did a little bit as we went. You couldn't level a field with horses like you can with the heavy equipment we have today. It took too long with horses. Now you can go out with land planes and level a field so it's easy to irrigate. In one field we had a carryall come in to level it. We made five-foot cuts and fills; it was just little rolling draws before. We leveled it right straight across. We took the top soil off and piled it around the edges of a fifteen-acre field. When it was leveled, we put the top soil back on six or eight inches deep. Then we put on manure a couple of times and added commercial fertilizer, nitrogen and phosphate. To get top production you have to use commercial fertilizer; it's the only way.

We got about all the fields leveled, at least we've gotten rid of the high spots. You reach a point where you get tired of picking rocks and would like to do something else. It's a lot of work and I guess there are only a few of us that are willing to devote all our time to it. You've got to have a special interest and desire to do it. Just like anything else, if you enjoy doing it, you don't mind the time it takes you to do it.

ROSAMOND ZETTERHOLM

SUMMER VACATION

Roz's house on top of Miller Mesa has a view of the whole Sneffels Range to the south. Roz is a quiet person who spends her time taking care of the ranch which has been in the family since her grandfather's time. The house is surrounded by beautiful flower gardens that she has worked on over the years. The flowers provide not only beauty, but also tasty snacks for wildlife.

Roz has memories of Ridgway based on visits each summer. Because the visits were special, she has a knack of seeing the ordinary that everyone else takes for granted. She saw Ridgway anew each year and, for that reason, remembers it and its changes well.

"We never went into the mountains. It was just something nobody ever did... I think once you got through the mountains in those days, you didn't push your luck until you had to leave."

My grandfather, Amos Walther, walked from Denver to Ouray as a teenager. He and this friend set out from Denver on foot to seek their fortune. They were headed for Cripple Creek which was a wide open mining town. On the way they ran into a man who asked them where they were headed. When Granddad answered, "to Cripple Creek," he said, "I don't think you boys will like Cripple Creek; why don't you go to Ouray?" So they did.

Granddad was always interested in business, and he got a job at the Merchants and Miners Bank, eventually becoming a teller. Later he went over to the Citizens State Bank and was still Chairman of the Board when he died. Granddad had owned a bank in Ridgway that was closed when Roosevelt closed all the banks in the thirties. That was just part of the reason the bank closed. The other part was that a man in Ridgway had stolen securities from Granddad's deposit box. He never kept it locked. I have notes that he wrote about that. Granddad wrote notes constantly. His handwriting never changed from the time he was a child until the day he died. He always wrote with a straight pen, a nib. In his notes he said, "The man must have needed the money"; he wasn't bitter about it.

I remember hearing a story about my mother when she was little. Someone gave her a piglet which she kept

A. E. Walther and family.

out behind the house in a bunny shed or chicken coop. For some reason it would always follow Granddad to the bank. Finally, he said, "This is very undignified to have a pig follow me to the bank every day."

Sometime in his teens, Granddad worked as an agent for the Ute Indians over in White River Junction. He kept a list of words that the Indians used, spelled phonetically. There was no dictionary of the Ute language. I still have that list somewhere.

My mother, Mary Elizabeth Walther, was born in Ouray. My father, Sterling Rohlfs, went to the School of Mines in Golden and then moved to Ouray to run a smelter. He met mother here, and after they were married, they moved to the ranch here in Elk Meadows. They formed the Sneffels Land and Cattle Company and operated the ranch until the market dropped out of the cattle business. My sister, Anna Louise, called Luanna, was born here.

My parents moved to New Mexico after that to manage the Vermejo Park, and that's where I was born in August 1923. My father was killed when I was five, and we moved to Cimarron, New Mexico.

I must have been seven or eight when we started coming to Ridgway for the summer. As soon as school was out, we'd drive over the narrow roads to Ridgway. The Million Dollar Highway was just wide enough for one car to pass. It was scary. We'd leave Cimarron about 5:30 in the morning and not arrive here until about 5:30 in the evening. Granny always had a nice dinner waiting for us. It always seemed to be a special highlight, looking forward to arriving, and knowing she was going to have fried chicken and chocolate cake. Their house was on Clinton Street which used to be the main highway through town. Granddad had the whole block except for a house on the corner. There were no other houses on the block. The street was tree-lined on both sides but terribly dusty. The street was low with irrigation ditches on both sides. When Granddad wanted to water the lawn of the house and the empty lots on either side, he just lifted a little gate in the ditch and flooded it. It was perfect. I did a lot of little sailboating in that ditch.

I don't know how my grandmother ever had time to sit down, but she had her time so well organized that she'd sit on the porch every afternoon. There was a quilting bee once a week over at the Holmes's place. They had a quilting frame that they put on the dining room table, and six or eight women would sit around it and quilt all afternoon. I would go over and just sit and watch. That was fun; it was a curiosity to me.

Grandmother used to can a lot of fruit during the season: peaches and apricots and everything. I don't think she ever got into vegetables. We never helped. I think she was afraid we'd get burned. She had a big wood stove in the kitchen that was there long after she died.

She was a wonderful cook; biscuits, real cakes, everything from scratch. We always had meat with meals; a beef roast, a pork roast, a lamb roast, or chicken or meat loaf. I can never remember having hamburgers. She always had salads and desserts, and she always had homemade biscuits. That's why I say I don't know how she had time to do all these things.

In the afternoon she'd rest after lunch and then go down on the porch with a big bowl of string beans or fresh peas. After she had finished stringing the beans or podding the peas, she would sit for a while; or maybe, go call on somebody. Then she'd come home and start dinner.

I don't ever remember Granddad working when we were coming to visit in the summer. I think he retired early from whatever he did. He had ranches as a hobby; he leased them out. Whenever we couldn't find Granddad, I'd ask Grandmother where he was and she'd say, "Oh, he's down at the pool hall." So I would go down and peek in through the swinging door, and he would be there. I don't ever remember a pool table there, but they had card tables and Granddad loved to play blackjack. He was lucky at cards. Granny used to say, "Aren't you ashamed that those children have to go to the pool hall to call you home?"

I never talked to Granddad about his trip from Denver to Ouray. You always think somebody is going to live forever. We have some of his notebooks, but I don't think they have anything about the trip over here. I do remember that he was a tremendous joker. One time when we were going to the Phillips' for dinner he said, "You go ahead, I'll catch up." We all went around and walked up the front street like proper people. After we got there, he came through the alley wearing an absolutely outlandish hat that he had found up in the attic that must have belonged to Granny or someone else.

The summers in Ridgway were always hot, and I don't think we knocked ourselves out doing much. I read constantly, two books a day. Granddad always liked to have Luanna and me go out and help work on the ranch. He thought running the stacker when they put up hay was fun for us little city kids. But I was very allergic to horses and hay, so when they'd get ready to go, I'd hide on the front porch behind the swing. The swing had a big blanket on it, and I would climb behind that until I thought they were gone. If I did go out there, by the time they got started, my eyes would be so blinded by hay fever that I couldn't see what I was doing. I hated it. Granddad couldn't understand why I disliked it so.

I played with the MacLean children who were about the same age. We'd go to each other's houses and play dolls. We had a pet prairie dog, which we named Chipeta, that we dressed up and fed with a little doll bottle. It tried so hard to hibernate upstairs in the attics. When we couldn't find it for awhile, we'd go up and look down in the bottom of those big wicker rag baskets to find him. He was always there.

Another thing I used to do was try to get up early enough to go up to Mrs. Sherbino's to watch her put up her hair for the day. She wore it in hundreds of little rolled curls. She'd sit there and roll up all these little curls. That fascinated me. She was a family friend, and I asked her how she did it. So she told me, and I used to run up to watch her. She did it every day.

We never went into the mountains. It was just something nobody ever did. I never remember going out toward the Cimarron Range or to Telluride or Silverton. I think once you got through the mountains in those days, you didn't push your luck until you had to leave. I know when we came, we always would come a different way. Mother liked to come over Cochetopa Pass, but she always tried to pick a different way. We did have friends in Durango, railroad people; so often, when we would leave, we'd stop in Durango for lunch before going on to New Mexico.

I don't remember going to Montrose much. The road to Montrose was a dirt road and it was never really much fun to go anyplace. Once a year Granddad always wanted to go up on Log Hill because he had a ranch up there. Mother dreaded it; we all dreaded it because it was so hot and dusty. We'd make this great big sacrifice and go up once a summer. I don't remember where the ranch was, but it was not in the ponderosas, it was in the pinions and scrub oak and stuff. Not a profitable ranch, I'm sure.

I do remember riding up to the Dallas Divide on the Galloping Goose. It seemed kind of funny to ride in an automobile on the railroad track.

We always went to Ouray for the 4th of July; that was a great thing. Our parents would fix big picnic dinners and we would go to the Box Canyon where they had tables and things. After the picnic supper, the fireworks would be right up above you.

We used to go to Ouray quite often because there were a number of old families that were good friends of my grandparents. Granny had been brought up in Ouray and

Granddad had worked there. When he was courting her, he would either take the train from Ridgway to Ouray and walk back or vice versa. We went to the Rices' for dinner a lot. We drove on the road to Ouray that went on the west side of the river. I can't remember when they put the bridge across the river here in Ridgway. It was a pretty hefty drive because the road was so narrow and dusty. The Rices lived up on Oak Street at the corner of Queen Street. It's the big house that is shingled now. It used to be a big, white board house with lovely trees in the front yard. We used to sit on their front porch and look with binoculars for mountain sheep in the Amphitheater. We usually found some.

After dinner we would swim in the pool in Ouray. The bathhouse had a corridor in it with little dressing rooms on each side. There was a men's wing on one side and a women's on the other. It seemed like there were loads of rooms, but I suppose there weren't more than twenty. The pool attracted a lot of people from the low country. As a matter of fact, almost everybody came up for their Saturday night bath.

We went to the Orvis Plunge often; that was a great summer thing. A lot of us young people would get together there. I suppose somebody's mother would drive us up. There was a big frame building over this great hot springs pool. There was a little annex that had a merry-go-round. You could stand up and pull on those poles to make it work its way around in a circle; it had the most awful squeak to it.

Once, on my birthday, a number of families went out

to the ranch on the Dallas for a picnic dinner on the river. While the women fixed dinner, the men fished. These picnic dinners were always great. We always had fried chicken, which was a great treat, and always chocolate cake. In those days the kids didn't run off and play; they just sort of sat around and talked with the old folksies. The mosquitoes were always terrible.

I just sort of remember what Ridgway was like then. There were at least three pool halls, and I always enjoyed going to Duckett's with my grandmother. Either Leland or Gilbert would meet us at the door with a basket. They'd walk around, up and down the aisles, and Granny would pick what she wanted off the shelf and put it in the basket, and then they would deliver it later in the day. They did the same thing at Carmichael's, too. We shopped at both places, but Duckett's stands out because they always had some luxury items, such as canned shrimp cocktail, that you couldn't get otherwise.

There was an enormous hardware store on the corner next to where the present hardware store is now. It was owned by Bill Binder whose son, Wilbur, still lives in Nucla. Next to the hardware was Max's drugstore; it was in the store that is now the hardware. Off and on the post office was in the back of that building. It had a soda fountain with the regular old soda fountain chairs. You could get ice cream cones, sodas, or milkshakes. The sodas cost ten or fifteen cents, but you always got a big dividend in the milkshake mixer. They always made more than your glass would hold, so they'd just put the container on the counter and you usually ended up with about three glasses of milkshake. Not little glasses, big ones.

When they got the first telephones in here, the office was upstairs above the drugstore. You cranked the phone and then had to give the operator the number you wanted. Often the operators would say, "Oh, they're not here, I heard them tell so and so they were going to Ouray" or somewhere. They knew absolutely everything. You had to be careful what you said on the phone.

We used to go down to the railroad station to watch the trains. There were lots of them. They had a big roundhouse where they did all the engine work. Trains would come in from Montrose and ore trains would come in from the Telluride area. Those trains had to go over trestles before you got to Telluride. Often the snow would come down in the winter and wash them out. I think it's a pity that none of that is evident now. There's nothing that tells you any history.

We went to the dances out at Cow Creek. They'd have a box supper. The girls would all fix boxes and decorate them. Then the men would bid on them. You ate your dinner with whoever bid the most for the box. It didn't make any difference if you were ten years old and the man who bought your box was fifty-five. I suppose it was a means of raising money to pay for the orchestra or the hall rental, or something like that. The dances were quite sedate, just country dances, not like today's. The Sherbinos had a group that played for the dances. Bess played the piano and Ambrose played the violin, and there were some other people in the orchestra. Sometimes the Carmichaels played for the dances, too.

They all played some kind of instrument. I remember going over to their house for musicals.

I didn't care much for dances much as a child. I had long hair and wore it around my head and looked rather sophisticated, but I was young. When people would ask me to dance, I'd say, "No, thank you, I don't dance." They'd say, "Well, does your little sister dance?" My sister, Luanna, who was older than me, would be furious. She was insulted.

Luanna had a lot more friends. I never have lived any place where I had friends my own age. In Santa Fe I never had anybody my own age except the kids I went to school with, but I never did anything with them. We sort of lived out of town and they didn't. I had little cars that I would take out and make roads in the dirt and ditches. I was a real tomboy.

Summertime in the thirties was a great time for tramps, just going through. They would come around to the back door and ask for something to eat. I suppose they had some kind of marking system because they would always come to the same houses. Once in a while they'd work, do something for you. But we didn't have work for everybody that showed up. Granny would always give them something to eat anyway. We had a fork, called the tramp's fork, and Luanna and I, whenever it was our turn to set the table, would try to put that fork at the other's place.

I remember running a nail in my head one summer. Granddad had gotten a horse and I was anxious to see it, so I ran down to the barn behind the house and didn't duck under a board that had a big nail in it. It went straight in and I just pulled back and put my hand up and rubbed it. When I went in the house, all this blood was shooting out. I remember somebody yelling, "Put her in the bathtub; she's bleeding." So to keep the blood from going all over the house they put me in the bathtub. When it had stopped bleeding, they took me down to the doctor's office and he sewed up my head with a curved needle that they sew horses with.

I also had blood poisoning one summer. I don't remember how I got it, but there was a red streak going up my arm. When they saw that they threw me in bed and put hot packs on my arm to draw the poison down. I would have thought it would have been cold. That was the same summer my sister was in New Mexico with typhoid fever. That was one summer we weren't together. They say when you have typhoid fever and lose your hair it comes back red and curly, but hers didn't.

In 1939 my sister graduated from high school, so my mother took her to Europe. While they were in Switzerland, the war started and they were told to leave. They were told to take the train to Paris, but when they got to the railroad station, there was a little Swiss excursion train that was shiny and clean so they got on that instead. Because they were late leaving, they had to go out through Italy instead.

While they were gone, I had to go back to Santa Fe to school, so I took the train to Ouray. Then I took the bus to Silverton and boarded the train for Durango and Chama. I remember everybody knew who I was because everybody knew everybody in those days, and I was Amos Walther's granddaughter. They took good care of me. The chairs were big, heavy plush velvet that just reeked of cigar smoke. That was a big excursion.

That was the summer that mother taught me how to drive. She took me down to the racetrack at the rodeo grounds in Ridgway and put me behind the wheel and just said, "Drive around." So all I did was drive around and around. After she left I drove my grandparents to Jackson Hole, Wyoming. I was old enough to have my driver's license, but I had never driven anywhere except around the racetrack. So off we went to Jackson Hole to fish; of course, there wasn't much traffic on the road then.

Mother had a four-door Cadillac convertible with isinglass windows that my father had custom made in New Mexico. It was a big touring car, high off the ground. We did everything in it. It was a lovely car. I guess Mother kept that car until about 1933 when we moved to Santa Fe, then we got better cars. I mean shinier, excitinger cars.

We kept coming to Ridgway every summer until I was in about the ninth grade. By that time we were living in Santa Fe, and I started working in the summers. My grandparents were spending their winters away from here, and then I went away to a girl's school in the East. After that things were never the same. Once you leave home, things are never the same.

Grandfather bought this ranch on Miller Mesa in about 1911 or 1912. We used to come up here to the cabin in the summer. It wasn't any place you stayed, but we always brought guests here and everybody wrote their names and the year they came on the wall. My sister and I own the ranch now, and I would come up in the summer. We always had tenants. Someplace along the way, I started taking more interest in the ranch. Mainly the water rights. If you let them slide, you've lost them forever, practically. That's what really brought me back. That and the county wanted to put a county road through the ranch. I filed a lawsuit to prove it was not a county road. They said it was, and I said, no, it wasn't. By the time you put so much money into something, you take a little more interest in it. It's funny, now that I've lived here this long I hardly imagine I ever lived any place else. I think about it a lot, but this is the first home I've ever had since I left home as a young person. It really is my home.